DATA RESOURCE UNDERSTANDING

UTILIZING THE

DATA RESOURCE DATA

MICHAEL H. BRACKETT

Published by:
Technics Publications, LLC
Post Office Box 161
Bradley Beach, NJ 07720 U.S.A.
www.technicspub.com

Cover design by Mark Brye

ISBN, print ed.   978-1-6346201-2-3

First Printing 2015
Library of Congress Control Number: 2014959271

Dedicated to those professionals desiring
to achieve maximum data resource understanding
with minimum effort.

CONTENTS AT A GLANCE

CONTENTS

FIGURES

SCENARIOS

PREFACE

The previous book on *Data Resource Data* explained the *What* about Data Resource Data. It provided a complete logical data resource model for the Data Resource Data. The current book is a companion book that explains the *How* of Data Resource Data. It describes how Data Resource Data are captured and maintained. The *Why* of Data Resource Data is explained in previous books *Data Resource Simplexity* and *Data Resource Design*.

Data Resource Understanding is the sixth book in the Data Resource Series written by the author. Previous books include *Data Resource Quality*, *Data Resource Simplexity*, *Data Resource Integration*, and *Data Resource Design*, and *Data Resource Data*. These books can be consulted for detailed explanations of the *How* and *Why* for developing and maintaining and high-quality data resource and the use of Data Resource Data.

Data Understanding Functions

The explanation of the use of Data Resource Data is presented as Data Understanding Functions, where a Function is a particular component of Data Resource Data. Each Function is oriented toward documenting and understanding a particular aspect of an organization's data resource through Data Resource Data, such as Data Stewardship Function or Data Inventory Function.

The Data Understanding Functions are presented in the general sequence that they might be used by an organization. However, an organization can use the Functions in any sequence that supports their need to understand their data resource, although some Functions must be performed before other Functions. Also, an organization may not use all of the Functions.

The description of each Data Understanding Function begins with an introduction and a data subject-relation diagram for that Function. The diagrams may or may not be identical to the diagrams presented in *Data Resource Data*, although they represent the same data resource architecture. They have just been packaged differently to represent the Function being described.

The beauty of documenting an organization's data resource as Data Resource Data is that any diagram can be produced, for any business function, for any audience. The Data Resource Data represent the overall data resource architecture, and can be extracted and packaged as necessary for an audience.

The description of each Data Understanding Function contains examples in the form of business scenarios. These scenarios do not cover all the possible uses of Data Resource Data, but give a general idea of how the Data Resource Data might be used to document and understand an organization's data resource. Previous books can be consulted for additional examples. A list of Scenarios is provided for a quick reference.

Book Contents

The current book is not a treatise on data resource modeling or on data resource design. It is intended only as a description of how the Data Resource Data are used to understand an organization's data resource. The reader must have some knowledge and skills about data resource modeling and data resource design to be able to fully utilize the Data Resource Functions.

The sequence of the chapters in the current book is shown below.

Chapter 1 describes the need to thoroughly understand all the data in an organization's data resource.

Chapter 2 describes the Responsibility Function.

Chapter 3 describes the Data Inventory Function.

Chapter 4 describes the Common Data Function.

Chapter 5 describes the Data Lexicon Function that supports the formal naming of Common Data.

Chapter 6 describes the Data Cross-Reference Function between Data Product Data and Common Data.

Chapter 7 describes the Data Protection Function for ensuring data privacy and confidentiality.

Chapter 8 describes the Data Access Function for documenting which business processes use the data.

Chapter 9 describes the Data Provenance Function for documenting the data path from their origin to the current destination and the changes made along that path.

Chapter 10 describes the Data Sharing Function where organizational units within an organization or across multiple organizations can cooperate on documenting, understanding, and sharing common data.

Chapter 11 describes Derived Data Function where data renormalized for analytical processing of analytical data, derived data hierarchies from operational and analytical processing, and derived spatial data subjects are documented.

Chapter 12 describes the Preferred Data Function for designating the preferred Common Data and documenting the physical implementation as preferred Data Resource Data.

Chapter 13 describes the Data Transform Function for creating the physical comparate data resource based on the preferred Common Data

Chapter 14 describes how to achieve the reality of a high quality data resource that supports the organization in its business endeavors.

Chapter 15 describes the Data Resource Development Cycle, the components of that cycle, and the Data – Information – Knowledge Cycle.

Chapter 16 describes the importance of relationships in developing an organization's data resource.

Chapter 17 describes the development of data resource architectures and data resource models.

Chapter 18 describes management of the data resource understanding process.

Appendix A describes the changes to Data Resource Data architecture since *Data Resource Data* was published.

Updated Versions

As with *Data Resource Data*, suggested revisions and additions can be sent to the author at MHBDiscuss@aol.com. Updated versions of *Data Resource Data* and *Data Resource Understanding* may be published when sufficient enhancements have been made.

Many people ask why I publish all these techniques with examples. Might someone take the techniques and compete with me? The answer is similar to the situation where a famous French chef, after 40 years of creating and preparing meals, published all of his recipes. People wanted to know why he published his secrets. Wouldn't someone use those recipes to compete with him? His reply was that he published the recipes, but not the 40 years of experience creating and preparing those recipes.

That's the same situation with me. I've published all the techniques and examples, but not the 50 years of experience developing and applying those techniques. In addition, people should take the techniques and examples and make them work for their organization to thoroughly understand the organization's data resource, resolve data resource disparity, and create a comparate data resource that fully supports the organization's business information demand.

Author Paradox

A paradox exists between the author, the publisher, and the reader. The publisher often wants smaller books which sell more readily than larger books. Many readers want smaller books because larger books seem overwhelming and often bring comments like larger books are good for door stops. Yet other readers complain about the necessity to buy multiple smaller books to get the material they need and often make comments about the author and publisher simply wants to sell more books. The author is caught in the middle of the paradox deciding how much material to put in a single book, versus the size of the book, versus how many books are needed to cover a particular topic.

That author's paradox existed with *Data Resource Simplexity* (637 pages), *Data Resource Integration* (580 pages pages), *Data Resource Design* (389 pages), and *Data Resource Data* (287 pages), and still exists with the current book on *Data Resource Understanding*. The author has opted for a smaller book covering just the Data Resource Understanding, but not covering the techniques for data integration or data design, or the design of Data Resource Data, or repeating all the examples of how the techniques are applied. Previous books can be consulted for those descriptions.

Michael Brackett
Olympic Mountains
January 2015

ACKNOWLEDGEMENTS

I thank all of the business professionals, data management professionals, professional friends, and personal friends that have a profound interest in understanding and documenting an organization's data resource. They have provided many insights, thoughts, ideas, suggestions, and criticisms that improved the quality of the book that has increased its usefulness.

I thank Steve Hoberman, yet again, for all of his support and encouragement through the development process and the publication process, and for discussing the Author's paradox with me. He has become a true professional friend as well as a close professional friend.

ABOUT THE AUTHOR

Mr. Brackett retired from the State of Washington in June 1996, where he was the State's Data Resource Coordinator. He was responsible for developing the State's common data architecture that spans multiple jurisdictions, such as state agencies, local jurisdictions, Indian tribes, public utilities, and Federal agencies, and includes multiple disciplines, such as water resource, growth management, and criminal justice. He is the founder of Data Resource Design and Remodeling and is a Consulting Data Architect specializing in developing integrated data resources.

Mr. Brackett has been in the data management field for over 50 years, during which time he developed many innovative concepts and techniques for designing applications and managing data resources. He is the originator of the Common Data Architecture concept, the Data Resource Management Framework, the data naming taxonomy and data naming vocabulary, the Five-Tier Five-Schema concept, the data rule concept, the Business Intelligence Value Chain, the Data Resource Data concept, the architecture-driven data model concept, and many new techniques for understanding and integrating disparate data. He has evolved to a recognized thought leader, a visionary thought leader, and is now considered a legend in data resource management.

Mr. Brackett has written ten books on the topics of application design, data design, and common data architectures. *Data Sharing Using a Common Data Architecture* and *The Data Warehouse Challenge: Taming Data Chaos* describe the concept and uses of a common data architecture for developing an integrated data resource. *Data Resource Quality: Turning Bad Habits into Good Practices* describes how to stop the creation of disparate data. *Data Resource Simplexity: How Organizations Choose Data Resource Success or Failure* describes the approach to data resource management that avoids the creation of disparate data. *Data Resource Integration: Understanding and Resolving a Disparate Data Resource* describes how to permanently resolve an organization's disparate data. *Data Resource Design: Reality Beyond Illusion* describes how to formally design an organizations data resource. *Data Resource Data: A Comprehensive Data*

Resource Understanding describes the complete data resource model for Data Resource Data. He has written numerous articles, including monthly articles for Dataversity.net. He is a well-known international author, speaker, and trainer on data resource management topics.

Mr. Brackett has a BS in Forestry (Forest Management) and a MS in Forestry (Botany) from the University of Washington, and a MS in Soils (Geology) from Washington State University. He was a charter member and is an active member of DAMA-PS, the Seattle Chapter of DAMA International established in 1985. He saw the formation of DAMA National in 1986 and DAMA International in 1988. He served as Vice President of Conferences for DAMA International; as the President of DAMA International from 2000 through 2003; and as Past President of DAMA International for 2004 and 2005. He was the founder and first President of the DAMA International Foundation, an organization established for developing a formal data management profession, and served as Past President of the DAMA International Foundation until 2013. He was the Production Editor of the DAMA-DMBOK released in April 2009.

Mr. Brackett received DAMA International's Lifetime Achievement Award in 2006 for his work in data resource management, the second person in the history of DAMA International to receive that award (Mr. Brackett presented the first award to John Zachman in 2003). He taught Data Design and Modeling in the Data Resource Management Certificate Program at the University of Washington and has been a member of the adjunct faculty at Washington State University and The Evergreen State College. He is listed in *Who's Who in the West*, *Who's Who in Education*, and *International Who's Who*.

Mr. Brackett is semi-retired and enjoys a variety of activities including back country hiking, cross-country skiing, snowshoeing, roller-blading, biking, dancing, and writing. He lives in a log home he built in the Olympic Mountains near Lilliwaup, Washington. He can be reached through the publisher.

Chapter 1

THE NEED TO UNDERSTAND

Organizations need to thoroughly understand their data resource.

The use of an organization's data resource to understand and support its business activities is only limited by one's imagination. When the data resource is comparate and well understood, then one's imagination can be limitless. However, when the data resource is disparate and not well understood, then imagination is severely constrained. Therefore, the best approach to fully support an organization's business activities is to develop a comparate data resource that is well understood by everyone in the organization.

Thomas Huxley made the following statement in the late 1800s:

Mathematics may be compared to a mill of exquisite workmanship, which grinds your stuff to any degree of fineness; but, nevertheless, what you get out depends on what you put in; and as the grandest mill in the world will not extract wheat flour from pea cods, so pages of formulae will not get a definite result out of loose data.

He was, of course, talking about the need to understand data and the quality of data, which was well before the age of computers and databases.

A DATA UNDERSTANDING STORY

We all thoroughly understand all the data we are using and all the results developed from the analysis of those data. Right?

I recently met a person who ran a company that provided results from the analysis of social media, like text messages, cell phone calls, and so on, including the location. He complained that no matter what topic or what media were analyzed that he always got a cluster of data in the Gulf of Guinea off the west coast of Africa. He had no idea what was located in the Gulf of Guinea and why he always had so many hits there.

I asked if he understood how locations were determined and he responded that latitude and longitude provided a location on the Earth, and the latitude and longitude were determined by the Global Positioning System (GPS)

1

satellites. Most social media devices have the ability to determine the location using the GPS satellites, which is basically correct.

I asked if he understood how latitude and longitude worked. He described something about latitude being north and south and longitude being east and west, which is basically correct. He said the latitude and longitude gave him a location, such as a city or an event, for the topic being analyzed. That's all he needed to meet his client's needs, except that a cluster of data always appeared in the Gulf of Guinea.

I explained that latitude was north and south from zero degrees at the Equator to 90 degrees at each pole, and longitude was east and west from Greenwich, England which establishes the Prime Meridian. Longitude goes 180 degrees east and west to where they meet at the International Date Line. Zero degrees latitude and zero degrees longitude is located where the Prime Meridian and the Equator meet, which is in the Gulf of Guinea. He had no idea what I had explained, but was still concerned about so much data coming from the Gulf of Guinea. Obviously there weren't very many people there.

So I asked him if he knew about default data values, which he did not. I explained that many social media devices do not have GPS capability and some devices that do have GPS capability cannot get a location because they are in a building or otherwise shielded from the GPS satellites. He did not know that.

Apparently someone or some application had inserted the values 0.0 degrees latitude and 0.0 degrees longitude when an actual latitude and longitude were not available. Since 0.0 / 0.0 are specific values designating a specific location, his analysis was considering that location as valid data. He did not know that either.

I further explained that when a value is not available, that an actual value should not be inserted. That's tantamount to saying that if a student's birth date is not known, then enter January 1, 1900 and people will certainly know that the actual birth date is not available. When real data are not available, the data field must remain blank (or null) so that people know that a value is not available and will plan accordingly. He did not know that.

So, his problem was 1) not understanding the real meaning of latitude and longitude data and 2) not understanding the real meaning of default data values. Therefore, the results of his analyses were basically flawed and he could be providing incorrect information to his customers. He was a bit upset at that conclusion, and vowed that he needed to better understand the data he was analyzing.

What about the rest of you?

UNDERSTANDING

Albert Einstein once said that if he had only one hour to solve a problem that he would spend fifty-five minutes defining the problem and only five minutes finding the solution. In other words, thoroughly understanding the problem is absolutely critical before that problem can be solved. Accordingly, understanding the data is absolutely critical before those data can be used to support an organization's business activities.

Uncertainty is a lack of understanding, and uncertainty about an organization's data results from a lack of understanding of those data. Since the data resource represents the business, any uncertainty about the data becomes an uncertainty about the business. Also, any uncertainty about the data leads to increased data disparity resulting in the data not adequately supporting the business needs.

Data resource quality can be no better than the understanding of the data in the data resource. Since the quality of the information produced from the data resource can be no better than the quality of the data resource, and the data resource quality depends on data understanding, then the information quality can be no better than the data understanding. In other words, information quality is commensurate with data resource quality, which is commensurate with data understanding.

As the data understanding increases, the understanding of the business increases. Also, as the data understanding increases, the data disparity decreases, and the data adequately support the business needs. Therefore, the need to thoroughly understand the data is critical for understanding the business and adequately supporting business needs.

DATA RESOURCE DATA

Data resource data are any data necessary for thoroughly understanding, formally managing, and fully utilizing the organization's data resource to fully support the current and future business information demand. Data Resource Data include data names, data definitions, data structures, data integrity rules, data source, data lineage, and so on. They are documentation of the existing disparate data resource and the specifications for a comparate data resource.

Data Resource Data are the means to thoroughly understand an organization's data. They are fully normalized to prevent any redundancy or anomalies. The Data Resource Data can be packaged and presented in any

3

manner, at any time, to any audience that has a need to understand the organization's data resource. The preparation and maintenance of dozens, or even hundreds, of individual data models, and the effort to keep those models updated and current, and to manage model check-in and check-out, is no longer necessary and is a total waste of an organization's resources.

Many concepts, principles, and techniques are available to create a data resource and a data architecture, including those in the Common Data Architecture Paradigm. The current book does not document those concepts, principles, or techniques, nor the quality of the application of those concepts, principles, and techniques. It only explains the documentation of the results of the application of those concepts, principles, and techniques as Data Resource Data.

The structure and content of business data vary widely across subject areas and organizations, and often within organizations. Data Resource Data are a fixed data structure that can be used to understand and document all forms of business data regardless of the structure of those business data. They are subject area independent and organization independent.

One perception of Data Resource Data provides the understanding and documentation of multiple perceptions of the business world across organizations and within an organization. In other words, Data Resource Data have no perception of the business world. They only document and organizations perceptions of the business world.

PERCEPTION AND REALITY

Data Resource Data represent a single version of reality about the organization's business data. Stephen Hawking states "We never have a model-independent view of reality. But that does not mean there is no model-independent reality." An organization's view of business world reality is a model-dependent reality as perceived by the organization. However, the business world reality, independent of an organization, is not model-dependent – it's a model-independent reality.

Organizations can never have a model-independent view of reality, because there is no model-independent test of reality. There may be an underlying reality, but the organization's perception of that reality is based on their perception and is model-dependent. The question is whether an organization's data resource agrees with observation (perception), not whether it is real. Therefore, the data resource is a model-dependent view of reality based on the organization's experience, and is the only reality the organization knows.

Organizations face two different types of reality pertaining to their data resource.

The first view is the data resource reality, which is how well the organization's data resource represents the business world as perceived by the organization. Each organization should have only one perception of the business world. However, an organization may consist of many different organization units and many people within those units, each of which has their own perception of the business world and their own data needs. The result is multiple individual data resource realities and the data resource often becomes disparate to support those individual realities. The data resource reality for an organization must be a collective reality of all the organization units and the people within those units, and the data resource must represent that collective reality.

The data resource reality across multiple organizations is by nature different because each organization perceives the business world differently. Those organizations may share common data, but the sharing of common data does not mean that the organizations need to maintain common data resources. Each organization's data resource is based on their perception of the business world.

The second view is the data resource understanding reality, which is how well the organization's data resource is documented and understood. Each organization should have only one data resource understanding reality. However, that reality is often incomplete and fragmented, resulting in a disparate understanding of the data resource. The data resource understanding reality for an organization must be a collective reality of all the understanding, in one location, readily available to anyone in the organization. The Data Resource Data provide that single, collective data resource understanding reality for an organization.

Both the data resource reality and the data resource understanding reality are critical for an organization to be successful in its business endeavors. The current book pertains only to the data resource understanding reality that is achieved through the Data Resource Data. However, as the data resource understanding reality improves, the data resource reality will improve. In other words, as people better understand the data resource, the data resource will better represent the business world, and the organization will be more successful in its business endeavors.

META-BUSINESS DATA

Meta-business data are any more detailed and less intricately structured business data that provide an understanding of more intricately structured business data. Meta-business data are not in any way considered to be meta-data or Data Resource Data. They are business data that provide a detailed understanding of more intricately structured business data, and are documented the same as any other business data using the Data Resource Data.

As the degree of data structuring increases the volume of meta-business data also increases. For example, voice is text with tonal inflections and are more intricately structured than pure text. Images of the person behind the voice contain all the non-verbal mannerisms, such as body movements, facial expressions, eye movement, and so on, and are more intricately structured than voice or text. The meta-business data provide data about the voice and images that are more detailed than the pure text.

Some concepts and techniques, such as Dublin Core, Digital Geospatial Meta-data, and so on, are really meta-business data because they describe in more detail the meaning of the more intricately structured data. They are not meta-data or Data Resource Data, but are documented as business data.

THE BOOK

Data Resource Data explained *What* needed to be documented about an organization's data resource to provide a thorough understanding. *Data Resource Understanding* explains *How* the Data Resource Data can be used to thoroughly understand an organization's data resource. It's not a set of data entry instructions for entering the Data Resource Data. It's a set of explanations about how the organization's data resource can be documented to provide a thorough understanding.

The Data Resource Data will be presented in a logical sequence of Data Understanding Functions for better understanding rather than in an alphabetical sequence for reference as was done in *Data Resource Data*. Each Data Understanding Function represents a cohesive segment of the Data Resource Data. However, the presentation sequence is not necessarily the sequence that the Data Resource Data may be entered by an organization. The data entry is usually driven by the availability of the data and any natural sequence, such as the Data Product Data and Common Data before any cross-referencing to the Common Data.

The data definitions provided in *Data Resource Data* will not be repeated in the current book, both because it would be redundant and would exceed the space limitation. Similarly, the material provided in *Data Resource Integration* and *Data Resource Design* will not be repeated in the current book. Those books can be consulted for detailed explanations about integrating disparate data and designing a comparate data resource.

A few major data integrity rules will be explained. However, not all the detailed data integrity rules will be explained due to space limitations. *Data Resource Data* can be referenced for the detailed data integrity rules.

PRESENTATION RULES

The following presentation rules apply throughout the current book and will not be repeated in each Data Understanding Function.

Definitions, Descriptions, and Comments

The Definition, Description, and Comment statements should always have the person's name that is responsible for the entry, whether or not the person responsible actually entered the statement, and a date for the entry. The statements should also have a source for the definition, description, or comment, such as personal knowledge, a design document, a meeting, and so on.

Old Definition, Description, and Comment statements are never deleted because they were part of the understanding process. New Definition, Description, and Comment statements are added to further the understanding process. In other words, the Definition, Description, and Comment data characteristics carry their own history.

Each organization can determine whether the Definition, Description, and Comment statements are listed in chronological order or reverse chronological order. Each sequence has advantages and disadvantages. However, an organization should pick one sequence that should be used consistently for all Data Resource Data.

Data Reference Sets

Data Reference Sets must have data characteristics for a Name, a Begin Date, and a Definition. A Code is optional. These data characteristics will not be listed for each Data Reference Set.

A Data Reference Item is never deleted because it is part of the understanding. In other words, Data Reference Items contain their own history.

Begin Dates are always required, but may be changed if found to be in error. End Dates are optional and show when a particular data occurrence is obsolete.

7

Obsolete Data Resource Data are never deleted. They are always retained for future reference because they are part of the understanding process. End Dates and status codes are used to show when a particular data occurrence became obsolete.

System Identifiers

The Data Resource Data contain System Identifier for the primary key of most data occurrences other than Data Reference Items. Each organization can use whatever equivalent is available in the particular database management system where the primary Data Resource Data are maintained.

The System Identifier, or its equivalent, is typically invisible to a person entering or using the Data Resource Data. They will not be shown in the list of data characteristics that need to be entered.

A System Identifier, or its equivalent, that is used as foreign key is typically invisible to a person entering or using Data Resource Data. The parent data occurrences are identified through the Name or some other unique data characteristic unless a unique data characteristic is not available. In that situation, the system identifier is shown.

Sequence

The data subjects within each Data Understanding Function are listed in alphabetical order. The data characteristic list within each data subject is slightly different than presented in *Data Resource Data*. The home data characteristics are listed first in alphabetical order, followed by the foreign data characteristics in alphabetical order. That sequence has proven useful for understanding the data within each data subject and the relationships to parent data subjects.

Required Data Characteristics

All required data characteristics are followed by an (R). A data characteristic may be required in some situations and prevented in other situations, in which case it is followed by (R/P) and an explanation is provided. If an (R) or (R/P) is not present, the data characteristic is optional.

Data Subject-Relation Diagrams

One or more data subject-relation diagrams are shown at the beginning of each major section within a chapter. These diagrams are oriented toward a description of the material presented in that major section and may appear different than the diagrams presented in *Data Resource Data*. However, the data structure is the same.

One of the major benefits of Data Resource Data is that data subject-relation diagrams can be produced directly from the Data Resource Data, given the appropriate diagramming software, based on the detail needed for a specific purpose and an intended audience. The need to maintain a multitude of different diagrams for different purposes and intended audiences is no longer necessary.

SUMMARY

Lack of understanding of the data resource leads to uncertainty about the data, which leads to disparate data, which do not adequately support the organization's business activities. The flip side is that thorough understanding of the data resource leads to certainty about the data, which leads to comparate data that adequately support the organization's business activities. Use of an organization's data resource is limited only by people's imagination, and that imagination is maximized with a thorough understanding of the data resource.

Organizations have two views of reality. The first view of reality is the data resource's representation of the business world and the second view of reality is a thorough understanding of the data resource. Data Resource Data document the second view of reality. It's the single version of reality about the data resource, compared to disparate data resource documentation. When the second view of reality is maximized, then the first view of reality is maximized and business activities are adequately supported.

Chapter 2

DATA RESPONSIBILITY

Data understanding is based on formal data responsibility.

Documenting the thorough understanding of an organization's data resource begins with the Data Responsibility Function consisting of the Organization Units and the Data Stewards that are responsible for finding and documenting the understanding about an organization's data resource. These two responsibilities are pervasive throughout the Data Resource Data.

The data subject-relation diagram for the Data Responsibility Function is shown in Figure 2.1. It contains two segments for Organization Unit and for Data Steward. Each of these segments is explained below.

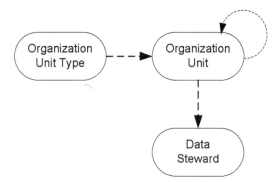

Figure 2.1. Data Responsibility.

ORGANIZATION UNITS

Organization Unit plays a critical role in finding and documenting the thorough understanding of the data resource. Organization Unit can represent any organizational unit within the organization whose data resource is being documented, or any external organizational unit from which data are received or which has knowledge about the data resource.

Organization Unit is recursive so that a hierarchy of Organization Units within an organization can be designated. However, the accurate documentation of an organization's structure is not required for the Data Resource Data, particularly for Organization Units outside the organization

11

whose data resource is being documented. Only the Organization Units involved with the understanding and documentation of an organization's data resource need to be documented.

The detail data for an Organization Unit are entered anytime an Organization Unit is identified.

> Organization Unit. Acronym
> Organization Unit. Begin Date (R)
> Organization Unit. Comment
> Organization Unit. Definition (R)
> Organization Unit. End Date
> Organization Unit. Name (R)
> Organization Unit. Organization Indicator (R)[1]
>
> Organization Unit Type. Name (R)
> "Parent" Organization Unit. Name

Organization Unit Type is a data reference set that qualifies an Organization Unit. Each organization implementing Data Resource Data can designate the data reference items to suit their particular needs, such as Branch, Department, Division, and so on. The data reference items can be added at any time.

An Organization Unit cannot reference itself as a "Parent" Organization Unit.

Several data subjects in the Data Resource Data are subordinate to Organization Unit, including Business Process, Business Process Steward, Data Site, Data Product, Data Steward, and Data Transform Process. Each of these subordinate data subjects will be explained in their respective Data Understanding Function.

Scenario 2.1. Internal Organization Unit

An organization is embarking on program to document their existing data and develop a comparate data resource. They want to start by documenting all the data stewards, but first need to document their organization units. The decision was made to document the top four levels of organization units and to assign data stewards to those organization units. The decision was also made to document only the basic data about each Organization Unit and to later tie those Organization Units to their existing formal organization unit structure of the organization.

---

[1] Organization Unit. Organization Indicator has been added since *Data Resource Data* was published. See Appendix A for details.

Scenario 2.2. External Organization Unit

An organization acquires considerable quantities of data from many different external organizations. They need the basic data about those external organizations so they can document the data stewards in those organizations, but do not need detailed documentation about those external organizations. The decision was made to only document the basic data about the highest organization unit in an external organization, or the highest organization unit at a specific location if the external organization had multiple sites.

DATA STEWARDS

Data Stewards have the primary responsibility for finding and documenting the thorough understanding of an organization's data resource. They can be responsible for any aspect of the organization's data resource for the welfare of the organization, including both Data Product Data and Common Data.

The detail data for a Data Steward are entered anytime a Data Steward is identified. Most of the Data Steward contact data are optional. Only the pertinent contact data need to be entered.

> Data Steward. Address City Name Complete
> Data Steward. Address Line 1
> Data Steward. Address Line 2
> Data Steward. Address Postal Code
> Data Steward. Address State Name Postal Abbreviation
> Data Steward. Begin Date (R)
> Data Steward. Cell Phone Number Complete
> Data Steward. E-Mail Address
> Data Steward. End Date
> Data Steward. Fax Number
> Data Steward. Name Complete (R)
> Data Steward. Office Phone Number Complete
> Data Steward. Responsibility Description (R)
> Data Steward. Title (R)
>
> Organization Unit. Name (R)

A Data Steward must belong to an Organization Unit, either within the organization whose data resource is being documented or in an external organization. That Organization Unit must be documented before the Data Steward can be documented.

Two data subjects are subordinate to Data Steward, including Data Product Steward and Data Subject Steward. Each of these subordinate data subjects will be explained in their respective Data Understanding Function.

13

Scenario 2.3. Internal Data Stewards

An organization desires to document all of their existing data product data and need to document all of the data stewards that have any knowledge or understanding about those data. Having already documented their basic organization units, they begin identifying anyone that has any insight about the existing data and documenting those people as data stewards. As data stewards are identified, they in turn identify additional people that have insight about the data, who are then documented as data stewards.

Scenario 2.4. External Data Stewards

An organization that acquires considerable data from external organizations needs to identify the knowledgeable people in those external organizations that can be contacted for insight about the acquired data. As those people are identified, they are documented as data stewards in their respective external organizations.

Data Stewardship Data Reference Sets

Data Steward Function is a data reference set that specifies the business function performed by the Data Steward, such as Database Administrator, Data Analyst, Data Architect, Knowledge Worker, and so on. Each organization implementing Data Resource Data can designate the data reference items to suit their particular needs. New data reference items can be added at any time.

Data Steward Level is a data reference set that specifies the organizational level of the Data Steward, such as Strategic, Tactical, or Detail. These three data reference items are part of the Common Data Architecture Paradigm, but could be adjusted to suit an organization's particular needs.

Data Steward Function and Data Steward Level do not directly qualify a Data Steward. They qualify specific Data Steward responsibilities for Data Products and Data Subjects. The details will be explained in those particular Data Understanding Functions.

SUMMARY

The Data Responsibility Function identifies the organizations and the data stewards within those organizations that have the primary responsibility for identifying, understanding, and documenting an organization's data resource. The data stewards may be within the organization whose data resource is being documented, or may be in an external organization that is in some way connected to the organization whose data resource is being documented. Either way, those data stewards must be formally documented and eventually connected to the data for which they have knowledge or responsibility.

Chapter 3

DATA INVENTORY

A formal data inventory begins the data understanding process.

The understanding process continues with the Data Inventory Function consisting of the documentation of all existing, often disparate, Data Product Data at an organization's disposal, whether whose data are from within the organization or from an external organization, so those data can be readily understood within the context of Common Data.

DATA INVENTORY OVERVIEW

The *data inventory concept* is that all data at the organization's disposal will be completely and comprehensively inventoried and documented in one location that is readily available to anyone in the organization so that the organization at large understands the content, meaning, and quality of those data.

The *data inventory objective* is to identify, inventory, and document all data that currently exist in the organization's data resource or are readily available to the organization so that those data can be readily understood and used to support the current and future business information demand.

The guiding philosophy for understanding and documenting Data Product Data is that *anything goes with existing data*. Many ingenious methods, and some not so ingenious methods, have been used to create disparate data. Sometimes considerable thought is needed to determine what the existing data really represent. The Definition, Description, and Comment data characteristics should be well used to provide an understanding of the Data Product Data.

Only the documentation of Data Product Data is explained in the current Chapter. The documentation of Common Data are explained in the Common Data Chapter and the cross-references to the Common Data are explained in the Data Cross-References Chapter.

The detailed techniques for documenting Data Product Data are explained in *Data Resource Integration* and will not be repeated here.

DATA INVENTORY APPROACH

The Data Inventory Function includes the sequence of the data inventory, the documentation of databases and data dictionaries, and the breakdown of combined Data Product Data.

Data Inventory Sequence

The existing Data Product Data can be inventoried in any sequence that is useful for the organization. One sequence is to conduct a high-level inventory for all the Data Product Data, followed with a more detailed inventory for the high priority or business critical data, and so on. Another sequence is to completely inventory all of the high priority or business critical data, then inventory lower priority or less critical data.

Many combined sequences could also be used based on the organization's needs. The only basic requirement is that Data Products must be documented before their subordinate Data Product Sets, which must be documented before their subordinate Data Product Units, which must be documented before their subordinate Data Product Codes.

Databases And Dictionaries

A database may have documentation associated with the database management system where the database resides. That documentation should be entered with the database documentation.

A database could also have documentation independent of the database management system where the database resides, such as an electronic or manual data dictionary. That independent documentation could either be entered with the database documentation, or it could be entered as a separate Data Product.

Entering the independent documentation with the database places all the documentation about the data in that database in one place, providing a better understanding of the data. However, the integrity of the independent documentation is lost.

Entering the independent documentation as a separate Data Product maintains the integrity of that independent documentation. However, the combined understanding of the data in the database is lost.

Entering independent documentation both with the database documentation and as a separate Data Product is an unnecessary redundant effort that is not recommended.

Either approach is acceptable and each organization can decide which approach to use. Ultimately, all the documentation about a database will come together through the data cross-referencing process to determine the preferred Common Data. When the data cross-referencing has been completed, the desired Data Product Data can be extracted through the Common Data and presented in a combined form to an intended audience.

Data Product Data Breakdown

The breakdown of combined Data Product Data is the first phase of understanding those existing data, and is explained in the current Chapter. The cross-referencing to Common Data is the second phase of understanding those existing data, and is explained in the Data Cross-References Chapter.

The breakdown of combined Data Product Data is done during the Data Inventory Function for several reasons. First, it helps people using the Data Product Data understand what those Data Product Data actually represent without having to develop the cross-references to the Common Data. Second, it keeps the Common Data less complex, which makes the Common Data and the designation of the preferred Common Data easier and more understandable. Third, it makes the creation of the data source rules that are defined for data transformation much simpler because the appropriate pieces of the Data Product Data can be referenced.

Data Resource Integration contains detailed explanations of the data variability that can be encountered with Data Product Data and how that variability can be broken down to understandable components during the data inventory.

DATA PRODUCT DATA

Data Product Data are the product of some development effort and can be either manual or automated data. They include the existing data resource, documentation of the existing data resource, and any insights people have about the existing data resource. They include any data at the organization's disposal, whether from within the organization or from external organizations.

Data Product Sets, Data Product Units, and Data Product Codes may have a subordinate Data Product Set Variation, Data Product Unit Variation, and Data Product Code Variation respectively. When a statement refers both to the basic unit or its variation the notation will be Data Product Set / Variation, Data Product Unit / Variation, and Data Product Code / Variation respectively.

The data subject-relation diagram for Data Product Data is shown in Figure

3.1. It contains five major segments for Data Site, Data Product, Data Product Set, Data Product Unit, and Data Product Code. Each of these segments is explained in the following sections.

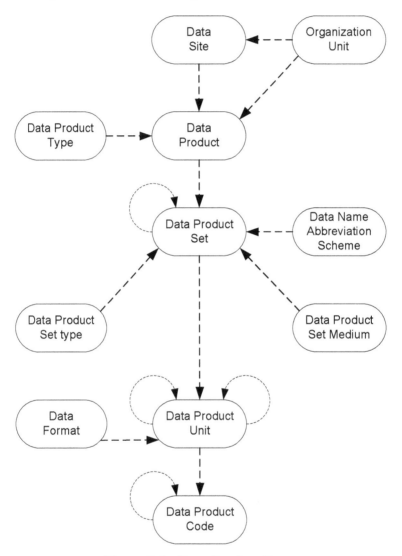

Figure 3.1. Data Product Data.

Data Site

A Data Site is any location where Data Product Data are stored or where documentation about the Data Product Data are stored. The Data Site may be manual or electronic, and may be within the organization whose data resource is being documented or in an external organization.

The detail data for a Data Site are entered anytime a Data Site is identified.

> Data Site. Comment
> Data Site. Description (R)
> Data Site. Name (R)
>
> Organization Unit. Name (R)

The name of the Data Site may or may not be readily apparent, particularly if the Data Site is in a distributed environment. If the name of the Data Site is readily apparent, that name should be entered. If the name is not readily apparent, a meaningful name can be created. The Data Site name must be unique within the parent Organization Unit.

A Data Site requires a parent Organization Unit that either contains the Data Site or is responsible for managing the Data Site. Organization Unit was described in the Data Responsibility Chapter.

Scenario 3.1. Internal Data Sites.

An organization has numerous major and minor data sites scattered throughout the organization ranging from their primary mainframe computer, to a variety of servers, to individual personal computers, as well as a variety of manual libraries where a large quantity of documents are stored. The decision was made to begin with the databases on the mainframe computer, then servers, then personal computers, and finally the manual libraries. The data sites would be documented as each new set of data was encountered.

Scenario 3.2. External Data Sites.

An organization that obtains data from many external organizations is not concerned about where those data are stored in the external organizations. Their only concern is documenting the initial location within their organization where those external data are stored when they are first received by the organization. Any downstream distribution of those data will be documented at a later time.

Data Product

A Data Product is a major independent set of documentation of any type that contains the names, definitions, structure, integrity, and so on, of the existing data. It can be an information system, a database, a data dictionary, a major project, a major data model that provides insight into the existing data.

Data Product has an Operational End Date, which can be used to indicate that the Data Product is Obsolete. There is no status code that indicates an obsolete Data Product.

Data Products are not deleted when they become obsolete and are no longer in use. They clarify the understanding and are retained for future reference.

The detail data for a Data Product are entered anytime a Data Product is identified.

> Data Product. Acronym
> Data Product. Comment
> Data Product. Definition (R)
> Data Product. Evolution Description
> Data Product. Hardware Description
> Data Product. Name (R)
> Data Product. Operational Begin Date (R)
> Data Product. Operational End Date
> Data Product. Preferred Common Indicator (R)
> Data Product. Record Count
> Data Product. Software Description
>
> Data Product Type. Name (R)
> Organization Unit. Name (R)
> Organization Unit. Name / Data Site. Name (R)

The data product name may or may not be readily apparent. If the name is not apparent, a suitable name can be created. The Data Product. Name must be unique within the parent Organization Unit.

The Data Site where the Data Product is stored does not necessarily belong to the same Organization Unit that is responsible for the Data Product. For example, the Organization Unit responsible for an off-site data storage is not the same Organization Unit that is responsible for managing the data resource.

Data Product Type is a data reference set that qualifies a Data Product. Each organization implementing Data Resource Data can designate the data reference items to suit their particular needs, such as Information System, Database, Data Dictionary, and so on. New data reference items can be added at any time.

Scenario 3.3. High Priority Databases.

An organization has designated their initial high priority databases that are either business critical or are used extensively throughout the organization. Each of those databases is documented as a Data Product. As additional high priority databases are discovered, they will be documented as Data

22

Products.

Scenario 3.4. External Data Documentation.

An organization determined that no useful documentation existed in their database management systems and decided to begin understanding their data resource through all the existing manual or electronic documentation outside the database management systems. At the same time, any insight of knowledge workers that became available would also be documented. The process began by identifying all the existing manual and electronic documentation and entering each as a Data Product.

Data Product Set

Data Product Set is a major grouping or cluster of closely related data within a Data Product, such as a data entity, a data table, a data record, a data record type, a screen, a report, a document, a computer program, and so on, that contain one or more data items or data fields.

A Data Product Set can have a subordinate Data Product Set Variation that documents multiple variations in a Data Product Set, such as a data record type, a data entity type, changes over time, or any other breakdown of a Data Product Set. Each of these variations would be documented as a Data Product Set Variation. Only one level of Data Product Set Variation is allowed.

Data Product Set has an End Date, which can be used to indicate that the Data Product Set is Obsolete. There is no status code that indicates an obsolete Data Product Set.

Data Product Sets are not deleted when Obsolete. They clarify the understanding of the existing data resource and are retained for future reference.

The detail data for a Data Product Set can be entered anytime a Data Product Set is identified within a Data Product. The parent Data Product must be documented before the Data Product Set can be documented.

> Data Product Set. Begin Date (R)
> Data Product Set. Comment
> Data Product Set. Cross Reference Comment
> Data Product Set. Data Integrity Rules
> Data Product Set. Definition (R)
> Data Product Set. End Date
> Data Product Set. Name (R)
> Data Product Set. Preferred Common Indicator (R)
> Data Product Set. Shared Indicator (R)

Data Product. Name ^ "Origin" Data Product Set. Name (R/P)
Data Name Abbreviation Scheme. Name (R)
Data Product. Name (R/P)
Data Product Set Medium. Name (R)
Data Product Set Type. Name (R)

The data product set name may not be readily apparent. If it's not readily apparent, a meaningful Data Product Set. Name can be created. The Data Product Set. Name must be unique within the parent Data Product.

A Data Product Set Variation cannot reference itself as the "Origin" Data Product Set.

A parent Data Product is required for a Data Product Set, but is prevented for a Data Product Set Variation. An "Origin" Data Product Set is required for a Data Product Set Variation, but is prevented for a Data Product Set.

A Data Name Abbreviation Scheme is required, even if that Data Name Abbreviation Scheme indicates no formal Data Name Word Set or formal Data Name Abbreviation Algorithm. The Data Name Abbreviation Scheme is explained in the Data Lexicon Chapter.

Data Product Set Medium is a data reference set that qualifies a Data Product Set. Each organization implementing Data Resource Data can designate the data reference items to suit their particular needs, such as Tabular Data, Book, Drawing, Photograph, and so on. New data reference items can be added at any time.

Data Product Set Type is a data reference set that qualifies a Data Product Set. Each organization implementing Data Resource Data can designate the data reference items to suit their particular needs, such as File, Document, Report, Screen, and so on. New data reference items can be added at any time.

The documentation of multiple database dictionaries can be done two different ways. First, the data dictionary and its location can be documented as a Data Site; each database within that data dictionary can be documented as a Data Product; and each data file within a database can be documented as a Data Product Set. Second, each database can be documented as a Data Product with a statement in the Definition specifying the data dictionary from which the material was taken.

Note that Data Product was not made recursive because it would unnecessarily complicate the structure of the Data Resource Data.

Scenario 3.5. High Priority Databases.

An organization has documented their high priority databases and are continuing to understand the data within each of those databases. The data records within each of the databases are identified and documented as Data Product Sets. When multiple data record types are encountered, such as an A Record, a B Record, and so on, a single Data Product Set is established and a Data Product Set Variation is established for each of the data record types. The Data Product Set would not contain any subordinate Data Product Units, but each of the Data Product Set Variations would contain their respective Data Product Units.

Scenario 3.6. Single Database Dictionaries.

An organization has multiple manual and electronic data dictionaries, each of which documents a single database. The data dictionary, which represents a database, is documented as a Data Product. The data files within that database, which represent data records, are documented as Data Product Sets within the Data Product.

Scenario 3.7. Multiple Database Dictionaries.

An organization has multiple manual and electronic data dictionaries, each of which documents multiple databases. The data stewards decide that the second option for documenting multiple database dictionaries would be used, which is to document each database as a Data Product with a statement in the Definition specifying the data dictionary from which the material was taken.

Data Product Unit

Data Product Unit is an individual data item or data field in a Data Product Set, such as a data attribute in a data model, a data column in a table, a data field on a screen or a report, and so on.

A Data Product Unit can have a subordinate Data Product Unit Variation that documents multiple variations in a Data Product Unit. For example, a Data Product Unit might represent a multiple valued data field, a variable meaning data field, and so on. Each of these individual facts would be documented as a Data Product Unit Variation. Only one level of subordinate Data Product Unit Variation is allowed.

Data Product Unit has an End Date, which can be used to indicate that the Data Product Unit is Obsolete. There is no status code that indicates an obsolete Data Product Unit.

Data Product Units are not deleted when Obsolete. They clarify the understanding and are retained for future reference.

The detail data for a Data Product Unit can be entered anytime a Data Product Unit is identified within a Data Product Set. The parent Data Product Set must be documented before the Data Product Unit can be documented.

> Data Product Unit. Accuracy Description (R)
> Data Product Unit. Begin Date (R)
> Data Product Unit. Comment
> Data Product Unit. Concatenated Indicator (R)
> Data Product Unit. Condition
> Data Product Unit. Conforming Indicator (R)
> Data Product Unit. Created Indicator (R)
> Data Product Unit. Cross Reference Comment
> Data Product Unit. Data Integrity Rules
> Data Product Unit. Decimal Places
> Data Product Unit. Definition (R)
> Data Product Unit. Denormalized Indicator (R)
> Data Product Unit. End Date
> Data Product Unit. Length (R)
> Data Product Unit. Mnemonic
> Data Product Unit. Name
> Data Product Unit. Null Indicator (R)
> Data Product Unit. Origin Description (R)
> Data Product Unit. Preferred Common Indicator (R)
> Data Product Unit. Preferred Source Indicator (R)
> Data Product Unit. Primary Key Indicator (R)
> Data Product Unit. Sequence
>
> Data Characteristic Variation. Name Complete
> Data Format. Name (R)
> Data Product. Name ^ Data Product Set. Name (R/P)
> Data Product. Name ^ Data Product Set. Name ^ {"Inherit" Data Product Unit. Name | "Inherit" Data Product Unit. Mnemonic}
> Data Product. Name ^ Data Product Set. Name ^ {"Origin" Data Product Unit. Name | "Origin" Data Product Unit. Mnemonic}

A data product unit name is usually apparent, although it may be in a variety of different physical notations and abbreviations. When a name is apparent, it is entered. In some situations a mnemonic is used rather than a name, and a name is not entered. Either a Name, or Mnemonic, or both are required.

A Data Product Unit can inherit the documentation of an identical Data Product Unit in another Data Product Set that has already been documented.

That inheritance eliminates the need to provide a detailed documentation of the current Data Product Unit.

A Data Product Unit Variation cannot reference itself as the "Origin" Data Product Unit.

A parent Data Product Set is required for a Data Product Unit, but is prevented for a Data Product Unit Variation. An "Origin" Data Product Unit is required for a Data Product Unit Variation, but is prevented for a Data Product Unit.

Data Format is a data reference set that qualifies a Data Product Unit. Each organization implementing Data Resource Data can designate the data reference items to suit their particular needs, such as Character, Integer, Floating Point, and so on. New data reference items can be added at any time.

Scenario 3.8. Variable Fact Data Field.

A textual data field named BD was encountered that contained either a birth date or a reason why no birth date was obtained. Clearly these are two different facts that need to be documented. A Data Product Unit is created to document BD with the definition that appears with the database and an additional notation that the data field can contain two different facts, but only one of those facts in any data record.

Then two subordinate Data Product Unit Variations are created, one for Birth Date and one for No Birth Data Reason with the appropriate definitions.

Scenario 3.9. Multiple Fact Data Field.

A textual data field named Comment was encountered that contained a series of different facts that were separated by a comma. Each of these facts needs to be documented. A Data Product Unit is created to document Comment with the definition that appears with the database and an additional notation that multiple facts are contained within Comment separated by a comma. The Sequence data characteristic indicates the sequence of the Comment data field within the data record.

Then subordinate Data Product Unit Variations are created for each fact within Comment and their respective definitions. The Sequence data characteristic in the Data Product Unit Variations indicates the sequence of the facts within the Comment data field.

Scenario 3.10. Identical Data Fields in a Data Record.

A data file has been identified that has multiple data record types, however the first several data fields of each data record type are identical. In this situation, the first data fields that are identical are documented as Data Product Units within the "Origin" Data Product Set. The unique data fields for each data record type are documented as Data Product Units within their respective Data Product Set Variation representing the specific data record type.

Note that an "Origin" Data Product Set can have subordinate Data Product Units as well as subordinate Data Product Set Variations.

Data Product Code

A Data Product Code is any coded data value that exists in a Data Product Unit or Data Product Unit Variation. It represents a specific data property of interest.

A Data Product Code can have a subordinate Data Product Code Variation that documents multiple variations in a Data Product Code. For example, a Data Product Code might represent multiple data properties or multiple data subjects. Each of these individual data properties would be documented as a Data Product Code Variation. Only one level of subordinate Data Product Code Variation is allowed.

Data Product Code has an End Date, which can be used to indicate that the Data Product Code is Obsolete. There is no status code that indicates an obsolete Data Product Code.

Data Product Codes are not deleted when Obsolete. They clarify the understanding and are retained for future reference.

The detail data for a Data Product Code can be entered anytime a Data Product Code is identified within a Data Product Unit. The parent Data Product Unit must be documented before a Data Product Code can be documented.

> Data Product Code. Begin Date
> Data Product Code. Comment
> Data Product Code. Created Indicator (R)
> Data Product Code. Cross Reference Comment
> Data Product Code. Definition
> Data Product Code. End Date
> Data Product Code. Name
> Data Product Code. Preferred Common Indicator (R)
> Data Product Code. Value

Data Product. Name ^ Data Product Set. Name ^ {Data Product. Unit. Name | Data Product Unit. Mnemonic} ^ {"Origin" Data Product Code. Value | "Origin" Data Product Code. Name}

Data Product. Name ^ Data Product Set. Name ^ {Data Product Unit. Name | Data Product Unit. Mnemonic} (R/P)

Data Product Codes may or may not have a formal name. In many situations a code could represent a coded data value and a name could represent the formal name. In other situations a code could represent the name and a name could represent a very short definition. A formal definition may or may not exist. Each organization, and the person documenting the Data Product Data, must determine what existing Data Product Code values represent the Code, the Name, and the Definition and document them accordingly.

A parent Data Product Unit is required for a Data Product Code, but is prevented for a Data Product Code Variation. An "Origin" Data Product Code is required for a Data Product Code Variation, but is prevented for a Data Product Code.

Scenario 3.11. Multiple Property Data Code.

Data codes for mgmt_lvl were encountered that consist of multiple data properties, such as E for Executive, M for Manager and Supervisor, and W for Lead Worker and Worker. The organization desires to separate these data codes into single data properties.

A Data Product Code is created for mgmt_lvl with the definition existing in the database and an explanation that the codes represent multiple data properties.

Then subordinate Data Product Code Variations are created for each of the individual data properties using the existing coded data values, such as E for Executive, M for Manager, M for Supervisor, L for Lead Worker, and W for Worker.

The duplicate codes for the different data properties will be resolved during data cross-referencing.

Scenario 3.12. Multiple Subject Data Code

Data codes for empl_typ were encountered that consist of gender, hair color, and eye color, such as 1 for Male, Blond Hair, Blue Eyes, 2 for Female, Blond Hair, Blue Eyes, and so on. The organization desires to separate these data codes into single subject and single property data codes.

A Data Product Code is created for empl_typ with the definition existing in the database and an explanation that the codes represent multiple data subjects.

Then subordinate Data Product Code Variations are created for each of the individual properties within their respective data subjects, such as 1 for Male, 1 for Blond Hair, 1 for Blue Eyes, 2 for Female, 2 for Blond Hair, 2 for Blue Eyes, and so on.

The duplicate codes for the different data subjects will be resolved during data cross-referencing.

DATA PRODUCT KEYS

Data Product Sets can have both Primary Keys and Foreign Keys, although their identification may be elusive and the process to identify them may be difficult. The Data Product Keys may be identified by the data name, by their use in computer applications, by the appearance of the same data name in another Data Product Set, by some type of indicator, by the data values, and so on. In many situations considerable investigation may be required to identify and document Data Product Keys.

The data subject-relation diagram for Data Product Keys is shown in Figure 3.2. It contains two major segments for Data Product Primary Keys and Data Product Foreign Keys. Each of these segments is explained in the following subsections.

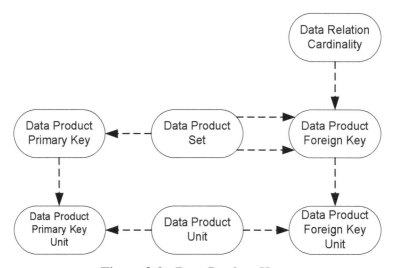

Figure 3.2. Data Product Keys.

Primary Keys

A Data Product Set can have one or more primary keys, each of which can be comprised of one or more Data Product Units / Variations. Generally, the primary key is comprised of Data Product Units, but could be comprised of Data Product Unit Variations where only a portion of the Data Product Unit is involved in the primary key.

The Data Product Primary Keys are usually documented in addition to the Data Product Unit. Primary Key Indicator.

The detail data for each Data Product Primary Key can be entered anytime a Data Product Primary Key is identified. The parent Data Product Set must be documented before the Data Product Primary Keys can be documented.

> Data Product Primary Key. Comment
> Data Product Primary Key. Explicit Indicator (R)
>
> Data Product. Name ^ Data Product Set. Name (R)

The detail data for each Data Product Primary Key Unit / Variation comprising a Data Product Primary Key can be entered when it is identified. The Data Product Units comprising the Data Product Primary Key must be documented before the Data Product Primary Key Units can be documented.

> Data Product Primary Key Unit. Comment
>
> Data Product Primary Key. System Identifier (R)
> Data Product. Name ^ Data Product Set. Name ^ {Data Product Unit. Name | Data Product Unit. Mnemonic} (R)

Scenario 3.13. Data Product Primary Key.

A primary key in emp was identified for employees that consist of emp-l-n and emp_l_ssn, which were identified as the employee's last name and the last four digits of their Social Security Number.

A Data Product Primary Key is created for the emp Data Product Set. Then two subordinate Data Product Primary Key Units are created with references to Data Product Units for emp_l_n and for emp_l_ssn.

Scenario 3.14. Unnecessary Data in Data Product Primary Key.

A primary key was identified that consists of std_id and std_admt_yr, representing the student's identifier and the calendar year in which the student was first admitted to the university. The determination was made that the student identifier was unique and that the calendar year they were first admitted was not necessary for unique identification.

31

A Data Product Primary Key is created with two subordinate Data Product Primary Key Units for std_id and std_admit_yr, because that is what the existing data actually contain. However, a comment is made in the Data Product Primary Key that the calendar year in which the student was first admitted is not necessary for unique identification.

Note that during data cross-referencing the appropriate Primary Key within the Common Data that provides unique identification will be documented.

Foreign Keys

A Data Product Set can have one or more foreign keys to a parent Data Product Set, each of which can be comprised of one or more Data Product Units / Variations. Generally, the foreign key is comprised of Data Product Units, but could be comprised of Data Product Unit Variations where only a portion of a Data Product Unit is involved in the foreign key.

The detail data for each Data Product Foreign Key can be entered anytime a Data Product Primary Key is identified. The "Local" and "Parent" Data Product Sets must be documented before the Data Product Foreign Keys can be documented.

> Data Product Foreign Key. Comment
> Data Product Foreign Key. Data Relation Name From
> Data Product Foreign Key. Data Relation Name To
> Data Product Foreign Key. Data Integrity Rules
> Data Product Foreign Key. Explicit Indicator (R)
>
> Data Product. Name ^ "Local" Data Product Set. Name (R)
> Data Product. Name ^ "Parent" Data Product Set. Name (R)
> Data Relation Cardinality. Name (R)

The "Local" Data Product Set and the "Parent" Data Product Set must not be the same Data Product Set.

Data Relation Cardinality is a data reference set that qualifies Data Product Foreign Key. Each organization implementing Data Resource Data can designate the data reference items to suit their particular needs, such as 1:1, 1:M, M:M, and so on.

The detail data for each Data Product Foreign Key Unit / Variation comprising a Data Product Foreign Key can be entered when identified. The Data Product Units comprising the foreign key must be documented before the Data Product Foreign Key Units can be documented.

> Data Product Foreign Key Unit. Comment
>
> Data Product Foreign Key. System Identifier (R)

Data Product. Name ^ Data Product Set. Name ^ {Data Product Unit. Name | Data Product Unit. Mnemonic} (R)

Scenario 3.15. Data Product Foreign Key.

A foreign key is identified in emp for the department where the employee works consisting of dpt_id.

A Data Product Foreign Key is created for the emp Data Product Set. Then a subordinate Data Product Foreign Key Unit is created with a reference to the Data Product Unit for dpt_id.

DATA PRODUCT STEWARD

Data Product Steward identifies the Data Stewards that are responsible for the Data Products, and the specific Data Steward Function and Data Steward Level for those Data Stewards. Data Steward, Data Steward Function, and Data Steward Level were explained in the Data Responsibility Chapter.

The data subject-relation diagram for Data Product Stewards is shown in Figure 3.3. It contains one major segment for Data Product Stewards, which is explained below the diagram.

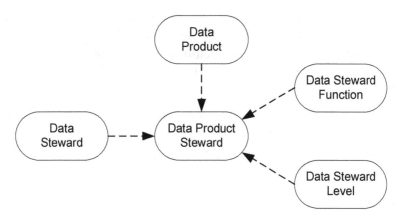

Figure 3.3. Data Product Stewards.

The detail data for each Data Product Stewards can be entered anytime a Data Product Steward is identified. The Data Steward must be documented before the Data Product Steward can be documented.

> Data Product Steward. Begin Date (R)
> Data Product Steward. Comment
> Data Product Steward. End Date
>
> Data Product. Name (R)
> Data Steward. Name Complete (R)

Data Steward Function. Name (R)
Data Steward Level. Name (R)

Data Steward Function and Data Steward Level are data reference sets that were explained in the Data Responsibility Chapter. The appropriate Data Reference Items for Data Steward Function and Data Steward Level can be assigned to Data Product Steward.

Scenario 3.16. Data Product Steward.

A data steward has been identified who has detailed knowledge about student data which has been acquired during their 25 years with the university. That person is documented as a Data Steward as explained in the Data Responsibility Chapter. That Data Steward is then assigned as a Data Product Steward to all Data Products that contain data about which that person has knowledge. As long as that Data Steward has knowledge about any of the data in a Data Product, they are documented as a Data Product Steward for that Data Product. Data Product Steward. Comment explains the type of knowledge that Data Steward has about that Data Product.

DATA PRODUCT MODEL

Existing Data Products may already be documented using some type of data model diagram or diagrams may be developed during the Data Inventory Function. Data Model Diagrams document the existence of these data model diagrams and the Data Products or Data Product Sets that are shown on those Data Model Diagrams.

The data subject-relation diagram for Data Product Models is shown in Figure 3.4. It contains three major segments for Data Model Diagram, Data Product Model, and Data Product Set Model. Each of these segments is explained below.

Data Model Diagram

Data Model Diagram contains the actual data model diagram or a reference to an external source where that data model diagram can be located. The detail data for each Data Model Diagram can be entered anytime a data model diagram is identified.

Data Model Diagram. Comment
Data Model Diagram. Description (R)
Data Model Diagram. Effective Date (R)
Data Model Diagram. External Reference
Data Model Diagram. Graphic
Data Model Diagram. Name (R)

34

Data Model Diagram. Obsolete Date

Data Model Diagram Type. Name (R)

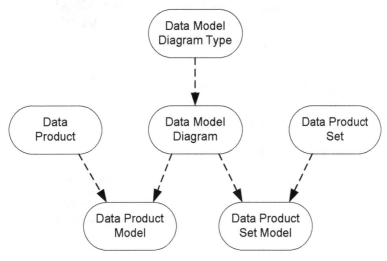

Figure 3.4. Data Product Models.

Data Model Diagram Type is a data reference set that qualifies Data Model Diagram.   Each organization implementing Data Resource Data can designate the data reference items to suit their particular needs, such as Strategic, Tactical, Detail, Analytical, and so on.

Scenario 3.17. Existing Data Model Diagrams.

An organization starts into the documentation of its disparate data resource and identifies major subject areas and their priorities.   When the documentation begins for a specific subject area, an inventory is made of all the data model diagrams that can be located that might represent the existing data in that major subject area.   Those data model diagrams are then documented as Data Model Diagrams.   Anytime additional data model diagrams are discovered, they are documented as Data Model Diagrams.

Scenario 3.18. New Data Model Diagrams.

During the disparate data documentation process, the organization finds many of the major subject areas that have no associated data model diagrams. To provide a pictorial overview of the major subject area, one or more Visio diagrams are developed and are revised whenever new insight is gained. A Data Model Diagram is created for each of those Visio diagrams.

Data Product Model

Data Product Model shows each Data Model Diagram where a Data Product appears. The detail data for each Data Product Model can be entered anytime a Data Product is identified on a Data Model Diagram. The Data Model Diagram must be documented before the Data Product Model can be documented.

> Data Product Model. Comment
> Data Model Diagram. Name (R)
> Data Product. Name (R)

Scenario 3.19. Data Product Models.

The organization documenting their disparate data identifies Data Model Diagrams that represent a high level view of their Data Products. A Data Product Model is created for each Data Model Diagram that contains insights about the Data Product.

Data Product Set Model

Data Product Set Model shows each Data Model Diagram where a Data Product Set appears. The detail data for each Data Product Set Model can be entered anytime a Data Product Set is identified on a Data Model Diagram. The Data Model Diagram must be documented before the Data Product Set Model can be documented.

> Data Product Set Model. Comment
> Data Model Diagram. Name (R)
> Data Product. Name ^ Data Product Set. Name (R)

Scenario 3.20. Data Product Set Models.

The organization documenting their disparate data identifies Data Model Diagrams that represent a detailed view of their Data Product Sets. A Data Product Set Model is created for each Data Model Diagram that contains insights about the Data Product Set.

SUMMARY

The Data Inventory Function documents all the existing, often disparate, data that the organization creates or acquires from outside the organization. It prepares the existing data for cross-referencing to the Common Data so they can be thoroughly understood in a common context. When they have been thoroughly understood and the preferred data designated, then the existing data can be transformed to a comparate data resource.

Chapter 4

COMMON DATA

Common data are the context within which all data are understood.

The data understanding process continues with the Common Data Function consisting of Common Data according to the concepts, principles, and techniques of the Common Data Architecture Paradigm. The Common Data must have formal data names, comprehensive data definitions, proper data structure, and precise data integrity rules. They must be developed in the sequence of business world perception, to business data schema, to logical data schema, to physical data schema.

COMMON DATA APPROACH

Common Data that are documented as Data Resource Data represent the logical data schema that are based on the organization's perception of the business world where it operates, and the data needed by the organization to operate successfully in that business world. Common Data are developed to fully support the current and future business information demand of the organization.

The approach to documenting Common Data includes the sequence of Common Data development, the development and enhancement of initial Common Data, the levels of detail for Common Data, and the formal names for Common Data.

Sequence

The initial Common Data can be developed before, during, or after the Data Inventory Function. Either approach is acceptable, but both Data Product Data and the initial Common Data must be completed for any specific subject area before data cross-referencing can be done. In other words, the Data Inventory and the development of initial Common Data are independent processes that need to be completed prior to data cross-referencing.

Initial Common Data

Initial Common Data documentation begins with the organization's perception of the business world where they operate. The major business objects and business events that are of interest to the organization and about which they capture and maintain data become the initial data subjects and data relations in the organizations subject-oriented data resource. A few major data characteristics, data definitions, and major data integrity rules may be documented, but the detail documentation will be done during data cross-referencing.

An organization must not attempt to document all of the Common Data prior to data cross-referencing. Many times an organization tries to document all of the Common Data before continuing with the data cross-referencing. That approach is a waste of time and effort. The initial Common Data will be more appropriately enhanced during data cross-referencing process.

Many organizations believe they already have their Common Data when, in fact, they do not have any Common Data. They believe that the more recently developed data can be documented as Common Data. That belief comes from the fact that more recently developed data are far better understood than older disparate data. However the more recently developed data usually do not meet the criteria for Common Data.

The same situation is true with most existing data models, data standards, predefined data models, and so on. They typically do not meet the criteria for Common Data, and seldom represent logical data. Most existing data are typically implemented from physical data models, and some may not even have the benefit of physical data models. In addition, most data models are incomplete because they lack formal data names, comprehensive data definitions, and precise data integrity rules.

The best approach is to treat all existing data and all existing data models as Data Product Data and document them accordingly. Then, during the data cross-referencing process, the Common Data are enhanced according to the established concepts, principles, and techniques of the Common Data Architecture Paradigm to accurately represent the Data Product Data.

The only exception is if an organization has developed data according to the concepts, principles, and techniques of the Common Data Architecture Paradigm, then those data can be documented as Common Data. However, a quick review should be made of those data to ensure that they meet the criteria for Common Data.

Levels of Detail

The Common Data Architecture Paradigm does not use the term *conceptual* because it is relatively meaningless to most people, and its development is often used as an excuse to jump directly to physical data modeling because the logical data modeling has been completed and accepted. The proper terms to use are *Strategic*, representing a 30,000 foot view of the data for executives; *Tactical*, representing a 10,000 foot view of the data for managers; and *Detail*, representing a ground level view of the data for knowledge workers. These terms are more meaningful and more understandable to business professionals.

The Data Subjects, Data Characteristics, and Primary Keys contain indicators for Strategic, Tactical, and Detail level data. Those indicators can be used to develop data resource models for those levels of detail. Those indicators are not used for foreign keys because the foreign key appearance on data resource models depends on both the local and parent data subject being present.

Common Data Names

All of the formal data name notations can be used when documenting Common Data. For example, Student can be used for the Student data subject; [Graduate] Student can be used for a data occurrence group representing graduate students; and "Tutor" Student can be used for a student who plays a role as a tutor to other students. Data version notations can be used for major changes in the definition of a data subject, such as Employee <Before 1991> and Employee <1991 to Present>. Any minor changes in the definitions are included in the comprehensive definitions and in the comments rather than in variations in the data subject.

Some software applications are unable to handle the notations and punctuations used in formal Data Naming Taxonomy, and use that excuse to claim that the formal Data Naming Taxonomy is flawed. However, the basic problem is with the software application that was developed in such a way that it does not allow special characters in a formal data name. No valid reason exists why software applications should not be able to handle the special characters in a formal data name according to the Data Naming Taxonomy.

COMMON DATA NUCLEUS

The Common Data Nucleus includes Basic Common Data, Common Data Reference Sets, Data Subjects, Data Characteristics, Data Characteristic

Variations, Data Reference Set Variations, Data Reference Items, and Data Subject Models.

Basic Common Data

The data subject-relation diagram for Basic Common Data is shown in Figure 4.1. It consists of Data Subject, Data Characteristic, Data Characteristic Variation, Data Reference Set Variation, Data Reference Item, and Data Subject Model. The recursive data relation for Data Subject indicates a Data Subject Variation.

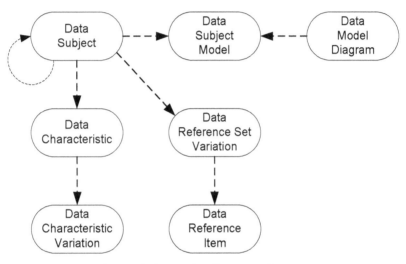

Figure 4.1. Basic Common Data.

Common Data Reference Sets

The data subject-relation diagram for the Common Data Status data reference set and the basic Common Data Subjects that it qualifies is shown in Figure 4.2.

Common Data Status is part of the Common Data Architecture Paradigm, such as Accepted, Obsolete, Proposed, and Rejected, but can be modified to suit an organization's particular needs. An Obsolete status should be used in conjunction with an End Data to indicate the date which the data became obsolete. Data Resource Data are not deleted, but are kept for thorough understanding of the data resource.

Data Subject

Data Subject is the highest level in the Basic Common Data hierarchy that represents a business object or event in the business world or a normalization of those business objects and events. It has a recursive data relation that shows derived data subjects, such as for spatial data, dimensional data analysis, data occurrence groups, and so on.

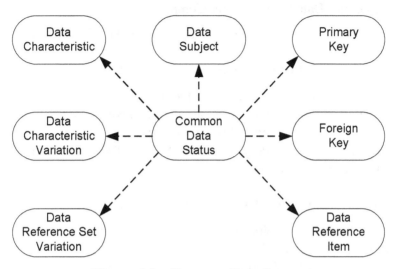

Figure 4.2. Common Data Status.

The detail data for a Data Subject can be entered anytime a Data Subject is identified, either during development of the initial Common Data or by enhancement during data cross-referencing. The data reference sets must be documented before a Data Subject can be documented.

Data Subject. Begin Date (R)
Data Subject. Comment
Data Subject. Data Focus Indicator (R)
Data Subject. Data Reference Set Indicator (R)
Data Subject. Definition (R)
Data Subject. Derived Indicator (R)
Data Subject. Detail Indicator (R)
Data Subject. End Date
Data Subject. Fundamental Indicator (R)
Data Subject. Image Indicator (R)
Data Subject. Multiple Version Indicator (R)
Data Subject. Name Abbreviated
Data Subject. Name Complete (R)
Data Subject. Preferred Data Integrity Rules
Data Subject. Spatial Indicator (R)
Data Subject. Strategic Indicator (R)
Data Subject. Tabular Indicator (R)
Data Subject. Tactical Indicator (R)
Data Subject. Temporal Indicator (R)

Data Subject. Textual Indicator (R)
Data Subject. Video Indicator (R)

Common Data Status. Name Complete (R)
"Origin" Data Subject. Name Complete

A derived Data Subject cannot reference itself as the "Origin" Data Subject.

Scenario 4.1. Initial Data Subject.

Business professionals in a university identify students, building units, staff, faculty, departments, and courses as major business objects that are of interest to the university and about which they capture and maintain data. Accordingly, Student, Building Unit, Staff, Faculty, Department and Course are created as Data Subjects.

Scenario 4.2. Data Subject From Data Cross-Referencing.

Data stewards are cross-referencing Data Product Data to the Common Data and identify data subjects for academic year and academic term that are not in the Common Data. Accordingly, Academic Year and Academic Term are created as Data Subjects.

Scenario 4.3. Data Occurrence Group.

An organization decides to document all of their data occurrence groups as Data Resource Data. Accordingly, any set of data occurrences routinely extracted from a Data Subject were documented as Data Resource Data. For example, [Pilot Certified] Employee was documented as a subordinate variation to the Data Subject for Employee and [Salvage] Vehicle was documented as a subordinate variation to the Data Subject for Vehicle. The data occurrence group is identified by the formal data name that uses [ ] to identify the specific nature of the data occurrence group.

Scenario 4.4. Data Occurrence Role.

The data stewards decide to document any data occurrence roles as Data Resource Data to prevent the development of disparate data occurrence roles. Accordingly, any role played by a data occurrence in a Data Subject is documented as Data Resource Data. For example, "Maintenance" Vendor was documented as a subordinate variation to the Data Subject for Vendor and "Customer Service" Employee was documented as a subordinate variation to the Data Subject for Employee. The data occurrence role is identified by the formal data name that uses " " to identify the specific nature of the data occurrence role.

Scenario 4.5. Levels of Detail.

Data stewards decide to document the levels of detail for the Common Data so that appropriate data resource models can be developed directly from the Data Resource Data for executives, managers, and knowledge workers. Accordingly, the Strategic Indicator, Tactical Indicator, and Detail Indicator were used on Data Subjects and Data Characteristics to indicate the level of the data resource model on which they would appear.

Note that Data Subjects and Data Characteristics can appear on multiple levels of data resource models, such as Strategic and Tactical, or Tactical and Detail, and so on. However, an effort should be made to assure that a Data Subject or Data Characteristic does not appear on a Strategic data resource model, not on a Tactical data resource model, then again on the Detail data resource model.

Data Characteristic

Data Characteristic is the second level in the Basic Common Data hierarchy that represents facts within a Data Subject. The Data Characteristic. Name Complete is a concatenation of the Data Subject. Name Complete and the fact name, such as Student. Birth Date. The Data Subject portion of the Data Characteristic. Name Complete must match the parent Data Subject. Name Complete.

The detail data for a Data Characteristic can be entered anytime a Data Characteristic is identified. The parent Data Subject and data reference sets must be documented before the Data Characteristic can be documented.

> Data Characteristic. Begin Date (R)
> Data Characteristic. Comment
> Data Characteristic. Conditional Data Source Rule
> Data Characteristic. Definition (R)
> Data Characteristic. Detail Indicator (R)
> Data Characteristic. Elemental Data Indicator (R)
> Data Characteristic. End Date
> Data Characteristic. Fundamental Indicator (R)
> Data Characteristic. Name Abbreviated
> Data Characteristic. Name Complete (R)
> Data Characteristic. Preferred Data Integrity Rules
> Data Characteristic. Primitive Indicator (R)
> Data Characteristic. Spatial Indicator (R)
> Data Characteristic. Strategic Indicator (R)
> Data Characteristic. Tactical Indicator (R)
> Data Characteristic. Temporal Indicator (R)

Common Data Status. Name (R)
Data Subject. Name Complete (R)

Scenario 4.6. Initial Data Characteristics.

The major facts for a student are identified, such as their complete name, birth date, permanent address, and so on. These facts are entered as Data Characteristics within the Student Data Subject.

Scenario 4.7. Data Characteristics From Data Cross-Referencing.

Data stewards are cross-referencing Data Product Data to the Common Data and identify facts for the length, surface width, number of lanes, and shoulder width for a road segment. These facts are entered as Data Characteristics within the Road Segment Data Subject.

Data Characteristic Variation

Data Characteristic Variation is the third level in the Basic Common Data Hierarchy that represents a variant of a fact that has been documented as a Data Characteristic. The Data Characteristic Variation. Name Complete is a concatenation of the Data Characteristic. Name Complete and the variant name, such as Student. Birth Date, CYMD. The Data Characteristic portion of the Data Characteristic Variation. Name Complete must match the parent Data Characteristic. Name Complete.

The detail data for a Data Characteristic Variation can be entered anytime a Data Characteristic Variation is identified. However, Data Characteristic Variations are seldom added when creating the initial Common Data. They are typically documented during data cross-referencing because that is when the variants are actually identified. The parent Data Characteristic and Data Reference Sets must be documented before the Data Characteristic Variation can be documented.

Data Characteristic Variation. Begin Date (R)
Data Characteristic Variation. Comment
Data Characteristic Variation. Definition (R)
Data Characteristic Variation. End Date
Data Characteristic Variation. Name Abbreviated
Data Characteristic Variation. Name Complete (R)
Data Characteristic Variation. Partial Fact Indicator (R)[2]
Data Characteristic Variation. Preferred Data Integrity Rules
Data Characteristic Variation. Preferred Indicator (R)

---

[2] Added since Data Resource Data was published. Refer to Appendix A for details.

Common Data Status. Name (R)
Data Characteristic. Name Complete (R)

Scenario 4.8. Date Fact Variants.

During data cross-referencing data stewards identify variants for a student's birth data in the form of m/d/y, cymd, and y/m/d, all of which are text fields. Data Characteristic Variations are created for Student. Birth Date, M/D/Y, Student. Birth Date, CYMD, and Student. Birth Date, Y/M/D.

Scenario 4.9. Measurement Fact Variants.

Data stewards identify variants for the measurement of well depths within the state, which include feet, yards, and meters, and one isolated case of fathoms. Data Characteristic Variations are created for Well. Depth, Feet, Well. Depth, Yards, Well. Depth, Meters, and Well. Depth, Fathoms.

Data Reference Set Variation

Data Reference Set Variation is a variation of a Data Subject that represents a data reference set. A data reference set is documented as a Data Subject, and any variation in that data reference set, such as a difference in the domain of data reference items, their names, their definitions, or their code values, are documented as a Data Reference Set Variation. The Data Reference Set Variation. Name Complete is a concatenation of the Data Subject. Name Complete and the variant name, such as Management Level; Personnel. The Data Subject portion of the Data Reference Set Variation. Name Complete must match the parent Data Subject. Name Complete.

The detail data for a Data Reference Set Variation can be entered anytime a Data Reference Set Variation is identified. Data Reference Set Variations are seldom added when creating the initial Common Data. They are typically added during data cross-referencing because that is when the variants are actually identified. The parent Data Subject and the data reference sets must be documented before the Data Reference Set Variation can be documented.

Data Reference Set Variation. Begin Date (R)
Data Reference Set Variation. Comment
Data Reference Set Variation. Definition (R)
Data Reference Set Variation. End Date
Data Reference Set Variation. Name Abbreviated
Data Reference Set Variation. Name Complete (R)
Data Reference Set Variation. Preferred Indicator (R)

Common Data Status. Name (R)

45

Data Subject. Name Complete (R)

The Data Reference Set Variation does not have any foreign keys to the Data Characteristic Variations that represent the Data Reference Item name, definition, or code. Data Reference Set Variations only document the domain and the values of the Data Reference Items, not the format of those values. The format applies only to the Data Product Data. Tracking the format of all the Data Reference Items would be too confusing and time consuming, and would not produce any material benefit.

Scenario 4.10. Gender Reference Set Variants.

A team in a school district is working on identifying and understanding disparate data, and identifies numerous variants for gender code throughout the organization, such as M / F / U used in Personnel, M / W / O used in state reporting, B / G / N used in student registration, and 0 / 1 that originated from Personnel, from the State, from the Registrar, and from an unknown source. Four Data Reference Set Variations are created for Gender; Personnel, Gender; State, Gender; Registration, and Gender; Other.

Scenario 4.11. Domain Reference Set Variants.

Data stewards documenting existing data files identify different domains of wetland classification, although each domain contains the same names, definitions, and coded values. The domains are different because the work groups managing wetlands deal with a different subset of wetlands. Three Data Reference Set Variations were created for Wetland Class; Roadway, Wetland Class; Recreation, and Wetland Class; Wildlife.

Data Reference Item

Data Reference Item is subordinate to Data Reference Set Variation and represents a data property. A complete Data Reference Item contains a Name and a Definition, and may contain a Code. An incomplete Data Reference Item may contain any combination of Name, Definition, and Code.

The detail data for a Data Reference Item can be entered anytime a Data Reference Item is identified, which is usually during data cross-referencing. However, preliminary documentation can be done prior to data cross-referencing when data reference sets are identified in the Data Product Data. The parent Data Reference Set Variation and data reference sets must be documented before the Data Reference Item can be documented.

Data Reference Item. Begin Date (R)

Data Reference Item. Code
Data Reference Item. Comment
Data Reference Item. Definition (R)
Data Reference Item. End Date
Data Reference Item. Name (R)

Common Data Status. Name (R)
Data Reference Set Variation. Name Complete (R)

Scenario 4.12. Data Property Codes and Long Names.

An existing set of data properties for timber stand species used by loggers includes a coded data value and a long name which is really a short definition of the coded data value. The Data Reference Set Variation is created for Timber Species; Logging that contains Data Reference Items for Timber Species. Code and Timber Species. Definition.

Scenario 4.13. Data Property Names and Definitions.

An existing set of data properties for measurement units used by field engineers includes a name and a definition, but no coded data value. The Data Reference Set Variation for Measurement Unit; Engineer is created and contains Data Reference Items for Measurement Unit. Name and Measurement Unit. Definition.

Data Subject Models

Data Model Diagram was explained in the Data Inventory Chapter. Data Subject Model shows each Data Model Diagram where a Data Subject appears. The detail data for each Data Subject Model can be entered anytime a Data Subject is identified on a Data Model Diagram. The Data Subject and Data Model Diagram must be documented before the Data Subject Model can be documented.

Data Subject Model. Comment
Data Model Diagram. Name (R)
Data Subject. Name Complete (R)

Scenario 4.14. Data Subject Models.

Data Model Diagrams are developed for each major subject area that is being documented by a Data Understanding Task Force. A Data Subject Model is created for each Data Model Diagram that contains a Data Subject within that major subject area so that the Task Force can readily identify all of the Data Model Diagrams containing a particular Data Subject.

COMMON DATA KEYS

The data subject-relation diagram for Common Data Keys, which include Primary Keys and Foreign Keys, is shown in Figure 4.3. Data Relation Cardinality is a data reference set that qualifies Foreign Key. Each organization implementing Data Resource Data can designate the data reference items to suit their particular needs, such as 1:1, 1:M, and M:M.

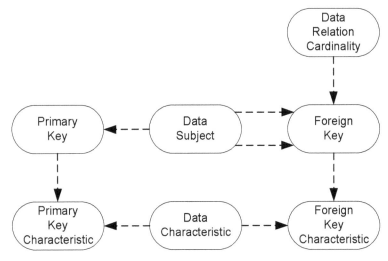

Figure 4.3. Common Data Keys.

The data subject-relation diagram for the data reference sets qualifying Primary Key is shown Figure 4.4. Primary Key is also qualified by Common Data Status, as shown in Figure 4.2.

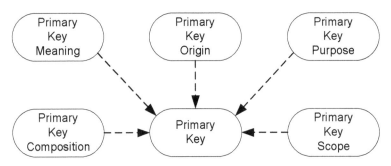

Figure 4.4. Primary Key Data Reference Sets.

Primary Key Composition qualifies Primary Key and is part of the Common Data Architecture Paradigm, such as Simple, Compound, and Complex, and should not be modified.

Primary Key Meaning qualifies Primary Key and is part of the Common Data Architecture Paradigm, such as Meaningful and Meaningless, and should not be modified.

Primary Key Origin qualifies Primary Key and is part of the Common Data Architecture Paradigm, such as Artificial and Natural, and should not be modified.

Primary Key Purpose qualifies Primary Key and is part of the Common Data Architecture Paradigm, such as Logical and Physical, and should not be modified.

Primary Key Scope qualifies Primary Key and is part of the Common Data Architecture Paradigm, such as General, Limited, and Specific, and should not be modified.

Primary Keys

Primary Key is a set of one or more Data Characteristics whose value(s) uniquely identify each data occurrence in a Data Subject. The detail data for a Primary Key can be entered anytime a Primary Key is identified. The parent Data Subject and data reference sets must be documented before the Data Primary Key can be documented.

> Primary Key. Begin Date (R)
> Primary Key. Comment
> Primary Key. Detail Indicator (R)
> Primary Key. End Date
> Primary Key. Preferred Indicator (R)
> Primary Key. Strategic Indicator (R)
> Primary Key. Tactical Indicator (R)
>
> Common Data Status. Name (R)
> Data Subject. Name Complete (R)
> Primary Key Composition. Name (R)
> Primary Key Meaning. Name (R)
> Primary Key Origin. Name (R)
> Primary Key Purpose. Name (R)
> Primary Key Scope. Name (R)

Scenario 4.15. Primary Key.

A student identifier is used to uniquely identify all K through 12 students within the state and is assigned by the State Public Instruction Supervisor's Office. The student identifier allows a student to move throughout the State's public school system and all records can be readily identified for that student. A Primary Key is established with all the appropriate data reference items.

Primary Key Characteristics

Primary Key Characteristics are the individual Data Characteristics that comprise a Primary Key. The detail data for Primary Key Characteristics can be entered anytime the Primary Key Characteristics are identified. The parent Primary Key and Data Characteristics must be documented before the Primary Key Characteristics can be documented.

> Primary Key Characteristic. Comment
>
> Data Characteristic. Name Complete (R)
> Primary Key. System Identifier (R)

Scenario 4.16. Primary Key Characteristics.

The Student. Statewide Identifier needs to be assigned to the Primary Key that was created in Scenario 4.15. A Primary Key Characteristic is created to make that assignment.

Foreign Keys

Foreign Key is one or more Data Characteristics whose value(s) uniquely identify a parent data occurrence in a parent data subject. The detail data for a Foreign Key can be entered anytime a Foreign Key is identified. The "Local" Data Subject, the "Parent" Data Subject, and data reference sets must be documented before the Foreign Keys can be created.

> Foreign Key. Begin Date (R)
> Foreign Key. Comment
> Foreign Key. End Date
> Foreign Key. Data Integrity Rules
> Foreign Key. Data Relation Definition
> Foreign Key. Data Relation Name From Parent
> Foreign Key. Data Relation Name To Parent
> Foreign Key. Preferred Indicator (R)
>
> Common Data Status. Name (R)
> Data Relation Cardinality. Name (R)
> "Local" Data Subject. Name Complete (R)
> "Parent" Data Subject. Name Complete (R)

Scenario 4.17. Foreign Key.

A student may enroll in many different public schools during their education years. Student Enrollment is created as the Data Subject for documenting the enrollment of a single Student in a single School. A Foreign Key is created with the "Local" Data Subject for School and the "Parent" Data Subject for

Student.

Foreign Key Characteristics

Foreign Key Characteristics are individual Data Characteristics that comprise Foreign Keys. The detail data for Foreign Key Characteristics can be entered anytime a Foreign Key Characteristic is identified. The parent Foreign Key and the Data Characteristic must be documented before the Foreign Key Characteristic can be created.

>Foreign Key Characteristic. Begin Date (R)
>Foreign Key Characteristic. Comment
>Foreign Key Characteristic. End Date

>Data Characteristic. Name Complete (R)
>Foreign Key. System Identifier (R)

Scenario 4.18. Foreign Key Characteristics.

The Student. Statewide Identifier needs to be assigned to the Foreign Key that was created in Scenario 4.17. A Foreign Key Characteristic is created to make that assignment.

DATA SUBJECT STEWARD

Data Subject Steward identifies the Data Stewards that are responsible for the Data Subjects, and is qualified with the specific Data Steward Function and Data Steward Level. Data Steward, Data Steward Function, and Data Steward Level were explained in the Data Responsibility Chapter.

The data subject-relation diagram for Data Subject Stewards is shown in Figure 4.5. It contains one major segment for Data Subject Steward, which is explained below the diagram.

The detail data for each Data Subject Stewards can be entered anytime a Data Subject Steward is identified. The Data Steward and the data reference sets must be documented before the Data Subject Steward can be documented.

>Data Subject Steward. Begin Date (R)
>Data Subject Steward. Comment
>Data Subject Steward. End Date

>Data Steward. Name Complete (R)
>Data Steward Function. Name (R)
>Data Steward Level. Name (R)
>Data Subject. Name Complete (R)

51

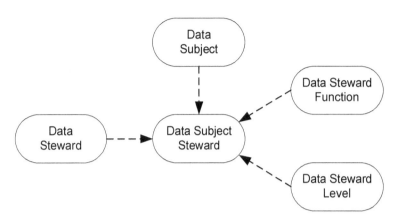

Figure 4.5. Data Subject Stewards.

Data Steward Function and Data Steward Level are data reference sets that were explained in the Data Responsibility Chapter. The appropriate Data Reference Items for Data Steward Function and Data Steward Level are assigned to Data Subject Steward.

Scenario 4.19. Data Subject Steward.

A business professional has been identified who has extensive knowledge about employee data and desires to organize all of the employee data for the organization. That person is documented as a Data Steward, as explained in the Data Responsibility Chapter. That Data Steward is then assigned as a Data Subject Steward to all Data Subjects that contain data about employees. Data Subject Steward. Comment explains the type of knowledge that the Data Steward has about the Data Subject.

DATA SUBJECT AREAS

Data Subject Areas provide a way to group Data Subjects for a variety of different purposes, such as for a data project, for printing specific data resource models, and so on. It consists of Data Subject Area, Data Subject Area Assignment, Data Subject Area Model, and a data reference set as shown in Figure 4.6.

Data Subject Area

Data Subject Area is any grouping of Data Subjects for a specific purpose. Data Subject Area Purpose identifies that purpose. Data Subject Area is recursive to allow the development of a hierarchy of Data Subjects when needed. The detail data for a Data Subject Area can be entered anytime a Data Subject Area is identified. The data reference set must be documented before a Data Subject Area can be created.

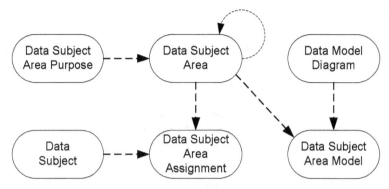

Figure 4.6. Data Subject Areas.

Data Subject Area. Begin Date (R)
Data Subject Area. Business Critical Indicator (R)
Data Subject Area. Comment
Data Subject Area. Definition (R)
Data Subject Area. End Date
Data Subject Area. Name (R)

"Parent" Data Subject Area
Data Subject Area Purpose. Name (R)

Data Subject Area Purpose is a data reference set that qualifies Data Subject Area. Each organization implementing Data Resource Data can designate the data reference items to suit their particular needs, such as Cluster, Discipline, Segment, and so on.

Scenario 4.20. Data Subject Area.

An organization is beginning a project for improving the affirmative action data for all of their employees. A Data Subject Area is created for Affirmative Action Project to contain all of the Data Subjects related to the Affirmative Action Project.

Scenario 4.21. Data Subject Area Hierarchy.

Data stewards decided to develop a Data Subject Area Hierarchy for printing data resource models from the Data Resource Data. They developed a three-tier hierarchy that consisted of Data Resource Models as the top tier, specific groupings of data resource models by business function as the second tier, and specific groupings of data resource models by level of detail as the third tier. Data Subjects were then assigned to the Data Subject Areas in the lowest tier.

Data Subject Area Assignment

Data Subject Area Assignment places Data Subjects in a Data Subject Area. The detail data for a Data Subject Area Assignment can be entered anytime a Data Subject is to be placed into a Data Subject Area. The Data Subject Area and Data Subject must be documented before the Data Subject Area Assignment can be documented.

> Data Subject Area Assignment. Begin Date (R)
> Data Subject Area Assignment. Comment
> Data Subject Area Assignment. End Date
>
> Data Subject. Name Complete (R)
> Data Subject Area. Name (R)

Scenario 4.22. Data Subject Area Assignment.

As the Affirmative Action Project in Scenario 4.16 evolves, data subjects that are needed for the Project are added to the Affirmative Action Data Subject Area through Data Subject Area Assignment, such as Employee, Department, and all of the data reference sets that qualify an employee and a department.

Data Subject Area Model

Data Model Diagram was explained in the Data Inventory Chapter. Data Subject Area Model shows each Data Model Diagram where a Data Subject Area Appears. The detail data for a Data Subject Area Model can be entered anytime a Data Subject Area appears on a Data Model Diagram. The Data Model Diagram and Data Subject Area must be documented before the Data Subject Area Model can be created.

> Data Subject Area Model. Comment
>
> Data Model Diagram. Name (R)
> Data Subject Area. Name (R)

Scenario 4.23. Data Subject Area Model.

Several data subject-relation diagrams were prepared for the Affirmative Action Project in Scenario 4.16. Data Subject Area Model entries are made for each Data Subject that appears on each of the Data Model Diagrams to help the team members identify the appropriate data subject-relation diagram.

SUMMARY

The Common Data Function provides the common context within which all of the organization's data are understood and is the base for designating the preferred data for the to-be comparate data resource. All existing data, which are seldom thoroughly documented or understood, can be thoroughly understood within the context of the Common Data. Once thoroughly understood, the preferred data can be designated for developing the comparate data resource.

Chapter 5

DATA LEXICON

The data lexicon provides formal words for Common Data names.

The data understanding process continues with the Data Lexicon Function consisting of the Common Words for naming Common Data, word abbreviations and abbreviation algorithms used for abbreviating Data Product Data and Common Data, synonyms and aliases for identifying formal data names, and business terms used in the organization.

COMMON WORDS

Establishing Common Words with denotative meanings and identifying those Common words through synonyms and aliases is crucial for formally naming Common Data. Thoroughly understanding an organization's data resource depends on the identification and use of Common Words.

Common Words are documented with a set of Data Name Common Words for each Data Resource Component Type, as shown in Figure 5.1. Each Data Name Common Word can have many synonyms or aliases that are documented in a Data Name Common Word Thesaurus.

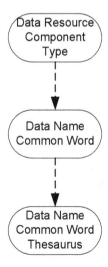

Figure 5.1. Data Name Common Words.

Data Resource Component Type

Data Resource Component Type is a data reference set containing data reference items identifying each component of the Data Naming Taxonomy that are formally named, such as Data Site, Data Subject (which includes Data Reference Set), Data Occurrence Group, Data Occurrence Role, Data Reference Set Variation, Data Characteristic, Data Characteristic Variation, Data Version, and Data Rule.

The data reference items for Data Resource Component Type are fixed within the Common Data Architecture Paradigm according to the Data Naming Taxonomy and should not be changed.

Data Name Common Word

A Common Word is any word that has consistent meaning whenever it is used in a formal data name, such as Date, Text, Code, Name, Quantity, Amount, and so on. A set of common words is established for each component of the Data Naming Taxonomy that is formally named. The *data naming vocabulary* is the collection of all the sets of common words for the components of the Data Naming Taxonomy.

The detail data for a Data Name Common Word can be entered anytime a common word is identified. The data reference set must be documented before the Data Name Common Word can be documented.

> Data Name Common Word. Begin Date (R)
> Data Name Common Word. Comment
> Data Name Common Word. Definition (R)
> Data Name Common Word. End Date
> Data Name Common Word. Phrase (R)
>
> Data Resource Component Type. Name (R)

Scenario 5.1. Data Subject Common Words.

An organization is having difficulty with the meaning of qualifying words used in Data Subject Names, such as Activity, History, Suspense, and so on. The determination was made that no qualifier would represent current data, such as Student; Activity would represent any incoming data, such as Student Activity; History would represent any non-current historical data that was saved, such as Student History; and Suspense would represent any data that failed the data integrity rules and was being held for correction, such as Student Suspense. These words and definitions were entered as Data Name Common Words for Data Subjects.

Scenario 5.2. Data Characteristic Common Words.

An organization is having difficulty with the meaning of words used in Data Characteristic names, such as Amount, Count, Number, Quantity, and so on. The determination was made that Amount would represent a monetary value, such as $43.54; Count would represent a counting of objects, such as 23 packages; Number would represent a numerical identifier, such as item 38541; and Quantity would represent a capacity, such as 135 gallons. These words and definitions were entered as Data Name Common Words for Data Characteristics.

Scenario 5.3. Paired Data Name Words.

An organization is having difficulty with the proper pairing of words, such as Begin, Start, Stop, End, and so on. The determination was made that Begin and End would be paired, Start and Stop would be paired, and Initiate and Terminate would be paired. These words and their definitions were entered as Data Name Common Words for Data Characteristics.

Data Name Common Word Thesaurus

A Data Name Common Word Thesaurus is a list of synonyms, aliases, and related business terms that help people find the appropriate Data Name Common Word to be used in a formal data name. It's a list of words and terms that point to a Data Name Common Word.

The detail data for a Data Name Common Word Thesaurus can be entered anytime an alias or synonym word is identified. The parent Data Name Common Word must be documented before the Data Name Common Word Thesaurus entry can be created.

> Data Name Common Word Thesaurus. Source Phrase (R)
>
> Data Name Common Word. Phrase (R)

Scenario 5.4. Common Data Name Word Aliases.

An organization is struggling with finding the appropriate Common Words to use in formal data names. The solution is to document a list of alias words and terms that point to possible Data Name Common Words, such as Money, Dollars, and Funds pointing to Amount. The documentation included similar alias words and terms for Price, Cost, Payment, and so on. The result was a complete set of Common Words relating to monetary data characteristics.

Multiple entries can be made to the Data Name Common Word Thesaurus that contain the same source phrase, where each source phrase points to a different Data Name Common Word. For example, People could be entered multiple times and point to Employee, Student, Faculty, and so on.

DATA NAME ABBREVIATION

The abbreviation of data names usually includes a set of formal data name abbreviations and a formal abbreviation algorithm. Much of the Data Product Data have informal word abbreviations and abbreviation algorithms created by an individual that may not be consistent with that individual or consistent across the organization. In some situations, Data Product Data have no formal data name abbreviations or abbreviation algorithm. Common Data should have one formal set of word abbreviations and one formal abbreviation algorithm.

Data name abbreviations are documented with a Data Name Word Set containing a set of Data Name Words, a Data Name Abbreviation Algorithm, and a Data Name Abbreviation Scheme consisting of one Data Name Word Set and one Data Name Abbreviation Algorithm, as shown in Figure 5.2.

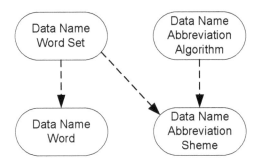

Figure 5.2. Data Name Abbreviations.

Data Name Word Set

A Data Name Word Set is a set of Data Name Words and their abbreviations that are used in naming data. Each set of words that are abbreviated differently become a separate Data Name Word Set. The abbreviations may or may not follow any formal abbreviation scheme.

The detail data for a Data Name Word Set can be entered anytime a different Data Name Word Set is identified.

> Data Name Word Set. Begin Date (R)
> Data Name Word Set. Comment
> Data Name Word Set. Definition (R)

Data Name Word Set. End Date
Data Name Word Set. Name (R)
Data Name Word Set. Unique Abbreviation Indicator (R)

Scenario 5.5. Common Data Name Word Set.

A data steward is faced with building a Data Name Word Set for formal abbreviations that will be used for all Common Data. The solution is to document a Data Name Word Set named Common Data Name Words that includes all the words and their definitions that will be used for naming all Common Data.

Scenario 5.6. Random Data Name Word Set.

A data steward realizes that some Data Product Data have been randomly abbreviated without any formal or consistent abbreviations or abbreviation scheme. The desire is to identify those Data Product Data as being randomly abbreviated. The decision was made to establish a Data Name Word Set called Random Data Name Words defined as words that are randomly abbreviated with no pattern or consistency. The Random Data Name Words would have no associated Data Name Words.

Data Name Word

A Data Name Word is any word that is used, or could be used, in a data name including the abbreviation of that word. Data Name Words with similar abbreviations, such as those done by one person or one group, are placed within a Data Name Word Set.

The detail data for a Data Name Word can be entered anytime a Data Name Word is identified. The parent Data Name Word Set must be documented before the Data Name Word can be documented.

Data Name Word. Begin Date (R)
Data Name Word. Comment
Data Name Word. Word Abbreviated (R)
Data Name Word. Word Complete (R)
Data Name Word. End Date

Data Name Word Set. Name (R)

Scenario 5.7. Formal Data Name Word.

A data steward wants to create a list of formal data name word abbreviations for use with all Common Data, which will be placed within Common Data Name Words in Scenario 5.5. The decision is made to abbreviate the root word and then abbreviate manifestations of that root word with a suffix, such as d for ed, n for sion, r for or, t for ment, and so on. Each word abbreviation will be unique so that the Common Data names can be automatically abbreviated and unabbreviated.

Data Name Abbreviation Algorithm

A Data Name Abbreviation Algorithm is a formal procedure for abbreviating a data name that specifies the sequence of the abbreviation, such as left to right for all words, and the format of the abbreviation, such as all uppercase with underscores between words.

The detail data for a Data Name Abbreviation Algorithm can be entered anytime a new data Name Abbreviation Algorithm is identified.

> Data Name Abbreviation Algorithm. Begin Date (R)
> Data Name Abbreviation Algorithm. Definition (R)
> Data Name Abbreviation Algorithm. End Date
> Data Name Abbreviation Algorithm. Name (R)

Scenario 5.8. Common Data Name Abbreviation Algorithm.

Data stewards determined that a Common Data Name Abbreviation Algorithm for Common Data would be that all words in a data name would be abbreviated and that the format of the abbreviated words would be all lower case with underscores between each word.

Scenario 5.9. Random Data Name Abbreviation Algorithm.

Data stewards determined that a Random Data Name Abbreviation Algorithm would be defined for the Data Product Data names that were abbreviated with no pattern or consistency and did not have a definable Data Name Abbreviation Algorithm.

Data Name Abbreviation Scheme

A Data Name Abbreviation Scheme is a combination of a specific Data Name Word Set and a specific Data Name Abbreviation Algorithm.

The detail data for a Data Name Abbreviation Scheme can be entered anytime a new abbreviation scheme is identified. The parent Data Name Abbreviation Algorithm and parent Data Name Word Set must be documented before the Data Name Abbreviation Scheme can be documented.

> Data Name Abbreviation Scheme. Begin Date (R)
> Data Name Abbreviation Scheme. Comment

Data Name Abbreviation Scheme. Description (R)
Data Name Abbreviation Scheme. End Date
Data Name Abbreviation Scheme. Name (R)
Data Name Abbreviation Scheme. Preferred Indicator (R)
Data Name Abbreviation Scheme. Random Indicator (R)

Data Name Abbreviation Algorithm. Name (R)
Data Name Word Set. Name (R)

Scenario 5.10. Common Data Name Abbreviation Scheme.

Data stewards determined that a Common Data Name Abbreviation Scheme would be defined consisting of the Common Data Name Words defined in Scenario 5.5 and the Common Data Name Abbreviation Algorithm defined in Scenario 5.8, and that it would be used for all Common Data.

Scenario 5.11. Random Data Name Abbreviation Scheme.

Data stewards determined that a Random Data Name Abbreviation Scheme would be defined consisting of the Random Data Name Words defined in Scenario 5.6 and the Random Data Name Abbreviation Algorithm defined in Scenario 5.9, and that it would apply to all Data Product Data for which no discernable pattern of abbreviations could be identified.

DATA SUBJECT THESAURUS

A Data Subject Thesaurus is a list of synonyms and related business terms that help people find the formal Data Subjects that support their business information needs. A Data Subject can have many synonyms and alias, and a synonym and alias can point to many Data Subjects, as shown in Figure 5.3

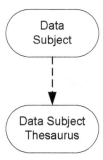

Figure 5.3. Data Subject Thesaurus.

The detail data for a Data Subject Thesaurus can be entered anytime an alias or synonym for the Data Subject name is identified. The Data Subject Thesaurus. Source Phrase is required and may be either an alias or synonym, or an established Data Subject Name. When the Source Phrase is an established Data Subject Name, the Target Phrase is prevented. When the Source Phrase is an alias or synonym, the Target Phrase is required. The Data Subject must be documented before the entry can be made.

> Data Subject Thesaurus. Source Phrase (R)
> Data Subject Thesaurus. Target Phrase (R/P)
>
> Data Subject. Name Complete (R)

Scenario 5.12. Data Subject Thesaurus.

Data stewards begin documenting the Data Subject Thesaurus phrases as soon as the Data Subjects are defined, and continue adding new Data Subject Thesaurus phrases for a Data Subject as they are identified. For example, a Timber Stand data subject could have Source Phrases for Forest, Timber, Woodlot, and so on, as well as a Source Phrase for Timber Stand with no Target Phrase.

BUSINESS TERMS

Business terms in an organization are often as confusing as data names, with many synonyms, homonyms, aliases, and abbreviations. Although not directly related to data names, an understanding of the business terms helps an organization understand the data and prepare appropriate formal names for the Common Data.

An organization can have many different Business Glossaries and each Business Glossary can contain many different Business Glossary Items, as shown in Figure 5.4. Business Glossary Item is recursive to reference another Business Glossary Item.

Business Glossary

A Business Glossary is specific set of business acronyms or business terms and their definitions that are used by the business. It can be a formal glossary published by an organization, or it can be an informal glossary of terms used in a particular business function. It does not contain any data definitions or data name words.

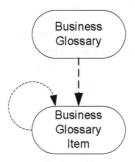

Figure 5.4. Business Terms.

The detail data for a Business Glossary can be entered anytime a new glossary of business terms is identified.

> Business Glossary. Begin Date (R)
> Business Glossary. Comment
> Business Glossary. Definition (R)
> Business Glossary. End Date
> Business Glossary. Name (R)
> Business Glossary. Publication Reference

Scenario 5.13. Business Glossary.

Several business professionals were amazed at how well the formal data names, common words, formal abbreviations, and thesauri were helping people identify the data they needed and understand those data. They wondered if something could be done for the plethora of disparate business terms and acronyms being used in the organization. The answer was to start building a Business Glossary for each set of business terms being used in the organization, such as medical terms, surveying terms, financial terms, and so on.

Business Glossary Item

A Business Glossary Item is a specific business acronym or business term used in the organization. Each Business Glossary Item belongs to a specific Business Glossary. Business Glossary Items representing acronyms reference another Business Glossary Item that represents the fully spelled out name and a definition. The reference can be within the same Business Glossary or in a different Business Glossary. Over time, the Preferred Indicators are used to identify the preferred business terms.

The detail data for a Business Glossary Item can be entered anytime a new Business Glossary Item is identified. The parent Business Glossary must be documented before the Business Glossary Item can be documented.

Business Glossary Item. Begin Date (R)
Business Glossary Item. Comment
Business Glossary Item. Definition (R)
Business Glossary Item. End Date
Business Glossary Item. Phrase (R)
Business Glossary Item. Preferred Indicator (R)

Business Glossary. Name (R)
Business Glossary. Name ^ "Reference" Business Glossary Item. Phrase

Scenario 5.14. Business Glossary Item.

After building the Business Glossaries from Scenario 5.13, the business professionals added Business Glossary Items to their respective Business Glossaries as they were identified, and eventually designated preferred business terms.

Scenario 5.15. Business Glossary Acronyms

Business professionals began a Business Glossary with Business Glossary Items for acronyms used in the business, but did not define those acronyms. Instead, a reference was made to a Business Glossary Item, either within that same Business Glossary or a different Business Glossary that contained the fully spelled out term and a comprehensive definition. When multiple acronyms appeared for the same term, one of the acronyms was designed the preferred acronym.

SUMMARY

The Data Lexicon Function directly supports the Common Data by providing a lexicon of words used in formal data names. The Lexicon consists of common words for naming data, word abbreviations, word abbreviation algorithms, synonyms and aliases for identifying formal data names, and business terms used by the organization. The formality of Common Data names provides the initial understanding of all data in the organization's data resource.

Chapter 6

DATA CROSS-REFERENCES

Data cross-references bring understanding to disparate data.

The data understanding process continues with the Data Cross-Reference Function consisting of cross-referencing the Data Product Data to the Common Data, particularly the Data Product Data representing the existing disparate data in the organization's data resource.

DATA CROSS-REFERENCE APPROACH

The *data cross-reference concept* is that the inventoried Data Product Data are cross-referenced to the Common Data to further increase the understanding of those disparate data within a common context. The initial understanding gained during data inventorying is increased through a cross-referencing of the inventoried Data Product Data to the Common Data.

The *data cross-reference objective* is to thoroughly understand the content, meaning, structure, and integrity of all data at the organization's disposal within the context of the Common Data.

The data cross-reference detail appears very small and could be presumed to be trivial, but cross-referencing is one of the most critical tasks for understanding the existing disparate data and creating a comparate data resource. The Data Cross-Reference Function should not be taken lightly.

Data Cross-Reference Difficulty

The data cross-referencing task can be very difficult. About 70% to 80% of the cross-references are relatively easy; about 10% to 15% of the cross-references are more difficult; and about 5% to 10% of the cross-references take some real thought and investigation. In some situations up to 5% of the Data Product Data cannot be cross-referenced to the Common Data because not enough understanding about the data is known to make even a reasonable determination of the Common Data equivalent.

Data Cross-Reference Sequence

The data cross-referencing does not have to be done in any particular sequence. Some individuals and teams prefer to make the easiest cross-references first to gain a success motivation. Other individuals and teams prefer to tackle the difficult cross-references first so that the remaining cross-references are easier. Still other individuals and teams prefer to work sequentially through a particular Data Product or Data Product Set and make cross-references or enter Comments about the cross-reference.

Data Cross-Reference Comments

Extensive use should be made of the Comment data characteristics in Data Product Set, Data Product Unit, and Data Product Code during data cross-referencing. Any problems, insights, thoughts, status, and so on, should be entered in the Comment. Many times the collective detail entered in the Comment by several people lead to an accurate cross-reference.

Data Cross-Reference Support

Support for data cross-referencing can come from a variety of sources. Business professionals and knowledge workers can provide insight into how the data are entered or used based on their knowledge of reports, screens, and documents. Database technicians can provide the domain of data values and histograms of data value frequency that provide insight into the data meaning. System analysts and programmers can provide insight into how the data are acquired, used, and stored. Collectively, these sources provide considerable insight into understanding the data enough to make an accurate cross-reference.

The reader should refer to *Data Resource Integration* for details on the data cross-referencing techniques.

DATA PRODUCT SET CROSS-REFERENCE

A Data Product Set may be cross-referenced to a Data Subject as shown in Figure 6.1. The recursive data relation for Data Product Set identifies a Data Product Set Variation.

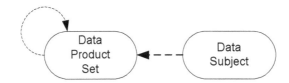

Figure 6.1. Data Product Set Cross-Reference

The Data Product Set cross-reference is made when a Data Product Set / Variation exactly matches a Data Subject. In other words, the Data Product

Set / Variation must contain Data Product Units that are cross-referenced to Data Characteristic Variations that are within the Data Subject to which the Data Product Set / Variation is being cross-referenced. The Data Product Set / Variation may not contain Data Product Units / Variations for all the Data Characteristics within a Data Subject to which the Data Product Set is being cross-referenced, but must contain Data Product Units / Variations that only represent Data Characteristics within the Data Subject to which the Data Product Set is being cross-referenced.

Typically, an existing disparate Data Product Set / Variation is not cross-referenced to a Data Subject. The cross-reference is usually made when the preferred Common Data are physically implemented, which is described in Preferred Data Chapter. However, situations do arise where an existing disparate Data Product Set matches a Data Subject.

Only the lowest level of a Data Product Set can be cross-referenced to a Data Subject. If a Data Product Set does not have a subordinate Product Set Variation, then it can be cross-referenced to a Data Subject. If a Data Product Set has a subordinate Data Product Set Variation, then it cannot be cross-referenced to a Data Subject. Only the subordinate Data Product Set Variation can be cross-referenced to a Data Subject.

The detail data for a Data Product Set / Variation cross-reference can be entered anytime a match is identified between a Data Product Set / Variation and a corresponding Data Subject. Typically, only the cross-reference to the Data Subject and the Cross Reference Comment are used during cross-referencing. The Data Subject must be documented before the cross-reference can be created.

> Data Product Set. Cross Reference Comment
> Data Subject. Name Complete (R)

Scenario 6.1. Data Product Set Cross-Reference.

Data stewards identify a Data Product Set containing Data Product Units that only apply to Student data. A Data Subject for Student has already been created, so a cross-reference is made to the Student Data Subject.

Scenario 6.2. Data Product Set Variation Cross-Reference.

Data stewards identify a Data Product Set that has multiple record types, so Data Product Set Variations are created for each of those record types. On further investigation one of those record types contains data unique to Road Segments. A Data Subject for Road Segment is created and the Data Product Set Variation is cross-referenced to that Data Subject.

Scenario 6.3. Data Cross-Reference Comment.

Data stewards encounter a Data Product Set that appears to match a Data Subject for Wetland. However, a Data Subject for Wetland has been created, but has no Data Characteristics, so the cross-reference is questionable. A comment is entered stating that there appears to be a cross-reference to Wetland, but cannot be verified. No actual cross-reference is made.

DATA PRODUCT UNIT CROSS-REFERENCE

A Data Product Unit is cross-referenced to a Data Characteristic Variation, as shown in Figure 6.2. The recursive data relation for Data Product Unit identifies a Data Product Unit Variation. The second recursive data relation for Data Product Unit representing inheritance is not shown because it is not relevant to data cross-referencing.

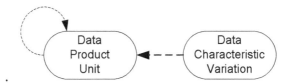

Figure 6.2. Data Product Unit Cross-References.

Only the lowest level of a Data Product Unit is cross-referenced to a Data Characteristic Variation. When a Data Product Unit does not have a Data Product Unit Variation, then the Data Product Unit is cross-referenced to the Data Characteristic Variation. When a Data Product Unit has a Data Product Unit Variation, then only the Data Product Unit Variation is cross-referenced to the Data Characteristic Variation, and the Data Product Unit cannot be cross-referenced.

The Data Product Unit cross-reference can be entered anytime that a cross-reference between a Data Product Unit and a Data Characteristic Variation is identified, or when difficulty is encountered in identifying a corresponding Data Characteristic Variation. Typically, only the cross-reference to the Data Characteristic Variation and the Cross Reference Comment are used during cross-referencing. The Data Characteristic and Data Characteristic Variation must be documented before the cross-reference can be created.

Typically no new Data Product Unit data or Data Product Units are added during the data cross-referencing. However, the opportunity can be taken to enter additional Data Product Unit data or Data Product Units as described in the Data Inventory Chapter if additional insight is gained.

Data Product Unit. Cross Reference Comment
Data Characteristic Variation. Name Complete (R)

Scenario 6.4. Data Product Unit Cross-Reference

Data stewards identified Data Product Units within a Data Product Set that represent individual facts for several Data Characteristics in different Data Subjects. Data Characteristic Variations were created as needed and the Data Product Units were then cross-referenced to the corresponding Data Characteristic Variations.

Scenario 6.5. Multiple-Subject Data Product Unit.

Data stewards identified Data Product Sets whose Data Product Units represented multiple Data Subjects, a situation that proved to be common in their existing data. The Data Product Sets and Data Product Units were documented and cross-references were made from the Data Product Units to the Data Characteristic Variations within the appropriate Data Subjects. The cross-referencing effectively assigned the Data Product Units to the Data Subjects they actually represented.

Scenario 6.6. Data Product Unit Variation Cross-Reference

Data stewards identified many Data Product Units within a Data Product Set that represented multiple facts. Data Product Unit Variations representing the single facts were created for those Data Product Units representing multiple facts. Data Characteristic Variations were identified or created for those single facts and cross-references were made between the Data Product Unit Variations and the respective Data Characteristic Variations.

Some Data Product Units may represent multiple facts and some may not, which is acceptable.

Scenario 6.7. Partial Fact Cross-Reference.

Data stewards identified several Data Product Units that represent partial facts. In other words, the complete fact is separated and stored in several different Data Product Units. A Data Characteristic is created for the complete fact and Data Characteristic Variations are created for each of the partial facts contained in the Data Product Units. The Data Characteristic Variation. Partial Fact Indicator is set to "Y" for each of those partial facts.

The Data Product Units representing portions of that fact are then cross-referenced to the appropriate Data Characteristic Variation. A comment is made for each cross-reference about the partial fact that is being cross-referenced and how the partial fact contributes to the combined fact represented by the parent Data Characteristic. A statement is added to the parent Data Characteristic definition that it contains Data Characteristic Variations representing partial facts.

DATA PRODUCT CODE CROSS-REFERENCE

A Data Product Code is cross-referenced to a Data Reference Set Variation, as shown in Figure 6.3. The recursive data relation for Data Product Code identifies a Data Product Code Variation.

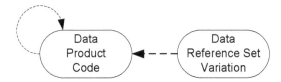

Figure 6.3. Data Product Code Cross-References.

The Data Reference Set Variation to which the Data Product Code is being cross-referenced must contain the exact set of codes that appear in the Data Product Unit containing the Data Product Code. The exact set means the same domain, the same codes, the same names, and the same basic definitions. The wording of the definition may not be the same, but the basic definition must be the same. Any difference in the domain, codes, names, or basic definitions becomes a separate Data Reference Set Variation.

Identifying the exact set of codes may be difficult in some situations, requiring further investigation. The domain of values, codes, names, and definitions in the Data Product Unit can be very helpful. The best approach is to err with too many Data Reference Set Variations rather than with too few Data Reference Set Variations. Data Reference Set Variations can easily be removed later and cross-references adjusted. However, adding new Data Reference Set Variations later and adjusting cross-reference adjustments can be very difficult.

The Data Product Codes could be cross-referenced to their respective Data Reference Items. However, there's a good chance that the Data Reference Set Variation containing the Data Reference Item may not be an exact match to the set of Data Product Codes. Therefore, the cross-reference is made to the Data Reference Set Variation to help ensure that the Data Reference Set Variation is an exact match to the set of Data Product Codes.

The Data Product Unit containing the Data Product Codes could be cross-referenced to the appropriate Data Reference Set Variation. However, the same problem exists as with the Data Product Codes being cross-referenced to the Data Reference Items. Therefore, the cross-reference is between the Data Product Codes and the Data Reference Set Variation.

Only the lowest level of a Data Product Code is cross-referenced to a Data Reference Set Variation. When a Data Product Code does not have a Data Product Code Variation, then the Data Product Code is cross-referenced to the Data Reference Set Variation. When a Data Product Code has a Data Product Code Variation, then only the Data Product Code Variation is cross-referenced to the Data Reference Set Variation, and the Data Product Code has no cross-reference.

The Data Product Code cross-reference can be entered anytime that a cross-reference between a Data Product Code and a Data Reference Set Variation is identified, or when difficulty is encountered in identifying a Data Reference Set Variation. Typically no new Data Product Codes are added during the data cross-referencing, although the opportunity can be taken to enter additional data according to the Data Product Code detail described in the Data Inventory Chapter.

> Data Product Code. Cross Reference Comment
> Data Reference Set Variation. Name Complete (R)

Scenario 6.8. Data Product Code Cross-Reference.

Data stewards encountered a set of codes for education levels that are single property, single subject codes. No Data Product Code Variations were needed and the Data Product Codes were cross-referenced to the appropriate Data Reference Set Variation with a parent Data Subject for Education Level.

Scenario 6.9. Data Product Code Variation Cross-Reference.

Data stewards encountered a set of codes for management levels where many of the codes represented multiple data properties. Data Product Code Variations representing single data properties were created for those codes representing multiple data properties. A Data Reference Set Variation was created for the set of single data properties and the Data Product Code Variations were cross-referenced to that Data Reference Set Variation.

Some of the Data Product Codes within a Data Product Unit may have Data Product Code Variations and some may not have Data Product Code Variations, which is acceptable. When a Data Product Code Variation exists, it is cross-referenced to the Data Reference Set Variation and the parent Data Product Code is not cross-referenced to the Data Reference Set Variation. When a Data Product Code Variation does not exist, the Data

Product Code is cross-referenced to the Data Reference Set Variation.

Scenario 6.10. Data Product Code Cross-Reference Comment.

Business professionals identified many existing Data Product Codes about which they had no explicit documentation or understanding for what those codes represented, but they had some ideas about what the codes might represent based on their understanding of the data use. These business professionals made cross-reference comments about their thoughts and ideas, even though they could not make the specific cross-references. Over time, the comments from many different business professionals led to an understanding of what the codes represented, Data Reference Set Variations were created, and cross-references were made to those Data Reference Set Variations.

Scenario 6.11. Exact Data Reference Set Variation.

An organization encountered what appeared to be a single set of codes for geographical regions in the Americas, consisting of N for North America and S for South America. However, on close examination of the definitions and the actual use of the codes, it became obvious that two distinctly different sets of codes existed. The first set includes Central America in North America and the second set includes Central America in South America. Clearly, two different sets of codes existed.

The situation was resolved by defining two Data Reference Set Variations for the two different sets of codes. Then the determination was made for each specific Data Product Unit about which set of codes was being used. Based on that determination, cross-references were made to the appropriate Data Reference Set Variation.

OF-TYPE CROSS-REFERENCE

A situation can arise where an organization decides to place several Data Product Sets into one Data Subject. For example, Data Product Sets exist for each specific type of Contractor, such as Carpenter, Electrician, Roofer, and so on. The organization desires to create a single Data Subject for Contractor with Contractor Type designating Contractor, Electrician, Roofer, and so on.

The situation is referred to as an Of-Type Cross-Reference because a Data Product Set is cross-referenced to Data Characteristic Variations within a Data Subject using an Of-Type designation. In other words, Data Product Sets represent subsets of a more encompassing Data Subject and those subsets are qualified with a type designation.

Scenario 6.12. Data Product Unit Of-Type Cross-References.

Data stewards encountered the situation where multiple Data Product Sets representing different Contractor Types were to be combined into a single Data Subject for Contractor.

The best way to document the understanding of contractors and contractor types was to create a Data Product Unit within the parent Data Product Set representing the Contractor Type. The Data Product Unit. Created Indicator is set to "Y" identifying the Data Product Unit as having been created and does not exist in the source data. The definition of the created Data Product Unit explains why it was created and that it does not exist in the Data Product Set. The Data Product Unit is cross-referenced to the appropriate Data Characteristic Variation

Scenario 6.13. Data Product Code Of-Type Cross-References.

That created Data Product Unit in Scenario 6.12 has a subordinate created Data Product Code designating the Contractor Type, such as C for Carpenter, E for Electrician, R for Roofer, and so on. The Data Product Code. Created Indicator identifies the Data Product Code as having been created and does not exist in the source data. The definition of the created Data Product Code explains why it was created and that it does not exist in the Data Product Set. The Data Product Codes are cross-referenced to the appropriate Data Reference Set Variation.

The cross-referencing of the created Data Product Codes to a Data Reference Set Variation is one exception to the rule that the Data Reference Set Variation must be an exact match to the domain, codes, names, and definitions. Since only one created Data Product Code is developed for each Data Product Set, but the collective set of created Data Product Codes for all the Data Product Sets representing Contractors, the Data Product Codes can be cross-referenced to the same Data Reference Set Variation. The exception is allowed because the set of Data Product Codes is being controlled, which eliminates the need to cross-reference the individual Data Product Codes to different Data Reference Set Variations.

OTHER CROSS-REFERENCES

The question always arises about cross-referencing the data on reports, screens, and documents to their respective Data Product Sets and Data Product Units. In other words, the reports, screens, and documents are documented as Data Products, Data Product Sets, and Data Product Units, and the databases are documented as separate Data Products, Data Product Sets, and Data Product Units. Should there be a cross-reference between the Data Product Units representing reports, screens, and documents and the Data Product Units representing their respective databases?

The answer is "No" for two reasons. First, creating cross-references within the Data Product Data is a monumental effort and likely provides no additional understanding of the data. In fact, such cross-referencing may create additional confusions. Second, the data on screens and reports is often derived data that are not represented in the databases. Therefore, the best approach is to make the cross-references between the Data Product Data and the Common Data. Then searches can be made from the Common Data to identify all the Data Product Data that correspond to those Common Data.

A better approach is to make use of the data use functions described in the Data Use Chapter. These functions describe how the data are used or produced by different business processes. Another approach is to make use of the derived data functions described in the Derived Data Chapter. These functions describe how the derived data are actually derived. Together these two functions provide more understanding of the data that any cross-references within the Data Product Data.

SPONTANEOUS INVOLVEMENT

The success that data stewards have with understanding the existing Data Product Data and cross-referencing those data to the Common Data often inspires others to become involved in the data understanding process. Their success, in turn, inspires others to become involved. The result is that many individuals in an organization, often spontaneously, become involved in understanding the data and documenting that understanding.

Scenario 6.14. Database Professional Involvement.

The database professionals in an organization saw the success of data stewards slowly working their way through the existing Data Product Data and documenting the understanding they had gained. The database professionals realized that they spent a significant portion of their time understanding the existing Data Product Data so they could be used effectively. However, much of that understanding was lost as the database professionals moved on to other problems.

The database professionals decided to start documenting their understanding of the data as they tackled each problem they encountered. Even though the documentation process took a little longer, the overall time saving not having to go through the understanding process again for the same data more than made up for the time spent documenting their understanding. Eventually, other database professionals started doing the same thing and even began making comments about possible definitions and cross-references, which ultimately led to appropriate definitions and cross-references.

Scenario 6.15. Knowledge Worker Involvement.

Knowledge workers in the same organization as the database professionals described in Scenario 6.14 realized they were having similar problems with the reports, screens, and documents they used in their daily activities, and were spending a significant amount of their time trying to understand the data.

They began documenting those reports, screens, and documents as Data Product Data and making cross-references to the Common Data. In many situations, one knowledge worker did not have enough insight into the data to make appropriate definitions or cross-references, so they began making comments about the definitions and cross-references. Eventually, enough comments were recorded that teams of knowledge workers would meet, go through the comments, and make appropriate definitions and cross-references.

The result was that many reports, screens, and documents were changed, many reports were eliminated, and some documents were changed. Based on the data understanding, the processes around those reports, screens, and documents were improved. The final result was a considerable saving in time and more efficient processing.

SUMMARY

The Data Cross-Reference Function connects the Data Product Data to their corresponding counterpart in the Common Data, specifically Data Product Sets, Data Product Units, and Data Product Codes. The cross-reference is to Common Data that exactly match each component of the Data Product Data. That cross-reference ultimately provides the thorough understanding of the Data Product Data.

Chapter 7

DATA PROTECTION

Data protection ensures the security and confidentiality of the data.

The data understanding process continues with the Data Protection Function consisting of the legal requirements for ensuring the privacy and confidentiality of the organization's data resource.

DATA PRIVACY AND CONFIDENTIALITY

Data privacy and confidentiality are an important, and growing, concern for most public and private sector organizations. The understanding and documentation of the criteria ensuring the privacy and confidentiality of the data is critically important. The criteria specify the data that are private and confidential and the conditions under which those data can be released. The criteria also specify the data that must be released and the conditions under which those data must be released. Each organization must understand, apply, and enforce the criteria for ensuring the privacy and confidentiality of their data.

The criteria do not specify the procedural controls for unauthorized access, alteration, or destruction of the data. Those controls are placed within business processes. Similarly, the controls for the appropriate backup and recovery of the data are placed within business processes.

The data privacy and confidentiality criteria apply only to the Common Data through Data Subjects and Data Characteristics. They do not apply directly to the Data Product Data. However, when the data cross-references have been made, the data privacy and confidentiality criteria apply to all Data Product Data that are cross-referenced to the Common Data.

The data subject-relation diagram for data privacy and confidentiality is shown in Figure 7.1. A Legal Regulation is promulgated by a specific Jurisdiction. The recursive data relation allows the documentation of a hierarchy of Legal Regulations that are promulgated by a specific Jurisdiction. A Data Privacy Regulation applies a Legal Regulation to either a Data Subject, which includes all the Data Characteristics in that Data Subject, or to specific Data Characteristics when it does not apply to all the

Data Characteristics in a Data Subject.

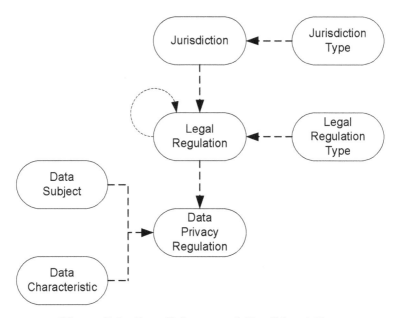

Figure 7.1. Data Privacy and Confidentiality.

Jurisdiction

Jurisdiction, as used here, is any legal entity that has the legal authority and right to develop, apply, and enforce laws and regulation pertaining to the privacy and confidentiality of the data.

The detail data for a Jurisdiction can be entered anytime a new Jurisdiction is identified.

> Jurisdiction. Begin Date (R)
> Jurisdiction. Comment
> Jurisdiction. Common Name (R)
> Jurisdiction. Definition (R)
> Jurisdiction. End Date
> Jurisdiction. Legal Name (R)
>
> Jurisdiction Type. Name (R)

Jurisdiction Type is a data reference set that qualifies a Jurisdiction. Each organization developing Data Resource Data can designate the types of jurisdiction based on their particular needs, such as City, County, State, Federal, and so on.

Scenario 7.1. Jurisdictions Promulgating Legal Regulations.

Business executives are extremely concerned about the release of privileged data and the legal impacts of such release. They want to implement a procedure to understand and document all the existing laws, regulation, court precedents, and so on, that pertain to any data that they capture and store in their data resource.

The data stewards tasked with that implementation begin by identifying all the legal entities that promulgate criteria for the privacy and confidentiality of their data. They discover that those legal entities include multiple Federal agencies, State agencies, a few County and City departments, Federal Courts, State Supreme Courts, and County Supreme Courts, professional organizations, and their own organizational policies. They document each of those legal entities as a Jurisdiction.

Legal Regulation

Legal Regulation is any law, ordinance, administrative code, policy, court order, and so on that is prepared, administered, or enforced by a Jurisdiction. Legal Regulation is recursive to identify a hierarchy of Legal Regulations within a specific Jurisdiction.

The detail data for a Legal Regulation can be entered anytime a new regulation pertaining to data privacy and confidentiality is identified. The parent Jurisdiction must be documented before the Legal Regulation can be documented.

> Legal Regulation. Comment
> Legal Regulation. Effective Date (R)
> Legal Regulation. Termination Date
> Legal Regulation. Text (R)
> Legal Regulation. Title (R)
>
> Jurisdiction. Legal Name (R)
> "Parent" Legal Regulation. Title
> Legal Regulation Type. Name (R)

Legal Regulation Type is a data reference set that qualifies Legal Regulation. Each organization developing Data Resource Data can designate the types of legal regulations that suit their particular needs, such as State Law, County Ordinance, Administrative Code, and so on.

Scenario 7.2. Legal Regulations Pertaining to Data.

When the data stewards have documented all the known Jurisdictions that promulgate Legal Regulations pertaining to data privacy and confidentiality, they continue by identifying and documenting all the specific Legal Regulations that pertain to data privacy and confidentiality. That task is often difficult and requires persistence to identify all the Legal Regulations pertaining to data privacy and confidentiality. Many Jurisdictions have search capability and people responsible for their Legal Regulations that the data stewards can use to identify Legal Regulations pertaining to data privacy and confidentiality. When an appropriate Legal Regulation is identified, it is documented.

Data Privacy Regulation

Data Privacy Regulation is the connection between Legal Regulation and the Common Data, specifically Data Subjects or Data Characteristics. Legal Regulation can apply to a Data Subject, which applies to all Data Characteristics within that Data Subject, or it can apply to specific Data Characteristics. Each Data Privacy Regulation connects one Legal Regulation to either a Data Subject or a Data Characteristic.

The detail data for a Data Privacy Regulation can be entered anytime the data covered by a Legal Regulation are identified. The Legal Regulation and the Data Subject or Data Characteristic must be documented before the Data Privacy Regulation can be documented.

> Data Privacy Regulation. Begin Date
> Data Privacy Regulation. Comment
> Data Privacy Regulation. End Date
> Data Privacy Regulation. System Identifier
>
> Data Characteristic. Name Complete (R/P)
> Data Subject. Name Complete (R/P)
> Legal Regulation. Title (R)

Scenario 7.3. Connecting Legal Regulation To Common Data.

When the data stewards have documented the Legal Regulations within each Jurisdiction that pertain to data privacy and confidentiality, they can begin connecting those Legal Regulations to the appropriate Data Subjects and Data Characteristics. The connection can be difficult since the names of the data specified in the Legal Regulation often do not match the names of the data in the organization's data resource, and often are broad groupings of data that require some degree of interpretation.

The data stewards need to work through these interpretations, and often use a Data Subject Thesaurus to help them identify the proper data subjects. That's one good reason to develop a comprehensive Data Subject Thesaurus when developing Common Data. When in doubt, it is usually best to opt for over-specifying data privacy and confidentiality rather than under-specifying.

When the Legal Regulations have been connected to Data Subjects and Data Characteristics, the data cross-references can be used to identify the specific data in the organization's data resource, or on screens, reports, and documents, that need to be protected.

SUMMARY

The Data Protection Function provides the detail necessary to ensure that all legal requirements are meant for protecting the privacy and confidentiality of the Common Data and any Data Product Data cross-referenced to those common data. The legal requirements produced by a jurisdiction are connected with Data Subjects or Data Characteristics to which those legal requirements apply. Business processes then enforce those requirements when processing the data.

Chapter 8

DATA ACCESS

Data access shows which business processes access the data.

The data understanding process continues with the Data Access Function consisting of the data accessed by business processes. Data access includes the creation, use, update, and deletion of the data. The understanding and documentation of the data access pertains to the Data Product Data, not to the Common Data.

DATA USE

The understanding of data access begins with understanding the use of the data by business processes. The data subject-relation diagram for the use of Data Product Sets and Data Product Units by Business Processes is shown in Figure 8.1. Data Product Set is recursive to document Data Product Set Variations, and Data Product Unit is recursive to document Data Product Unit Variations.

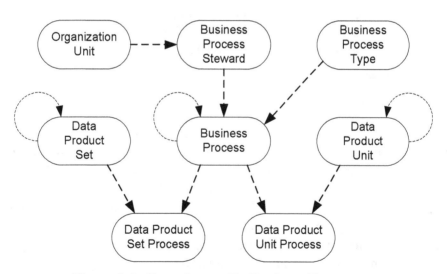

Figure 8.1. Data Access By Business Processes.

Business Process Steward

Business Process Steward is a person responsible for maintaining some aspect of creating, altering, or managing the organization's business activities for the welfare of the organization. A Business Process Steward has responsibilities for business processes much like a Data Steward has responsibilities for data. Business Process Stewards are part of a Business Activity Architecture, but are included within the Data Architecture because of their knowledge and insight about the data.

The detail data for a Business Process Steward can be entered anytime a business process steward is identified. The Organization Unit must be created before the Business Process Steward can be created. Organization Unit was described in the Data Responsibility Chapter.

> Business Process Steward. Address City Name Complete
> Business Process Steward. Address Line 1
> Business Process Steward. Address Line 2
> Business Process Steward. Address Postal Code
> Business Process Steward. Address State Name Postal Abbreviation
> Business Process Steward. Begin Date (R)
> Business Process Steward. Cell Phone Number Complete
> Business Process Steward. E-Mail Address
> Business Process Steward. End Date
> Business Process Steward. Fax Number
> Business Process Steward. Name Complete (R)
> Business Process Steward. Office Phone Number Complete
> Business Process Steward. Responsibility Description (R)
> Business Process Steward. Title (R)
>
> Organization Unit. Name (R)

Scenario 8.1. Business Process Steward.

An organization has been considering establishing business process stewards for the management of their business processes, but have been delaying their establishment due to time constraints. However, realizing that the business professionals were having difficulty understanding much of the data used by the business processes, and realizing that business process stewards could assist with that process as well as assist with the understanding and document of the business processes, the organization decided to proceed with establishing Business Process Stewards.

Initially, the Business Process Stewards were tasked with helping understand the use of data by business processes. As more data understanding was gained and documented, the Business Process Stewards began to identify and understand problems with the business processes and ultimately set about resolving the business process problems.

Business Process

Business Process is any manual or automated process that captures, creates, stores, uses, or manipulates the data in any manner. Business Process is recursive to document a hierarchy of Business Processes, such as information systems, application programs, subroutines, and so on. Business Process is part of the Business Activity Architecture, but is included within the Data Architecture for the purpose of understanding the data used by Business Processes.

The detail data for a Business Process can be entered anytime a Business Process is identified. Parent Business Processes may be documented as an understanding of the Business Activity Architecture, however only the Business Processes that use the data need to be documented for an understanding the use of data.

> Business Process. Definition (R)
> Business Process. Name (R)
>
> "Parent" Business Process. Name
> Business Process Steward. Name Complete (R)
> Business Process Type. Name (R)

Business Process Type is a data reference set that qualifies Business Process. Each organization implementing Data Resource Data can designate the Business Process Types that suit their particular needs, such as Manual, Automated, Computer, and so on.

Scenario 8.2. Business Process

The Business Process Stewards begin by identifying the business processes that use the data and document them as Business Processes. In some situations, parent Business Processes are documented to understand the hierarchy of business processes within a Business Activity Architecture. In other situations, parent Business Processes are not documented.

Data Product Set Process

Data Product Set Process identifies the access of a Data Product Set by a Business Process. If a Business Process accesses the entire Data Product Set, then that Data Product Set is connected to the Business Process, whether or not the Business Process actually uses all the data in the Data Product Set. It's the access to the data that's important to document. The detailed documentation of the business process describes how that business process actually uses the data.

The detail data for a Data Product Set Process can be entered anytime the use of a Data Product Set by a Business Process is identified. The Business Process and Data Product Set must be documented before the Data Product Set Process can be documented.

> Data Product Set Process. Comment
>
> Business Process. Name (R)
> Data Product Set. Name (R)

Scenario 8.3. Data Product Set Use.

Business process stewards identify the Data Product Sets where all the data in the Data Product Set are accessed by the business process. The Data Product Sets are connected to the Business Processes. Comments are made about the connection to further understand the data that are used by the Business Process.

Data Product Unit Process

Data Product Unit Process identifies the individual Data Product Units that are accessed by a Business Process. If the Business Process accesses a subset of the Data Product Units in a Data Product Set, then only those Data Product Units, rather than the entire Data Product Set, are connected to the Business Process, regardless of whether the Business Process actually uses those data. It's the access to the data that's important to document.

The detail data for a Data Product Unit Process can be entered anytime the use of a subset of Data Product Units in a Data Product Set by a Business Process is identified. The Business Process and Data Product Unit must be documented before the Data Product Unit Process can be documented.

> Data Product Unit Process. Comment
> Data Product Unit Process. Data Create Indicator[3]
> Data Product Unit Process. Data Delete Indicator
> Data Product Unit Process. Data Update Indicator
> Data Product Unit Process. Data Use Indicator
>
> Business Process. Name (R)
> Data Product Unit. Name (R)

---

[3] The four indicators were added since *Data Resource Data*. See Appendix A for details.

Scenario 8.4. Data Product Unit Use.

Business process stewards determine that most of the business processes access only a small subset of the data in a Data Product Set, commonly known as a data view. They decide to document only the Data Product Units within a Data Product Set that are accessed and used by the Business Process. The Data Use Indicator is set to "Y".

Scenario 8.5. All Data Product Units Regardless of Access.

A team of business process stewards and application developers decide to document all of the Data Product Units in a Data Product Set that is being accessed by a Business Process. The primary reason for that decision is to document how the data are being used by each Business Process, which is placed in the Comment data characteristic. That insight will be used during the process to designate the preferred Common Data. The secondary reason for that decision is that the Business Process can be easily changed at any time to access more or fewer Data Product Units within a Data Product Set, therefore it's best to document all the Data Product Units. The tertiary reason is that the use of data by Business Processes changes over time and the team wants to monitor the trends in the use of data.

DATA CREATION, UPDATE, AND DELETION

Business processes can also create, update, and delete the data. The same technique is used to document the creation, updating, and deletion of data as was used for documenting the use of the data. Data Product Unit Process is used to document all the data accessed by a business process, and in addition. The Data Creation Indicator, Data Update Indicator, and Data Delete Indicator are set as necessary to indicate if the Business Process can create, update, or delete the data.

The technique for documenting when a Business Process can create, update, or delete data is time consuming. However, the benefits of knowing what Business Processes can alter the data is a great benefit when resolving the disparity in the data resource or in business activities.

Scenario 8.6. Data Creation, Update, and Deletion.

Business process stewards and data stewards are working together within an organization to identify and resolve both the disparity in their data resource and the disparity in their business activities. They discovered that the disparity in the business activities was at least as serious as the disparity in the data resource, and in many situations more serious. They decided to embark on a major initiative to resolve both the data resource disparity and the business activity disparity.

The first step in the initiative was to identify and document the Data Product Units that each Business Process created, used, updated, and deleted. As the team moved through the data and business processes, a constraint was placed on the business processes that if any changes were made to the data that the business process created, used, updated, or deleted, that the team must be notified first so that the changes could be documented.

The result was a thorough understanding of the data that was created, used, updated, and deleted by business processes. Based on the understanding, informed decisions could be made about the resolution of data resource disparity and business activity disparity.

SUMMARY

The Data Access Function documents the data that are accessed and used by business processes. The Data Product Data access and use are documented rather than the Common Data because the Common Data are not actually used by business processes. However, they do help identify the Data Product Data that are accessed and used by business processes.

Chapter 9

DATA PROVENANCE

Data provenance tracks data back to their origin.

The data understanding process continues with the Data Provenance Function consisting of tracking the movement of data along a pathway from their source to their present location and any changes made to those data along that pathway.

DATA PROVENANCE ORIGIN

Provenance comes from the French provenir, meaning *to come from*. It represents the origin or source of something, the history of ownership, or the current location of an object. The primary purpose of provenance is to confirm or gather evidence as to the time, place, and business entity responsible for the creation, production, or discovery of something. Provenance is accomplished by tracing the history of something from its origin to the present.

Data provenance is provenance applied to the organization's data resource. It includes the source of data, how the data were captured, the meaning of the data when first captured, where the data were stored, the path of those data to the current location, how the data were moved along that path, and how those data were altered along that path. It ensures the authenticity of those data and their appropriateness for supporting the business, and provides the base to evaluate data resource quality.

Data provenance includes data heritage and data lineage. Data heritage is documentation of the source of the data and their original meaning at the time of capture. Data lineage is a description of the pathway from the data source to their current location and the alterations made along that pathway.

Data tracking is the process of documenting the data provenance. External data tracking deals with the flow of data between data sites in different organizations. Internal data tracking deals with the flow of data between applications and data files within an organization.

Data tracking often results in a network of data movement and changes to the data. Seldom are the data flows linear with minimal changes to the data. The data are often moved, split, merged, and altered in their pathway from the initial source to the current location.

DATA PROVENANCE

The data subject-relation diagram for data provenance is shown in Figure 9.1. The data provenance data apply to the Data Product Data, not to the Common Data. The external data provenance data are not intended for identifying the detail Data Product Data along the pathway from their origin to an organization, but only for identifying the changes to the data along that pathway. They are driven by the data an organization receives, not necessarily by the data that move along a pathway but never reach an organization. The internal data provenance data are intended for identifying the detail Data Product Data within the organization.

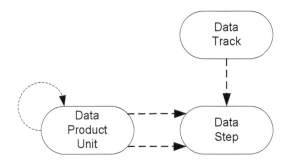

Figure 9.1. Data Provenance.

The detail about the Data Product Data is contained in Data Product Unit, which was described in the Data Inventory Chapter. Data Product Unit is recursive to show Data Product Unit Variations, and is subordinate to Data Product Set, which is subordinate to Data Product, which is subordinate to both Organization and Data Site.

Data Track

A Data Track is pathway that a unit of data follows from its origin to its current location. The detail data for a Data Track can be entered anytime a Data Track is identified.

> Data Track. Begin Date (R)
> Data Track. Comment
> Data Track. Description (R)
> Data Track. End Date

Data Track. Name (R)[4]

Scenario 9.1. Data Tracks.

An organization receives data from many different data sources, analyzes those data, and provides comments and recommendations to their clients about business actions they should take based on the result of the data analysis. The organization has become increasingly concerned about the original source of the data and the meaning of those data, particularly since the data have very few definitions or integrity rules. The major concern is that the organization is providing incorrect or inappropriate comments and recommendations to their clients.

The organization establishes a team of data stewards to identify the source, meaning, integrity, and quality of the data they receive from the external sources. The data steward team begins by identifying the data units they receive and the sources from which each unit of data is received. As they identify each source, they ask where that source acquired the data. In many situations, the process continues through multiple sources, and the data from one source were often combined from multiple previous sources. The team decided they needed to start defining the Data Tracks for each data unit moving from its source to the organization.

Data Step

A Data Step is one increment in a Data Track from the creation of data to its current location that documents any changes to the data. It represents incoming data and outgoing data and any changes to those data. The changes to the data are documented in the Data Product Unit represented by the Data Step, such as definitions, integrity rules, and so on. The data characteristics in Data Step document the process of the Data Step, not the detail of changes to the data.

> Data Step. Begin Date (R)
> Data Step. Comment
> Data Step. Description (R)
> Data Step. End Date
> Data Step. Sequence Number (R)[5]
>
> "Incoming" Data Product Unit. Name (R)
> "Outgoing" Data Product Unit. Name (R)
> Data Track. Name (R)

---

[4] The data characteristic was added since *Data Resource Data*. See Appendix A for details.
[5] The data characteristic was added since Data Resource Data. See Appendix A for details.

Scenario 9.2. Data Steps.

The data steward team established in Scenario 9.1 discovered that most of the data they received from external sources were not well defined when initially collected, were seldom edited by more than simple format integrity rules, had likely been altered since their collection, and were the result of analysis of other source data that was not formally documented.

They decided to document each step for each data unit they received as Data Steps in the pathway from the original source to their organization. They flagged all the data that were in question and eliminated most of those data from their analyses and recommendations. The result was a greater confidence in the comments and recommendations that were being provided to their clients.

SUMMARY

The Data Provenance Function tracks data from their source, along a pathway to their destination, and documents any changes to the data long that pathway. The Data Product Data are tracked, specifically the Data Product Units. The tracking provides insight for both the understanding of the data and the quality of the data.

Chapter 10

DATA SHARING

Data sharing requires a robust data clearinghouse.

The data understanding process continues with the Data Sharing Function that consists of a data clearinghouse for the sharing data between organizations, and data projects for the cooperation between organizations to acquire and manage data common to those organizations.

DATA CLEARINGHOUSE

Data Clearinghouse is a central location for the collection, classification, and distribution of data pertaining to the understanding organizations have about their business data. Those data can be readily shared between organizations belonging to the Data Clearinghouse, resulting in the possible sharing of the business data, which is often less expensive than each organization collecting their own data. The data subject-relation diagram for the Data Clearinghouse is shown in Figure 10.1.

Basically, the Data Clearinghouse has a central Data Clearinghouse Item that pertains to a set of data maintained by some Organization. That Data Clearinghouse Item can have multiple authors that are assigned to the Data Clearinghouse Item through the Data Clearinghouse Item Author.

A Data Clearinghouse Item can be referenced by many different Data Clearinghouse Topics that are assigned to the Data Clearinghouse Item by the Data Clearinghouse Item Topic. Each of the Data Clearinghouse Topics can be referenced by many different Data Clearinghouse Keywords that are assigned to the Data Clearinghouse Topic by Data Clearinghouse Topic Keyword.

A Data Clearinghouse Item can represent one or more Spatial Areas that are assigned to the Data Clearinghouse Item by Data Clearinghouse Item Area.

Data Steward and Organization were described in the Data Responsibility Chapter. A Data Steward is the liaison between a Data Clearinghouse Item and an Organization that either contributes to or uses the Data Clearinghouse. It's the person that populates the Data Clearinghouse for the

Organization and can be contacted for any details about the data stored in the Data Clearinghouse by the Organization's business data.

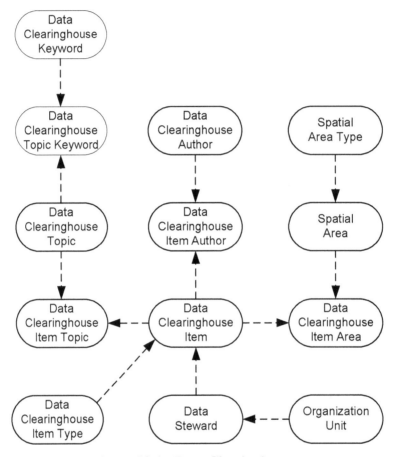

Figure 10.1. Data Clearinghouse.

The Data Clearinghouse has no specific sequence for entering the data, other than the parent data need to be entered before subordinate data can be entered. Each Data Steward can determine the sequence in which they enter the data into the Data Clearinghouse.

Data Clearinghouse Item

Data Clearinghouse Item is the heart of the Data Clearinghouse. It is any material that is published or unpublished, that describes or explains the business data meaning, how the business data were captured, how the business data were edited, how the business data are stored, or how the business data might be used. It is a reference to the existence of business data and does not contain the actual business data.

The detail data for a Data Clearinghouse Item can be entered anytime a Data Clearinghouse Item is identified. The parent Data Steward must be documented before the Data Clearinghouse Item can be documented.

> Data Clearinghouse Item. Acronym
> Data Clearinghouse Item. Definition (R)
> Data Clearinghouse Item. Name Complete (R)
> Data Clearinghouse Item. Publication Date
> Data Clearinghouse Item. Publication Identification
>
> Data Clearinghouse Item Type. Name (R)
> Data Steward. Name Complete (R)

Data Clearinghouse Item Type is a data reference set that qualifies Data Clearinghouse Item. Each organization implementing Data Resource Data can designate the data reference items to suit their particular needs, such as Book, Journal, Article, Presentation, and so on.

Scenario 10.1. Data Clearinghouse Establishment.

A state government agency receives funding to promote data sharing between other government agencies within and without the state and between government agencies and the private sector to the extent that such data sharing is allowed. The task is so large considering all the data available in each government agency that could be shared that a process is needed to make the existence of the data readily known to all interested government agencies.

The solution was to develop a Data Clearinghouse, invite other government agencies and private sector companies to document the data they have available in that Data Clearinghouse, and to make access to the Data Clearinghouse readily available. The project was slow getting started, but with persistent advertising and encouragement for government agencies to join the Data Clearinghouse became highly successful.

Scenario 10.2. Data Stewards For The Data Clearinghouse.

Each Organization that joins the Data Clearinghouse, whether government agency or private sector company, designates one or more of their Data Stewards to be the liaison between the Organization and the Data Clearinghouse Items representing the business data maintained by that Organization. These Data Stewards are responsible for populating the Data Clearinghouse and for answering questions about the business data maintained by their Organization. They enter their vitae as Data Stewards into the Data Clearinghouse.

Scenario 10.3. Data Clearinghouse Items

After the Data Steward vitae are entered into the Data Clearinghouse, those Data Stewards begin identifying the data their Organization has that may be of interest to other Organizations. They identify any documents that exist, or prepare documents, describing each set of data that their Organization has and enter that data into the Data Clearinghouse Items.

Data Clearinghouse Author

Data Clearinghouse Author is any person who is involved in developing material pertaining to the business data that are maintained by their Organization and are documented as Data Clearinghouse Items, whether or not their name appears on the material and whether or not the material is formally published.

The detail data for a Data Clearinghouse Author can be entered anytime an author is identified. The Data Clearinghouse Author is not necessarily the same as the Data Steward, however if the Data Steward prepares any documents that are entered as Data Clearinghouse Items, they should also enter themselves as a Data Clearinghouse Author.

> Data Clearinghouse Author. Description (R)
> Data Clearinghouse Author. Family Name (R)
> Data Clearinghouse Author. Individual Name (R)

Scenario 10.4. Data Clearinghouse Authors.

The Data Stewards entering the Data Clearinghouse Items determine if that item has any known authors. Many of the Data Clearinghouse Items are formal publications describing specific data, such as wetlands, drainage basins, public land survey, and so on. These formal publications generally have authors. Many of the Data Clearinghouse Items are informal publications that may or may not have known authors. In these situations no Data Clearinghouse Authors are documented. The Data Stewards enter the know authors as Data Clearinghouse Authors.

Data Clearinghouse Item Author

Data Clearinghouse Item Author is the connection between Data Clearinghouse Authors and Data Clearinghouse Items. One entry is made for each Data Clearinghouse Author that prepared a Data Clearinghouse Item.

The detail data for a Data Clearinghouse Item Author can be entered anytime the Data Clearinghouse Authors and Data Clearinghouse Items have been created. When multiple authors appear on a Data Clearinghouse Item, the Sequence Number is used to show the sequence of those authors. Both the Data Clearinghouse Item and Data Clearinghouse Author must be created before the connection can be made.

> Data Clearinghouse Item Author. Comment
> Data Clearinghouse Item Author. Sequence Number
>
> Data Clearinghouse Author. System Identifier (R)
> Data Clearinghouse Item. Name Complete (R)

Scenario 10.5. Data Clearinghouse Item Author.

The Data Stewards connect the Data Clearinghouse Authors to the Data Clearinghouse Items as soon as each is created in the Data Clearinghouse. The purpose for making the connection is that Organizations interested in finding all the material prepared by a specific author can readily search for those authors and find the material they prepared.

Data Clearinghouse Topic

Data Clearinghouse Topic is a particular subject area that can be used to search Data Clearinghouse for relevant Data Clearinghouse Items, such as roads, timber stands, hydroelectric dams, and so on.

The detail data for a Data Clearinghouse Topic can be entered anytime a specific topic is identified.

> Data Clearinghouse Topic. Begin Date (R)
> Data Clearinghouse Topic. Description (R)
> Data Clearinghouse Topic. End Date
> Data Clearinghouse Topic. Phrase (R)

Scenario 10.6. Data Clearinghouse Topics.

Each Data Steward entering Data Clearinghouse Items identifies the major topic for the data represented by the Data Clearinghouse Item. More than one major topic can be identified for a Data Clearinghouse Item, however all the aliases for those major topics should not be entered. The Data Stewards generally coordinate the designation of major topics to be entered as Data Clearinghouse Topics before they are entered to provide a meaningful set of major topics.

Data Clearinghouse Item Topic

Data Clearinghouse Item Topic is a connection between Data Clearinghouse Items and Data Clearinghouse Topics. One entry is made for each relevant

Data Clearinghouse Topic that pertains to a Data Clearinghouse Item.

The detail data for a Data Clearinghouse Item Topic can be entered anytime the Data Clearinghouse Items and Data Clearinghouse Topics have been created. Both the Data Clearinghouse Item and Data Clearinghouse Topic must be entered before the connection can be made.

> Data Clearinghouse Item Topic. Comment
> Data Clearinghouse Item Topic. Phrase (R)
> Data Clearinghouse Topic. Phrase (R)
>
> Data Clearinghouse Item. Name Complete (R)

Scenario 10.7. Data Clearinghouse Item Topic.

The Data Stewards connect all the relevant Data Clearinghouse Topics to the Data Clearinghouse Items. New connections are made anytime additional Data Clearinghouse Topics are created, and can be removed when Data Clearinghouse Topics are removed or changed. The Data Stewards work closely together to maintain a meaningful set of Data Clearinghouse Topics and connect them to the Data Clearinghouse Items.

Data Clearinghouse Keyword

Data Clearinghouse Keyword is a synonym or alias for a Data Clearinghouse Topic. Data Clearinghouse Keywords are created to help identify the major Data Clearinghouse Topics, and to keep the list of Data Clearinghouse Topics relatively small and meaningful.

The detail data for a Data Clearinghouse Keyword can be entered at any time. Generally, the more aliases and synonyms that can be identified and entered as Keywords for a major Data Clearinghouse Topic help Organizations searching for specific data find the data relevant to their needs. For example, Creek, Stream, Brook, Canal, and so on may be entered as Data Clearinghouse Keywords for a River.

> Data Clearinghouse Keyword. Begin Date (R)
> Data Clearinghouse Keyword. Definition (R)
> Data Clearinghouse Keyword. End Date
> Data Clearinghouse Keyword. Phrase (R)

Scenario 10.8. Data Clearinghouse Keywords.

Data Stewards work through the major Data Clearinghouse Topics and identify as many aliases and synonyms as possible, and enter them as Data Clearinghouse Keywords. For example, public works data stewards identify keywords for Road such as Street, Alley, Highway, Avenue, Boulevard,

Court, and so on. Similarly, environmental data stewards identify keywords for Wetlands such as marsh, swamp, bog, and so on. All of these aliases are entered as Data Clearinghouse Keywords.

Data Clearinghouse Topic Keyword

Data Clearinghouse Topic Keyword is a connection between Data Clearinghouse Topics and their alias or synonym Data Clearinghouse Keywords. The connection allows Organizations to search for relevant Data Clearinghouse Topics, which can be used to search for relevant Data Clearinghouse Items.

The detail data for Data Clearinghouse Topic Keyword can be entered anytime the Data Clearinghouse Topics and Data Clearinghouse Keywords have been created. Both the Data Clearinghouse Topic and Data Clearinghouse Keyword must be created before the connection can be made.

> Data Clearinghouse Keyword. Phrase (R)
> Data Clearinghouse Topic. Phrase (R)
> Data Clearinghouse Topic Keyword. Comment

Scenario 10.9. Data Clearinghouse Topic Keywords.

Data Stewards connect the Data Clearinghouse Topics to the Data Clearinghouse Keywords to provide the link from Data Clearinghouse Keyword to Data Clearinghouse Topic to Data Clearinghouse Item. The tasks of creating the Data Clearinghouse Keywords and connecting them to the Data Clearinghouse Topics are often done at the same time while the terms are fresh in the Data Steward's minds. New connections are made anytime new Data Clearinghouse Keywords are identified, and Data Clearinghouse Keywords can be removed or changed. The Data Stewards work closely together to create a set of Data Clearinghouse Keywords to identify the major Data Clearinghouse Topics.

Spatial Area

Spatial Area is any point, line, two-dimensional area, or three-dimensional area such as a coordinate location, a road, a geographical area, a political area, an underground aquifer, and so on. Spatial area can represent the Earth (geospatial), another planet like Mars (ariespatial), a building (structo-spatial), an organism (biospatial), space (astrospatial), and so on, depending on the base for the measurement.

The detail data for a Spatial Area can be entered anytime a Spatial Area is identified.

Spatial Area. Begin Date (R)
Spatial Area. Comment
Spatial Area. Definition (R)
Spatial Area. End Date
Spatial Area. Name (R)

Spatial Area Type. Name (R)

Spatial Area Type is a data reference set that qualifies Spatial Area. Each organization implementing Data Resource Data can designate the data reference items to suit their particular needs, such as Coordinate System, Road, City, Drainage Basin, underground oil deposit, and so on.

Scenario 10.10. Spatial Areas.

Data Stewards across multiple government agencies work together to identify all of the spatial areas that are commonly used by those agencies, such as USGS Quadrangles, States, Counties, Cities, Drainage Basins, all forms of Districts, and so on. When those spatial areas are identified, they are defined and entered into the Data Clearinghouse. As additional spatial areas are identified, they are defined and entered into the Data Clearinghouse. The Data Stewards coordinate the Spatial Area identification and definition to ensure that all Spatial Areas are identified and that none of them are identified redundantly.

Data Clearinghouse Item Area

Data Clearinghouse Item Area is a connection between Data Clearinghouse Items and Spatial Areas that identify the spatial location of the data represented by a Data Clearinghouse Item.

The detail data for a Data Clearinghouse Item Area can be entered anytime a Spatial Area is identified that contains data represented by the Data Clearinghouse Item. Both the Data Clearinghouse Item and the Spatial Area must be created before the connection can be made.

Data Clearinghouse Item Area. Comment
Data Clearinghouse Item. Name Complete (R)
Spatial Area. Name (R)

Scenario 10.11. Data Clearinghouse Item Area.

The Data Stewards that are familiar with the Data Clearinghouse Items that they entered which pertain to Spatial Areas begin making the connection between those Data Clearinghouse Items and Spatial Areas. In many situations the Data Stewards find that a Data Clearinghouse Item is, or can be, relevant to many different Spatial Areas, such as Stream data can be relevant to a Drainage Basin, a USGS Quadrangle, a County, and so on.

The Data Stewards determine that initially connections will be made to all of the relevant Spatial Areas for a Data Clearinghouse Item so that other government agencies can readily identify the Data Clearinghouse Item. However, as geographic information systems become common across multiple government agencies, those geographic information systems can readily identify all the relevant Spatial Areas for a Data Clearinghouse Item when it has been connected to one Spatial Area.

DATA PROJECTS

Data Project is any formal or informal project that is related to the data resource of an Organization in any way. Documenting Data Projects helps Organizations with similar needs coordinate their efforts and maximize resources. Data Project is not intended to be a project management system, but only to make Organizations aware of the existence or desire of other Organizations to establish a Data Project.

The data subject-relation diagram for Data Project is shown in Figure 10.2. Data Steward and Organization Unit were described in the Data Responsibility Chapter.

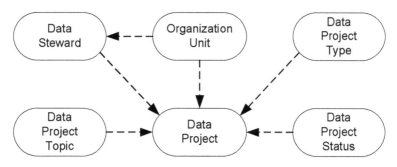

Figure 10.2. Data Project.

Data Project Status is a data reference set that qualifies Data Project. Each organization implementing Data Resource Data can designate the data reference items to suit their particular needs, such as Abandoned, Completed, Desired, and so on.

Data Project Topic is a data reference set that qualifies Data Project. Each organization implementing Data Resource Data can designate the data reference items to suit their particular needs, such as Financial, Geospatial, Water Infrastructure, and so on.

Data Project Type is a data reference set that qualifies Data Project. Each organization implementing Data Resource Data can designate the data reference items to suit their particular needs, such as Development, Documentation, Integration, Sharing, and so on.

The detail data for a Data Project can be entered anytime a Data Project is identified. The Data Project Status can be changed at any time to reflect the status of the Data Project.

> Data Project. Acronym
> Data Project. Actual End Date
> Data Project. Begin Date (R)
> Data Project. Comment
> Data Project. Description (R)
> Data Project. Name (R)
> Data Project. Planned End Date (R)
>
> Data Project Status. Name (R)
> Data Project Topic. Name (R)
> Data Project Type. Name (R)
> Data Steward. Name Complete (R)
> Organization Unit. Name (R)

Scenario 10.12. Data Projects.

The government agency that received funding to promote data sharing, described in Scenario 10.1, also implemented Data Project to help coordinate that data sharing effort and encourage Organizations to cooperate on data projects that are common to multiple Organizations. The intent is that any Organization that is conducting, planning, or desiring a Data Project should create an entry for that Data Project.

Organizations that are planning any type of data project should consult Data Project to determine if another Organization is already conducting or has planned a similar data project. The opportunity may exist to cooperate on the data project or to acquire the data resulting from the data project.

Scenario 10.13. Cooperation On Desired Data Projects.

Data Stewards discovered that many Organizations were listing Data Projects that they desired to conduct, but did not have the resources to conduct. They made a concentrated effort to identify identical or similar Data Projects that were desired and to connect the Organizations desiring to conduct those data projects. The result was that many of the data projects could be accomplished with cooperation between Organizations.

While reviewing the desired Data Projects the Data Stewards identified several Organizations that were conducting identical Data Projects. They notified these Organizations, which resulted in a coordinated effort and a saving of resources. The Data Stewards decided to make routine searches for desired Data Projects and identical or similar Data Projects.

SUMMARY

The Data Sharing Function provides a robust data clearinghouse to assist organizations in sharing data and sharing projects related to the data resource. The sharing can be done within an organization or between multiple organizations. Data Projects related to the data resource are also documented so that organizations can share in both the effort to conduct the project and the results of the project.

Chapter 11

DERIVED DATA

Derived data must be documented so they can be understood.

The data understanding process continues with the Derived Data Function that consists of documenting the data that have been renormalized for the analytical processing of evaluational data, derived data hierarchies resulting from operational processing and from analytical processing, and derived spatial data subjects.

DERIVED DATA OVERVIEW

The data subject-relation diagram for derived data is shown in Figure 11.1. Data Subject and Data Characteristic are shown vertically in the center of the diagram. The two data subjects on the left pertain to the contributors to a derived data subject and the assignment of foreign data characteristics to a derived data subject. The three data subjects on the right pertain to the documentation of a derived data hierarchy, the data subject sets within that hierarchy, and the data characteristics within those data subject. The details are described in the following sections.

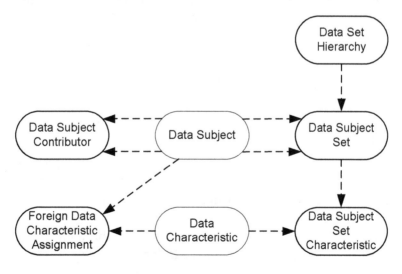

Figure 11.1. Derived Data.

EVALUATIONAL DATA

Evaluational data, often referred to as dimensional data, multi-dimensional data, data warehouse data, and so on, are a renormalization of operational data for the purpose of performing different forms of analyses on those data. The renormalization process alters the structure of the operational data to make those data easier to analyze by a wide variety of processes. Evaluational data are historical data, although the time delay from operational data to historical data can vary from quarterly or longer to near real time, known as trickle feeds.

A set of similar evaluational data form a data perspective that consists of a data focus and surrounding data dimensions. Data are typically drawn down from the data dimensions into the data focus where the analytical processing occurs. The Derived Data Function documents the data focus and its surrounding data dimensions.

Data Focus

Data focus is the data subject that contains the data from surrounding data dimensions that are being stored and used for analysis. A data focus is derived from an operational data subject and contains the common data subject word Focus. For example, if statistics are being developed about students, the data focus would be named Student Statistic Focus.

Manifestations of that data focus based on different selection criteria and different primary keys are identified with the data subject name followed by a number. For example, manifestations of Student Statistic Focus would be Student Statistic Focus 1, Student Statistic Focus 2, and so on.

A data focus is documented as a Data Subject, as described in the Common Data Chapter, with the definition describing the basic data subject, such as Student, and the type of analyses that are performed, such as Statistic. The Data Focus Indicator is set to "Y". The foreign keys identify the surrounding data dimensions. The manifestations of the data focus are documented as Data Subject Variations of that Data Subject.

The data dimensions have typically been documented as operational Data Subjects and do not need to be documented again. However, if a data dimension has been restructured during data renormalization, such as data drawn down from a parent data dimension, then it is documented as a Data Subject Variation. For example, if State data were brought down to County then County 1 would be created as a Data Subject Variation of County.

Scenario 11.1. Data Focus.

Business professionals in a county wanted to compile statistics about students within that county so they could make plans for the forthcoming school year. They decided that school district, school, academic year, race, and grade level were the categories about which they wanted to compile statistics.

An evaluational data resource model was created with Student Analytics Focus as the data focus and surrounding data dimensions for School District, School, Academic Year, Race, and Grade Level. The complete primary key for Student Analytics consists of School District. Identifier, School. Identifier, Academic Year. Number, Race. Code, and Grade Level. Number.

A Data Subject is documented for Student Analytics Focus with the Data Focus. Indicator = "Y". The complete primary key is documented for Student Analytic Focus.

Scenario 11.2. Data Dimensions.

The data dimensions in Scenario 11.1, which include School District, School, Academic Year, Race, and Grade Level, are already documented as operational Data Subjects and do not need to be further documented.

Scenario 11.3 Restructured Data Dimension.

The data in Scenario 11.1 are for a specific County, so County does not appear as a data dimension. However, the business professionals wanted to include County in their analyses in case the data were ever combined with other counties for state level data. Therefore, County was added as a parent of School District, and County. Code and County. Name were added to School District. The new restructured School District was documented as a Data Subject Variation for School District 1.

Foreign Data Characteristic Assignment

Foreign Data Characteristic Assignment is the assignment of operational Data Characteristics to a data focus. Specifically, it's the assignment of a Data Characteristic that is foreign to that Data Subject. The fact that the Data Characteristic is foreign to a Data Subject is shown by the Data Subject Name for the foreign Data Characteristic. For example, a data dimension for Student Statistic Focus might be Ethnicity. The Ethnicity. Name and Ethnicity. Code might be assigned to Student Statistic Focus.

The detail data for Foreign Key Characteristic Assignment can be entered anytime a Foreign Data Characteristic appears in a data focus. The parent

Data Subject representing the data focus and Data Characteristics must be created before the assignment can be made.

> Foreign Data Characteristic Assignment. Comment
> Data Characteristic. Name Complete (R)
> Data Subject. Name Complete (R)

Scenario 11.4. Foreign Data Characteristic In A Data Focus.

The Student Analytics Focus in Scenario 11.1 has data dimensions for School District, School, Academic Year, Race, and Grade Level. The business professionals wanted to be able to perform their analyses using either the data values or the data names, so both were brought down from the data dimensions to the data focus.

The result is foreign data characteristics for County. Code, County. Name, School District. Identifier, School District. Name, School. Identifier, School. Name, Academic Year. Number, Race. Code, Race. Name, Grade Level. Number, and Grade Level. Name within Student Analytics Focus. Each of these data characteristics are documented as a Foreign Data Characteristic within Student Analytic Focus.

Scenario 11.5. Foreign Data Characteristic In A Data Dimension.

The placement of County. Code and County. Name in the data dimension for School District described in Scenario 11.3 are documented as foreign data characteristics in the School District 1 Data Subject Variation.

Analytical Processing

As the analytical processing continues many different manifestations of the Student Analytics Focus are created based on the selection criteria and the primary keys. Each specific manifestation of a data focus, meaning each different set of selection criteria and each different set of primary keys are documented as a manifestation of the data focus. Only the set of primary keys is important for the manifestation of a data focus. The sequence of the primary keys is not important.

Scenario 11.6. Data Focus Manifestations For Different Primary Keys.

The Student data described in Scenario 11.1 are analyzed using different data dimensions, meaning different sets of primary keys. Analyses were conducted for:

> School District ^ Grade Level ^ Academic Year ^ Race
>
> School ^ Academic Year ^ Race

School District ^ School ^ Academic Year ^ Grade Level ^ Race

Each of the data subject sets in these analyses has a different set of primary keys, as listed below.

School District is the top of the hierarchy and has no parents, so the primary key is School District. Identifier. It is designated Student Analytics 1.

School is the top of a hierarchy with the primary key of School. Identifier. It is designated Student Analytics 2.

School has a parent of School District with the primary key of School District. Identifier and School. Identifier. It is designated Student Analytics 3.

Grade Level has a parent of School District with the primary key of School District. Identifier and Grade Level. Number. It is designated Student Analytics 4.

Grade Level has parents of School District, School, and Academic Year with the primary key of School District. Identifier, School. Identifier, Academic Year. Number, and Grade Level. Number. It is designated Student Analytics 5.

Academic Year has parents of School District and Grade Level with the primary key of School District. Identifier, Grade Level. Number, and Academic Year. Number. It is designated Student Analytics 6.

Academic Year has parents of School District and School with the primary key of School District Identifier, School. Identifier, and Academic Year. Number. It is designated Student Analytics 7.

Race has parents of School District, Grade Level, and Academic Year with the primary key of School District. Identifier, Grade Level. Number, Academic Year. Number, and Race. Code. It is designated Student Analytics 8.

Race has parents of School and Academic Year with the primary key of School. Identifier, Academic Year. Number, and Race. Code. It is designated Student Analytics 9.

Race has parents of School District, School, Academic Year, and Grade Level with the primary key of School District. Identifier, School. Identifier, Academic Year. Number, Grade Level. Number, and Race. Code. It is designated Student Analytics 10.

Each of these data subject sets is documented as a Data Subject Variation of the Data Subject representing Student Analytics Focus. Only the set of primary keys is important, not the sequence of the primary keys. The set of primary keys, representing the sequence of the parent, grandparent, and so on, can be arranged in any sequence without altering the meaning of the data set.

Scenario 11.7. Data Focus Manifestation For Primary Key Sequence.

The Student data described in Scenario 11.1 are analyzed with the same set of primary keys, but the primary keys are in a different sequence. Analyses were conducted for:

> Grade Level ^ Academic Year ^ School District ^ Race
>
> Academic Year ^ School District ^ Grade Level ^ Race

The set of primary keys for Race in both analyses is the same even though the sequence is different. Therefore, Race is not a different manifestation of Student Analytics Focus.

However, different manifestations of Student Analytics Focus are created for Grade Level, Academic Year, and School District. Each of these need to be documented as Data Subject Variations for Student Analytics Focus, as described in Scenario 11.6.

Scenario 11.8. Data Focus Manifestations for Selection Criteria.

The Student data described in Scenario 11.1 are analyzed with different selections of data, meaning different sets of data were used for the analyses. The different sets may be a different range of Academic Years, a subset of Race, and so on. Each different set of data used in the analyses, even within the same set of primary keys, becomes a different manifestation of the data focus. The data integrity rules for the data focus manifestation describe the selection criteria used for the analysis.

Using the hierarchy below, data were analyzed for the last five academic years, the last 10 academic years, and the last 15 academic years. These three different selections of data result in different manifestations of Student Analytics Focus for Academic Year, School District, Grade Level, and Race, which could be named Student Analytics 11, Student Analytics 12, Student Analytics 13, and Student Analytics 14 respectively.

> Academic Year ^ School District ^ Grade Level ^ Race

The techniques described above may seem very detailed and time consuming, and the tendency may be to not do the detailed documentation. However, when many different analyses are performed on a particular data focus, and those analyses are not properly documented, the results can become quite confusing. Many organizations have found that they do not thoroughly understand the result of their analyses because they have not properly documented those analyses. Therefore, it is most prudent to thoroughly document each analysis that is performed.

DERIVED DATA HIERARCHY

The results of analyses performed on evaluational data typically produce a hierarchy of nested data sets. The hierarchy may be displayed as an actual hierarchy of nested data sets, or as a table of data with rows, columns, horizontal and vertical totals, cross-footing, and so on. To put it the other way around, any table, screen, or report of data can be documented as a hierarchy of nested data sets. The reader can refer to *Data Resource Design* for specific examples.

A hierarchy of nested data sets can be easily documented using the Data Set Hierarchy, Data Subject Set, and Data Subject Set Characteristic, as described below. When properly documented, the hierarchy can be easily printed to show the structure of the data resulting from analysis.

Data Set Hierarchy

Data Set Hierarchy is a hierarchy of nested data sets where each data set in that hierarchy represents the manifestation of a data focus. The nesting of data sets shows the relationship between the data sets. The Data Set Hierarchy has a name and each of the nested data sets in that hierarchy are named according to the manifestation of the data focus they represent.

The detail data for a Data Set Hierarchy can be entered anytime the hierarchy has been identified.

> Data Set Hierarchy. Begin Date (R)
> Data Set Hierarchy. Comment
> Data Set Hierarchy. Description (R)
> Data Set Hierarchy. End Date
> Data Set Hierarchy. Name (R)

Scenario 11.9. Data Set Hierarchy.

The sequence of data subjects in Scenario 11.6, which are shown below, can be documented as three different Data Set Hierarchies. Each of the Data Set Hierarchies has a unique name and a description that explains the meaning of the Data Set Hierarchy.

> School District ^ Grade Level ^ Academic Year ^ Race

113

School ^ Academic Year ^ Race

School District ^ School ^ Academic Year ^ Grade Level ^ Race

Data Subject Set

Data Subject Set is a Data Subject that appears as a data set in a Data Set Hierarchy. It may have a variety of parent, peer, or subordinate Data Subject Sets. However, only the parent Data Subject Sets are important for identifying the Data Subject Set. Specifically, the set of primary keys identifying the parent Data Subject Sets is important, regardless of the sequence of those primary keys.

The detail data for a Data Subject Set, which is the "Child" Data Subject Set, can be entered anytime a Data Set Hierarchy is being created. The Data Set Hierarchy, "Parent" Data Subject, and "Child" Data Subject must be created before the Data Subject Set can be created.

> Data Subject Set. Comment
> Data Set Hierarchy. System Identifier (R)
> "Child Set" Data Subject. Name Complete (R)
> "Parent Set" Data Subject. Name Complete (R)

Scenario 11.10. Data Subject Set.

Using the first data hierarchy in Scenario 11.9, which is shown below and documented in Scenario 11.6, Data Subject Sets are created within the Data Set Hierarchy for School District at the top, Grade Level within School District, Academic Year within Grade Level, and Race within Academic Year.

> School District ^ Grade Level ^ Academic Year ^ Race

> School District is designated Student Analytics 1.
> Grade Level is designated Student Analytics 4.
> Academic Year is designated Student Analytics 6.
> Race is designated Student Analytics 8.

Data Subject Set Characteristic

Data Subject Set Characteristic is the assignment of Data Characteristics to a Data Subject Set. These are the Data Characteristics that appear, either as identifiers or as derived data, within a specific Data Subject Set in a Data Set Hierarchy. The identifier Data Characteristics are typically documented as operational data, such as School. Name and Race. Code. The derived Data Characteristics can be documented with the Data Focus, such as Student Analytics Focus. Total Student Count, Student Analytics Focus. Average Student

Cost, and Student Analytics Focus. Student Failure Count, or they can be documented with the manifestations of the Data Focus, such as Student Analytics 1. Total Student Count, Student Analytics 1. Average Student Cost, Student Analytics 1. Student Failure Count, and so on. That determination depends on the organization's desires.

The detail data for Data Subject Set Characteristic can be entered anytime a Data Subject Set has been created. The Data Characteristics and Data Subject Set must be created before the Data Subject Set Characteristics can be assigned.

> Data Subject Set Characteristic. Comment
> Data Characteristic. Name Complete (R)
> Data Subject Set. System Identifier

Scenario 11.11. Specific Derived Data Characteristics.

Specific derived data characteristics can be placed in the Data Subject Sets on a Data Set Hierarchy. Specific means that the derived data characteristics are specific to the Data Subject Set within which they are placed. In other words, they are specific to the primary key of the Data Subject Set.

The specific derived data characteristics from Scenario 11.9 might be Student Analytics 1. Total Student Count, Student Analytics 1. Average Student Cost, Student Analytics 1. Student Failure Count, and so on. They are documented with the manifestations of the Data Focus and are specifically defined based on the place within the Data Set Hierarchy where they appear.

Scenario 11.12. Specific Data Subject Set Characteristics.

Specific derived data characteristics can be placed in the Data Subject Sets in a Data Set Hierarchy. The first set of data from Scenario 11.9 is:

> School District ^ Grade Level ^ Academic Year ^ Race

The Data Subject Set Characteristics for School District might be School District. Identifier and the specific derived data might be Student Analytics 1. Total Student Count and Student Analytics 1. Student Failure Count.

The Data Subject Set Characteristics for Grade Level might be Grade Level. Number and Grade Level. Name, and the specific derived data might be Student Analytics 4. Total Student Count and Student Analytics 4. Student Failure Count.

The Data Subject Set Characteristics for Academic Year might be Academic Year. Number, and the specific derived data might be Student Analytics 6. Total Student Count and Student Analytics 6. Student Failure Count.

115

The Data Subject Characteristics for Race might be Grade Level. Number and Grade Level. Name, and the specific derived data might be Student Analytics 8. Total Student Count and Student Analytics 8. Student Failure Count.

These specific Data Subject Set Characteristics are assigned from their respective Data Focus manifestations.

Scenario 11.13. General Derived Data Characteristics

General derived data characteristics can be placed in the Data Subject Sets on a Data Set Hierarchy. General means that the derived data characteristics are general to the Data Subject Sets within which they are placed. In other words, they are independent of the primary key of the Data Subject Set.

The general derived data characteristics from Scenario 11.9 might be Student Analytics Focus. Total Student Count, Student Analytics Focus. Average Student Cost, Student Analytics Focus. Student Failure Count, and so on. They are documented with the Data Focus and are generally defined independent of their place within the Data Set Hierarchy where they appear. Their specific interpretation depends on their location within the Data Set Hierarchy.

Scenario 11.14. General Data Subject Set Characteristics.

General derived data characteristics can be placed in the Data Subject Sets in a Data Set Hierarchy. The first set of data from Scenario 11.9 is:

School District ^ Grade Level ^ Academic Year ^ Race

The Data Subject Set Characteristics for School District might be School District. Identifier and the general derived data might be Student Analytics Focus. Total Student Count and Student Analytics Focus. Student Failure Count.

The Data Subject Set Characteristics for Grade Level might be Grade Level. Number and Grade Level. Name, and the general derived data might be Student Analytics Focus. Total Student Count and Student Analytics Focus. Student Failure Count.

The Data Subject Set Characteristics for Academic Year might be Academic Year. Number, and the general derived data might be Student Analytics Focus. Total Student Count and Student Analytics Focus. Student Failure Count.

The Data Subject Characteristics for Race might be Grade Level. Number and Grade Level. Name, and the general derived data might be Student Analytics Focus8. Total Student Count and Student Analytics Focus. Student Failure Count.

These general Data Subject Set Characteristics are assigned from the Data Focus.

DERIVED SPATIAL DATA SUBJECT

A spatial data layer, such as contained in a Geographic Information System, represents a particular theme, such as a base layer for the geographic coordinates; a hydrology layer for lakes, rivers, and so on; a transportation layer for roads, streets, and so on; and a topographic layer for elevations. These spatial data layers become data subjects within the organization's data resource.

The elemental spatial data layers, such as described above, can be combined or aggregated to produce derived data layers. For example, a hydrology data layer and a transportation data layer can be combined to show the spatial relations between water and roads. These combined spatial data layers become derived data subjects in the organization's data resource.

The derived data subjects, representing the derived spatial data layers, have contributing data subjects, representing the contributing spatial data layers. Each of these data subjects contains data characteristics describing the features of the spatial data layer.

Data Subject Contributor

Data Subject Contributor is an elemental data subject or a derived data subject that contributes to a new derived data subject. The contribution of elemental and derived data subjects to additional derived data subjects often forms a network of derived data subject.

The detail data for Data Subject Contributor can be entered anytime one or more elemental or derived data subjects are combined to form an additional derived data subject. The "Contributor" Data Subject and the "Derived" Data Subject must be created before the Data Subject Contributor can be created.

> Data Subject Contributor. Comment (R)
>
> "Contributor" Data Subject. Name Complete (R)
> "Derived" Data Subject. Name Complete (R)

Scenario 11.15. Data Subject Contributor.

Geographic information system (GIS) professionals determine that they need to document both the primitive spatial data layers and the development of derived spatial data layers to ensure the quality of all data layers. They are concerned that the creation, combination, and documentation of the spatial data layers may not be done formally and may be leading to low quality data.

117

The GIS professionals begin by documenting all the primitive spatial data layers within the organization as data subjects. When competing primitive data layers are identified, an official primitive spatial data layer is designated. Next, they document the combination of the spatial data layers to create derived spatial data layers, then the combination of derived spatial data layers to create additional spatial data layers. Any derived spatial data layer that is based on an unofficial primitive spatial data layer is questionable, as is any derived spatial data layer based on an unofficial derived spatial data layer.

The result of the documentation was the identification of questionable spatial data layers, which were removed, and the streamlining and formal documentation of the derived spatial data layers.

OPERATIONAL DATA HIERARCHIES

The data hierarchies that exist in operational data are not the same as the derived data hierarchies described above. They are typically a data occurrence hierarchy or a data subject hierarchy that do not represent derived data. Each of these hierarchies is described below to show the difference from the derived data hierarchies.

Data Occurrence Hierarchy

A data occurrence hierarchy is a single data subject that has a recursive many-to-many data relation. The data occurrences within that data subject form the hierarchy based on the parent-child relationships between the data occurrences. That hierarchy could be printed or displayed at any point in time based on the parent – child relationship represented by the recursive data relation.

For example, Organization Unit is a data subject with a recursive one-to-many data relation. The data occurrences within Organization Unit represent the hierarchy of the organization units based on the parent – child relationships defined by the recursive data relation. The Org Chart could be printed or displayed based on the parent – child relationships.

Data Subject Hierarchy

A data subject hierarchy is a hierarchy of different data subjects, or data subject types, based on the data relations between those data subjects or data subject types. It's basically a classification scheme for data subjects or data subject types, with the major classifications at the top and minor classifications progressing toward the bottom, with one-to-one data relations between the data subjects or data subject types.

For example, wells might have a classification scheme with Well at the top. The second layer of the classification might be Well Type, which designates whether the well is a Water Well, Geothermal Well, Petroleum Well, and so on. The third layer of the classification scheme might be Well Class, such as Withdrawal or Recharge for Water Well, Crude Oil or Natural Gas for Petroleum Well, and so on.

A data subject hierarchy can be displayed as the hierarchy described above with Well at the top, or it could be displayed as a data subject-relation diagram with the sequence of classifying data subjects, such as Well Type, Well Class, and so on, progressing down from the top and Well at the bottom.

SUMMARY

The Derived Data Function documents the data that have been renormalized for evaluational and analytical processing, derived operational data hierarchies, and derived spatial data. Derived data are part of an organization's data resource the same as primitive data and need to be documented so they can be thoroughly understood. Since an organization's business activities depend on derived data for making management decisions, it's mandatory that those derived data are thoroughly understood and documented.

Chapter 12

PREFERRED DATA

Preferred data represent the to-be comparate data resource.

The data understanding process continues with the Preferred Data Function that consists of designating the preferred Common Data and documenting the physical implementation of those preferred Common Data as Data Product Data.

PREFERRED COMMON DATA

The *preferred data architecture concept* is that the redundancy and variability of disparate data will be resolved through the designation of a preferred data architecture and the transformation of disparate data to comparate data according to that preferred data architecture.

The *preferred data architecture objective* is to designate the preferred representation of all data at the organization's disposal so those data can be readily understood and shared within and without the organization. The objective is to take a common data architecture that was enhanced to cover the data cross-references and designate preferred components that will become a pattern for transforming disparate data to comparate data.

The Preferred Data Function uses a portion of the data structure described in the Common Data Chapter and Data Inventory Chapter. It is the portion of the Common Data that becomes the to-be design of the comparate data resource for the organization and will be physically implemented. Designating and documenting the preferred Common Data is done before the documentation of the preferred physical data are documented as Data Product Data, which is done before the data transformation process.

Preferred Data Characteristic Variations

The preferred Common Data process begins with identifying and documenting the preferred Data Characteristic Variation for each Data Characteristic. Each Data Characteristic can have only one preferred Data Characteristic Variation. When the data cross-referencing process has been completed for a particular subject area, the Data Characteristic Variations for each Data Characteristic in that subject area are reviewed to determine which variant is the most acceptable for developing the compare data resource.

If an existing Data Characteristic Variation that is acceptable to the business cannot be identified, then one is created that is acceptable to the business. When an acceptable Data Characteristic Variation is identified, the Data Characteristic Variation. Preferred Data Indicator is set to "Y".

In some situations a Data Characteristic is not used in the preferred Common Data architecture and a preferred designation is not made. The Data Characteristic. End Date is entered, the Common Data Status. Code is changed, and the Data Characteristic Variation. Preferred Indicators for that Data Characteristic remains "N".

Scenario 12.1. Existing Preferred Data Characteristic Variations.

Data stewards and business professionals work through the Data Characteristic Variations for each Data Characteristic and determine which variation is most acceptable for the business. The data definitions, data integrity rules, and Data Product Units cross-referenced to each Data Characteristic Variation are reviewed to make that determination.

General rules were made for designating the preferred Data Characteristic Variations, such as all dates will be in the Century / Year / Month / Day format, and all measurement units will be metric.

Scenario 12.2. Creating Preferred Data Characteristic Variations.

The data stewards and business professionals occasionally encounter a few situations where the existing Data Characteristic Variations were not acceptable to the business and a new Data Characteristic Variation was created that was acceptable to the business.

For example, all the existing data definitions were short truncated phrases less than 20 characters. All preferred data definitions were memo data that allowed for comprehensive data definitions.

Scenario 12.3. Obsolete Data Characteristic Variations.

The data stewards and business professionals encounter several Data Characteristics representing physical data that will not become part of the organization's comparate data resource. They enter an end date for those Data Characteristics, enter obsolete status codes, and leave all the Data Characteristic Variation. Preferred Indicators = "N".

Preferred Data Reference Set Variations

The preferred Common Data process continues with identifying and documenting the preferred Data Reference Set Variation for each Data Reference Set, which is documented as a Data Subject with the Data Reference Set Indictor = "Y".

Each Data Reference Set can have only one preferred Data Reference Set Variation. When the data cross-referencing process has been completed for a particular subject area, the Data Reference Set Variations for each Data Reference Set in that subject area are reviewed to determine which Data Reference Set Variation is the most acceptable for developing the comparate data resource.

If an existing Data Reference Set Variation is not acceptable to the business, then one is created that is acceptable to the business. When an acceptable Data Reference Set Variation is identified, the Data Reference Set. Preferred Data Indicator is set to "Y".

In some situations a Data Subject designated as a Data Reference Set is not used in the preferred Common Data architecture and a preferred Data Reference Set Variation designation is not made. The Data Subject. End Date is entered, the Data Reference Set Variation. Preferred Indicators for that Data Subject remain "N", and an obsolete status code is entered.

Scenario 12.4. Existing Preferred Data Reference Set Variations.

Data stewards and business professionals work through the Data Reference Items within the Data Reference Set Variations for each Data Subject designated as a data reference set and determine which set of Data Reference Items is most acceptable for the business. The domain of data reference items, data definitions, data names, coded data values, and data cross-references are reviewed to make that determination.

General rules were made for designating the preferred Data Reference Set Variations, such as all the Data Reference Items will have a formal name that is capitalized and any coded data values will be upper case or numeric.

Scenario 12.5. Creating Preferred Data Reference Set Variations.

The data stewards and business professionals occasionally encounter a few situations where the existing Data Reference Set Variations were not acceptable to the business and a new Data Reference Set Variation was created that was acceptable to the business.

For example, no existing Data Reference Set Variation existed for all the world regions where the organization operated. A new Data Reference Set Variation was created that included all the world regions where the organization operated and any world region where they might possible operate in the future.

Scenario 12.6. Obsolete Data Reference Set Variations.

The data stewards and business professionals encounter several Data Subjects representing data reference sets resulting from existing physical data that will not become part of the organization's compare data resource. They enter Data Subject. End Date, enter an obsolete status code, and leave all the Data Reference Set Variation. Preferred Indicators = "N".

Preferred Data Definitions

After the preferred Data Characteristic Variations and preferred Data Reference Set Variations are designated, the preferred data definitions are established for the Data Subjects, Data Characteristics, and Data Reference Items that are part of the preferred Common Data architecture. Some data definitions exist in the Common Data and some data definitions may exist in the Data Product Data that are cross-referenced to those preferred Common Data.

All of the Data Product Data definitions are brought across the data cross-references from the Data Product Data and added to the Common Data to provide a substantial base for making the comprehensive preferred data definitions.

All of the existing definitions for a Data Subject that contain one or more preferred Data Characteristic Variations are reviewed, as well as all the Data Characteristics within that Data Subject, to prepare a comprehensive data definition for that Data Subject that will become the preferred data definition.

All of the existing definitions for a Data Characteristic, including the definitions for all the Data Characteristic Variations within that Data Characteristic, are reviewed to prepare a comprehensive data definition for that Data Characteristic that will become the preferred data definition.

All of the existing definitions for a Data Subject that represent a data reference set are reviewed and contains one or more preferred Data Reference Set Variations, as well as all the Data Reference Set Variation Definitions within that Data Subject, to prepare a comprehensive data definition for that Data Subject that will become the preferred data definition.

All of the existing definitions for the Data Reference Items in each preferred Data Reference Set Variation are reviewed, and possibly the Data Reference Items in the non-preferred Data Reference Set Variations within the same Data Subject, to prepare comprehensive data definitions for each Data Reference Item that will become the preferred data definitions.

Scenario 12.7. Preferred Data Subject Definitions.

Data stewards and business professionals review each Data Subject to determine which ones have one or more preferred Data Characteristic Variations, meaning that Data Subject will become part of the organization's compare data resource. They then develop a comprehensive data definition for that Data Subject based on existing definitions in the Data Subject and its subordinate Data Characteristics and Data Characteristic Variations and the needs of the business professionals.

Any Data Subject that does not have preferred Data Characteristic Variations will not become part of the organization's compare data resource. An End Date and an obsolete status code are entered for those Data Subjects.

Scenario 12.8. Preferred Data Characteristic Definitions.

Data stewards and business professionals review each Data Characteristic to determine which ones have one or more preferred Data Characteristic Variations, meaning that Data Characteristic will become part of the organization's compare data resource. They then develop a comprehensive data definition for that Data Characteristic based on existing definitions in the Data Characteristic and its Data Characteristic Variations and the needs of the business professionals.

Any Data Characteristic that does not have a preferred Data Characteristic Variation will not become part of the organization's compare data resource. An End Date and an obsolete status code are entered for those Data Characteristics.

Comprehensive data definitions were not developed for each Data Characteristic Variation, or even for the preferred Data Characteristic Variations. It's the Data Characteristic that's important for the compare data resource and that definition will be used. The preferred Data Characteristic Variation only indicates the preferred variant of the Data Characteristic.

Scenario 12.9. Preferred Data Reference Set Definitions.

Data stewards and business professionals review the Data Reference Set

Variations for each Data Reference Set and develop a comprehensive definition for the Data Subject representing the Data Reference Set. They review the Data Subject definitions and all of the Data Reference Set Variation definitions, the Data Reference Items, and the business needs to develop a comprehensive data definition.

Scenario 12.10. Preferred Data Reference Item Definitions.

Data stewards and business professionals review all of the Data Reference Items in each preferred Data Reference Set Variation and develop comprehensive data definitions for each Data Reference Item. The comprehensive definition is based on the existing definitions of the Data Reference Items within the preferred Data Reference Set Variation, the Data Reference Items in the non-preferred Data Reference Set Variations, and the business needs of the organization.

Preferred Data Integrity Rules

After the preferred data definitions are prepared, the preferred data integrity rules are established for Data Subjects and Data Characteristics. Some data integrity rules exist in the Common Data and some data integrity rules may exist in the Data Product Data that are cross-referenced to those preferred Common Data.

All of the Data Product Data integrity rules are brought across the data cross-references from the Data Product Data and added to the Common Data to provide a substantial base for making the preferred data integrity rules. In most situations, the data integrity rules are sorely lacking in the Data Product Data, and only a few data integrity rules have been added to the Common Data. Therefore, the process of defining the data integrity rules and designating the preferred data integrity rules can be a substantial task.

All of the existing data integrity rules for a Data Subject that contains one or more preferred Data Characteristic Variations are reviewed to prepare the preferred data integrity rules for that Data Subject.

All of the existing data integrity rules for a Data Characteristic that contain a preferred Data Characteristic Variation are reviewed, as well as the data integrity rules for each Data Characteristic Variation of that Data Characteristic, to prepare the preferred data integrity rules for that Data Characteristic.

Scenario 12.11. Preferred Data Subject Integrity Rules.

Data stewards and business professionals review any existing data integrity rules for each Data Subject and the needs of the business to determine the preferred data integrity rules. They find that very few data integrity rules exist for Data Subjects, and most of those data integrity rules are simple rules. They needed to define all of the data integrity rules for that Data Subject and for relationships between Data Subjects.

Scenario 12.12. Preferred Data Characteristic Integrity Rules.

Data stewards and business professionals review the existing data integrity rules for each Data Characteristic within a Data Subject and the needs of the business to determine the preferred data integrity rules for the preferred Data Characteristic. They find that only a few, rather simple, data integrity rules exist, such as the domain of values and requirement. They needed to define all of the data integrity rules for each preferred Data Characteristic and for relationships between Data Characteristics.

Preferred Data Name Abbreviations

After the preferred data integrity rules are prepared, the preferred Data Name Abbreviation Scheme is designated and formal data name abbreviations are applied to the Data Subjects containing preferred Data Characteristic Variations and preferred Data Reference Item Variations, to Data Characteristics containing preferred Data Characteristic Variations, to Data Characteristic Variations, and to Data Reference Set Variations. If a Data Name Abbreviation Scheme does not exist that is acceptable to the organization, a new one is developed that is acceptable to the organization.

When the preferred physical data are prepared that represent the preferred Common Data, only the Data Subject and Data Characteristic formal data name abbreviations will be used, as described in the Preferred Physical Data section. The variant portion of the data name is rarely used in the physical data, so the preparation of physical data names for Data Reference Set Variations and Data Characteristic Variations could be skipped.

Scenario 12.13. Preferred Data Name Abbreviation Scheme.

Data stewards, business professionals, and database professionals review the formal data names for the Common Data and develop a set of Data Name Words with their unique abbreviations and a Data Name Abbreviation Algorithm that will form their preferred Data Name Abbreviation Scheme.

Scenario 12.14. Preferred Physical Data Names.

The data stewards that helped develop the preferred Data Name Abbreviation Scheme in Scenario 12.13 apply that scheme to all of the

127

preferred Common Data to develop formal physical data names. Those formal physical data names are then used to name the Data Product Data that are developed to represent the physical implementation of the preferred Common Data.

Preferred Data Keys

After the preferred data name abbreviations have been prepared and applied, the preferred data keys are established for each Data Subject containing a preferred Data Characteristic Variation. The primary key that will become the physical primary key for the preferred physical data is designated as the preferred Data Product Primary Key. The foreign keys that refer to that preferred primary key are designated as the preferred Data Product Foreign Key.

Scenario 12.15. Preferred Primary Keys.

Data stewards, business professionals, and database professionals work together to identify the Primary Key for each Data Subject in the Common Data that will be used as the preferred Data Product Primary Key. The Data Product Primary Key may well be a system identifier or equivalent. In that case, a business primary key is identified that is meaningful to the business professionals and is designated as an additional Data Product Primary Key. However, that Data Product Primary Key is not implemented in the database as a primary key, but is used in programming to help the business professionals identify a unique data occurrence.

Scenario 12.16. Preferred Foreign Keys.

Data stewards, business professionals, and database professionals use the Data Product Primary Keys identified in Scenario 12.15 to identify and document the Data Product Foreign Keys. The physical Data Product Primary Key implemented in the database will have a corresponding physical Data Product Foreign Key. The business Data Product Primary Key that is not implemented in the database will have a corresponding business Data Product Foreign Key.

Preferred Data Sources

After the preferred data keys are designated, the preferred data sources are designated and the data source rules for obtaining data from those preferred data sources are developed. Specifically, the Data Product Unit. Preferred Source Indicator identifies the preferred source for existing data and the Data Characteristic. Conditional Data Source Rule provides the rules for obtaining data from those preferred data sources.

The designation of preferred data sources and data source rules are necessary for the data transformation process described in the Data Transform Chapter. It is often very difficult to designate all the preferred data sources and data source rules when designating the preferred Common Data and the corresponding preferred Data Product Data. The preferred data sources and data source rules are often adjusted and enhanced during the Data Transform Function. However, it is appropriate to make initial designations during the Preferred Data Function.

Scenario 12.17. Preferred Data Sources.

Data stewards, business professionals, and database professionals work together to identify the preferred data source for each Data Characteristic. They review the Data Product Data corresponding to the Data Characteristic and make an initial determination which Data Product Unit or Data Product Units will be used for sourcing the data for each Data Characteristic. The Data Product Unit. Preferred Source Indicator is set to "Y" for each Data Product Unit that has been designated as a preferred data source.

The identification of initial preferred data sources is done during development of the preferred Data Resource Data while the data understanding is fresh in their minds. They realize that during the actual Data Transform Function that additional insight may be gained and the preferred data sources may well be adjusted.

Scenario 12.18. Data Source Rules.

The data stewards, business professionals, and database professionals that identified the initial preferred data sources in Scenario 12.17 continue with the development of the initial data source rules for each Data Characteristic. Those data source rules are documented as the Data Characteristic. Conditional Data Source Rules. Those data source rules will likely be enhanced during the Data Transform Function, and will be used for transforming the disparate physical data to the compare physical data.

PREFERRED PHYSICAL DATA

After the preferred data designations have been made, the preferred physical data can be designed and documented based on the preferred Common Data. The design consists of the denormalization of the preferred Common Data according to formal data denormalization rules for the operating environment where the data will be stored. The documentation consists of entering those preferred physical data as Data Product Data.

The preferred physical data uses a portion of the data structured described in the Data Inventory Chapter. It is the portion of the Data Product Data that documents the to-be design of the comparate data resource for the organization. It needs to be done before the data transformation process.

Data Denormalization

The preferred Common Data represent the logical design of the organization's comparate data resource. The development of the preferred Common Data follows the formal rules for data normalization and usually needs to be formally denormalized before implementation into an operating environment. The data denormalization process is based on formal data denormalization rules that structure the data for optimum processing in an operating environment without compromising the logical design.

Scenario 12.19. Denormalization Of Preferred Common Data.

The database professionals work with the data stewards to formally denormalize the preferred Common Data for the intended operating environment. Decisions are made about changes to the Common Data that are appropriate for optimum operational processing without compromising the logical nature of the Common Data. A balance needed to be made between peak physical performance of the database and applications, and the integrity of the logical structure of the Common Data.

Preferred Data Product Data

After the preferred Common Data have been denormalized for an operating environment, that design is entered as preferred Data Product Data. Those Data Product Data represent the physical implementation of the preferred Common Data. The process proceeds from Data Products, to Data Product Sets, to Data Product Units, to Data Product Codes.

The preferred Data Product Data are identified with the Preferred Common Indicator = "Y", meaning that those Data Product Data are implementations of the preferred Common Data for the organization's comparate data resource. Typically all of the Data Product Data that represent the preferred Common Data must have the indicator set to "Y". It is inappropriate and very confusing to intermingle Data Product Data that are preferred and non-preferred. In other words, a preferred Data Product must have Preferred Data Product Sets, which must have preferred Data Product Units, which must have preferred Data Product Codes.

In some situations where the disparate data are being transformed to comparate data, it may be acceptable to intermingle preferred and non-preferred Data Product Data on an interim basin. However, in the long term, all of Data Product Data subordinate to a preferred Data Product must be preferred.

The Data Product Data follow the descriptions presented in the Data Inventory Chapter. Readers can refer to that Chapter for the detailed Data Subjects and Data Characteristics comprising Data Product Data.

Preferred Data Products

The process begins with creation of a preferred Data Product that typically represents a database or database management system. The denormalized data are reviewed to determine what databases or database management systems will be used. Each of those databases or database management systems will be defined as a Data Product

Typically, a data dictionary is not defined for the Common Data, the preferred Common Data, or the preferred Data Product Data since the Data Resource Data are essentially that data dictionary.

Scenario 12.20. Preferred Data Product.

The data stewards and database professionals review the denormalized data and determine how the data will be stored on database management systems. The process includes a review of the applications that will be accessing the databases and the types of processing that will be performed. When the database management systems were determined, they were documented as Data Products.

Preferred Data Product Sets

After the preferred Data Products are created for the databases or database management systems, the preferred Data Product Sets within those preferred Data Products can be created. Each preferred Data Product Set typically represents a Data Subject, or a Data Subject as modified by formal denormalization.

Since the preferred Data Product Data has been formally normalized and formally denormalized, no recursions are needed to document Data Product Set Variations. Therefore, only one level of preferred Data Product Set is created. When it appears that a preferred Data Product Set Variation might need to be created, the data normalization and data denormalization processes should be reviewed, which will likely resolve the need to create a preferred Data Product Set Variation.

Scenario 12.21. Preferred Data Product Set

Data stewards and database professionals review the preferred Data Subject as they existed in the Common Data or were modified by denormalization and determine the data tables that will contain those data. After that determination was made, preferred Data Product Sets are created for each of those data tables.

Preferred Data Product Units

After the preferred Data Product Sets are created, the preferred Data Product Units within those Data Product Sets can be created. Each preferred Data Product Unit typically represents a Data Characteristic that will become a data field / data column in a database.

Data Product Unit Variations are not needed for the preferred Data Product Units. Therefore, only one level of preferred Data Product Unit is created. Similarly, references to another preferred Data Product Unit are not needed because the data disparity should have been eliminated with the preferred Data Product Data.

Scenario 12.22. Preferred Data Product Units.

Data stewards and database professionals review the preferred Data Characteristics as they existed in the Common Data and determine the preferred Data Product Units that will represent those Data Characteristics. After that determination was made, preferred Data Product Units are created for each of those Data Characteristics.

Preferred Data Product Codes

After the preferred Data Product Units are created, the preferred Data Product Codes can be created for those preferred Data Product Units that contain coded data values or represent data reference items within a data reference set. Data Product Code Variations are not needed for the preferred Data Product Codes. Therefore, only one level of preferred Data Product Code is created.

An organization may determine that creation of the Data Product Codes for the Data Reference Items in the preferred Data Reference Set Variation is not necessary, since the documentation is contained in the Common Data. No physical implementations will be developed for those Data Reference Items, therefore it is not necessary to create the preferred Data Product

Codes.

Scenario 12.23. Preferred Data Product Code.

Data stewards and database professionals review the Data Reference Items within the preferred Data Reference Set Variation, and determine that it is not necessary to re-document all of those Data Reference Items as preferred Data Product Codes. Business professionals can easily access the Common Data for that detail.

Preferred Data Product Data Names

The formally abbreviated Common Data names that were created from the preferred Data Name Abbreviations Scheme are used for the preferred Data Product Data.

> The preferred Data Product. Name is created since it does not have a counterpart in the Common Data.

> The preferred Data Product Set. Name is the corresponding Data Subject. Name Abbreviated, except as modified during formal denormalization.

> The preferred Data Product Unit. Name is the corresponding Data Characteristic Name Abbreviated. The Data Characteristic Variation. Name, is not used because the variant portion of the name is not necessary. The preferred Data Product Unit. Name represents the preferred Data Characteristic Variation. Name even though the variant name is not shown.

> The preferred Data Product Code. Name, if entered, is the formal name of the Data Reference Item. It is not abbreviated.

> The Data Reference Set Variation. Name Abbreviated does not appear in the Data Product Data since it is only a variant of the parent Data Subject. Name.

Scenario 12.24. Preferred Data Product Data Names.

Data stewards enter the appropriate physical data names as they are creating the preferred Data Product Data. Having already prepared the formally abbreviated Common Data names, the entry of those names in the preferred Data Product Data is a relatively simple task.

Preferred Data Product Data Definitions

Preferred physical data definitions are prepared based on the preferred data definitions in the Common Data and on the formal data denormalization. If the data are not denormalized, then the Common Data preferred data definitions can be entered into the preferred Data Product Data. If the data are denormalized, then the Common Data preferred data definitions are adjusted according to the denormalization and entered into the preferred Data Product Data.

An organization can choose whether the data definitions are entered into the Data Product Data or whether they remain solely with the Common Data. The choice depends on whether the organization desires people to find the definitions with the preferred Data Product Data or navigate to the Common Data to find the definitions. One aspect of that decision is whether the preferred Data Product definitions would be adjusted to contain the abbreviated data names.

Scenario 12.25. Preferred Data Product Data Definitions.

Data stewards decide that since the Common Data were substantially denormalized before the preferred Data Product Data were created, that the adjusted data definitions resulting from the denormalization would be entered into the preferred Data Product Data. The data definitions were also adjusted to include the physical data names.

Scenario 12.26. No Preferred Data Product Data Definitions.

Data stewards decide that since the Common Data were not denormalized, except for the data reference sets, that it was not necessary to enter the data definitions into the preferred Data Product Data. The application they developed for access to the Data Resource Data could easily retrieve the data definitions from the Common Data.

Preferred Data Product Data Integrity Rules

Preferred physical data integrity rules are based on the preferred data integrity rules in the Common Data and on the formal data denormalization. If the data are not denormalized, then the Common Data preferred data integrity rules can be entered into the preferred Data Product Data. If the data are denormalized, then the Common Data preferred data integrity rules are adjusted according to the denormalization and entered into the preferred Data Product Data. One aspect of that decision is whether the preferred Data Product integrity rules would be adjusted to contain the abbreviated data names.

Scenario 12.27. Preferred Data Product Data Integrity Rules.

Data stewards decide that since the Common Data were substantially denormalized before the Data Product Data were created, that the adjusted data integrity rules resulting from the denormalization would be entered into the preferred Data Product Data. The data integrity rules were also adjusted to include the physical data names.

Scenario 12.28. No Preferred Data Product Data Integrity Rules.

Data stewards decide that since the Common Data were not denormalized, except for a few data reference sets, that it was not necessary to enter the data integrity rules into the preferred Data Product Data. The application they developed for access to the Data Resource Data could easily retrieve the data integrity rules from the Common Data.

Preferred Data Product Data Keys

The preferred physical data keys that will be used for searching and navigation in the database are based on the preferred primary keys and foreign keys in the Common Data and on the formal data denormalization. If the data are not denormalized, then the Common Data preferred primary keys and foreign keys can be entered into the preferred Data Product Data. If the data are denormalized, then the Common Data primary keys and foreign keys are adjusted according to the denormalization and entered into the preferred Data Product Data.

Scenario 12.29. Preferred Data Product Data Keys.

Data stewards decode that since the Common Data were denormalized, that the adjusted primary keys and foreign keys would be entered into the preferred Data Product Data to accurately represent the physical implementation of the data. The physical data names are used for the Data Product Primary Keys and Data Product Foreign Keys.

Scenario 12.30. No Preferred Data Product Data Keys.

Data stewards decide that since the Common Data were not denormalized that it was not necessary to enter the Data Product Primary Keys and Data Product Foreign Keys. The application they developed for access to the Data Resource Data could easily use Primary Keys and Foreign Keys from the Common Data.

Preferred Data Product Data Cross-References

The preferred Data Product Data may or may not be cross-referenced to the Common Data depending on the organization's desires. In some situations, an organization may desire to cross-reference the preferred Data Product

Data to the Common Data to provide a ready reference between the Data Product Data and the Common Data. In other situations, an organization may desire not to cross-reference the preferred Data Product Data to the Common Data and to rely on the formal abbreviated data name to make a connection between the preferred Data Product Data and the Common Data.

The preferred Data Product Data can stand on their own since the Preferred Common Indicators are set to "Y", the preferred data definitions are readily available, and the preferred data integrity rules are readily available. Whether all the understanding is stored as preferred Data Product Data or is obtained from the Common Data by an application, the preferred Data Product Data can stand on its own and provide a thorough understanding of the data.

The preferred Data Product Sets could be cross-reference to a Data Subject when it exactly matches the Data Subject, depending on the organization's desires. A preferred Data Product Set could be created to represent a Data Occurrence Group, and could be cross-referenced to the appropriate Data Subject Variation, depending on the organization's desires.

Scenario 12.31. Preferred Data Product Data Cross-References.

Data stewards decide that minimum data should be stored in the preferred Data Product Data, and cross-references would be created to the corresponding Common Data. They believe that multiple definitions for the logical and the physical data may become out of synch over time and want to avoid that situation.

Scenario 12.32. No Preferred Data Product Data Cross-References.

Data stewards decide that all documentation should be placed in the preferred Data Product Data so that anyone using those data could easily find all the documentation. Minimum cross-references would be created to the Common Data, and those cross-references would be through the formally abbreviated data name.

Multiple Physical Implementations

The Common Data can be formally denormalized different ways for implementation in different operating environments and different types of processing. They can be formally denormalized any time that new technology evolves and new processing techniques are developed. The Common Data are the stable logical data that can have multiple formal denormalizations for different operating environments and processing techniques.

Each formal denormalization of Common Data is documented as a different set of Data Product Data as described above. In other words, each formal data denormalization results in a different set of Data Product Data representing that formal denormalization.

Scenario 12.33. Multiple Physical Implementations

Data stewards establish a policy that the Common Data must always go through a formal denormalization process before any physical implementation. If that formal denormalization process creates a different set of denormalized data that has not already been documented as preferred Data Product Data, then that set of denormalized data is documented as a different set of preferred Data Product Data before physical implementation.

SUMMARY

The Preferred Data Function designates the preferred Common Data that will be used to develop the organization's comparate data resource. Those preferred data are then implemented, and are documented as Data Product Data with the Preferred Indicator = "Y". Anyone in the organization using those preferred physical data can thoroughly understand those data and use them appropriately.

Chapter 13

DATA TRANSFORMATION

Data transformation creates the physical comparate data.

The data understanding process concludes with the Data Transformation Function that consists of defining the data translation algorithms and defining the data transformation rules. When the comparate data resource (the to-be data resource) has been defined through the preferred Common Data and preferred Data Product Data, the translation and transformation of the existing disparate data resource to the new comparate data resource can be defined.

DATA TRANSFORMATION OVERVIEW

Organizations need to transform their existing, usually low quality and redundant, disparate data to higher-quality comparate data so those data can be readily understood and used to support the organization's current and future business information demand.

The *data resource transformation concept* states that all data transformation, whether disparate data to comparate data or comparate data to disparate data, will be done within the context of a common data architecture, using the preferred data architecture designations, according to formal data transformation rules. The best existing disparate data are extracted and transformed to comparate data to create a single, high quality version of truth about the business.

The *data resource transformation objective* is to transform the best of the existing disparate data to a high quality comparate data resource so it can support the current and future business information demand. It's a precise, detailed, and very rigorous process that creates a high quality comparate data resource. The data transformation process includes a formal Extract-Transform-Load sequence that consists of three extract processes, five transform processes, and three load processes. The reader can refer to *Data Resource Integration* for the details.

DATA TRANSLATION

Data translation is the conversion of data values between Data Characteristic Variations and between Data Reference Items in different Data Reference Set Variations. Typically, the data translation is between preferred and non-preferred data values, but can be between non-preferred data values if necessary.

The data subject-relation diagram for data translation is shown in Figure 13.1. The data subjects on the left show the data translation between Data Characteristic Variations. The recursive data relation shows that an existing Data Characteristic Translation can be referenced rather than redefining the same translation algorithm. The data subjects on the right show the data translation between Data Reference Items, which must be between two different Data Reference Set Variations within the same Data Reference Set that is defined as a Data Subject. The recursive data relation shows that an existing Data Reference Item Translation can be reference rather than redefining the same translation algorithm.

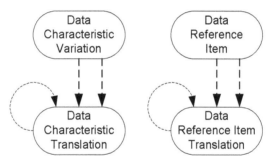

Figure 13.1. Data Translation.

Data Characteristic Translation

Data Characteristic Translation is the conversion of data values between two Data Characteristic Variations. Typically, two algorithms are defined for going from the preferred Data Characteristic Variation to the non-preferred Data Characteristic Variation, and going from the non-preferred Data Characteristic Variation to the preferred Data Characteristic Variation. The Data Characteristic Variations must be within the same Data Characteristic.

Algorithms are not typically defined between non-preferred Data Characteristic Variations unless absolutely needed. However, if the translation algorithms for moving data across existing bridges within existing databases are desired, then those algorithms can be defined.

The detail data for a Data Characteristic Translation can be created anytime that the translation algorithm is known. The parent Data Characteristic Variations must be documented before the Data Characteristic Translation can be created. Any referenced Data Characteristic Translation must be documented before the reference can be made.

Data Characteristic Translation. Algorithm (R)
Data Characteristic Translation. Begin Date (R)
Data Characteristic Translation. Comment
Data Characteristic Translation. Description (R)
Data Characteristic Translation. End Date
Data Characteristic Translation. Fundamental Indicator (R)

"Reference" Data Characteristic Translation. System Identifier
"Source" Data Characteristic Variation. Name Complete (R)
"Target" Data Characteristic Variation. Name Complete (R)

Scenario 13.1. Data Characteristic Translation.

Data stewards work with business professionals to identify the preferred Data Characteristic Variations for each Data Characteristic in a major subject area. They then work with both the business professionals and database professionals to define the algorithms to translate both the non-preferred Data Characteristic Variations to the preferred Data Characteristic Variations and the preferred Data Characteristic Variations to the non-preferred Data Characteristic Variations. The defined algorithms are then entered as Data Characteristic Translations.

The data stewards decide that data translation algorithms will not be developed between two non-preferred Data Characteristic Variations unless those data translation algorithms are needed to support data bridges and cross-walks while applications are being adjusted to the comparate data resource.

Data Reference Item Translation

Data Reference Item Translation is the conversion of data values between two Data Reference Items in different Data Reference Set Variations within the same Data Reference Set, which is defined as a Data Subject. Typically, two algorithms are defined for going from the Data Reference Items in the preferred Data Reference Set to Data Reference Items in the non-preferred Data Reference Set, and going from the Data Reference Items in the non-preferred Data Reference Set to the Data Reference Items in the preferred Data Reference Set. The Data Reference Sets must be within the same Data Subject.

Algorithms are not typically defined between Data Reference Items in two non-preferred Data Reference Sets unless absolutely needed. However, if the translation algorithms for moving data across existing bridges and cross-walks for existing databases and applications are desired, then those algorithms can be defined.

The detail for a Data Reference Item Translation can be created anytime that the translation algorithm is known. The parent Data Reference Items must be documented before the Data Reference Item Translation can be created. Any referenced Data Reference Item Translation must be documented before the reference can be made.

> Data Reference Item Translation. Algorithm
> Data Reference Item Translation. Begin Date (R)
> Data Reference Item Translation. Comment
> Data Reference Item Translation. Description (R)
> Data Reference Item Translation. End Date
> Data Reference Item Translation. Fundamental Indicator (R)
> Data Reference Item Translation. General To Specific Indicator (R)
>
> "Reference" Data Reference Item Translation. System Identifier
> "Source" Data Reference Item. Name (R)
> "Target" Data Reference Item. Name (R)

Scenario 13.2. Data Reference Item Translation.

The data stewards work with business professionals to identify the preferred Data Reference Set Variations for each Data Subject representing a Data Reference Set in a major subject area. They then work with both the business professionals and database professionals to define the algorithms to translate both the non-preferred Data Reference Items to the preferred Data Reference Items, and the preferred Data Reference Items to the non-preferred Data Reference Items. The algorithms are then entered as Data Reference Item Translations.

The data stewards decide that data translation algorithms will not be developed between the Data Reference Items in two non-preferred Data Reference Set Variations unless those data translation algorithms are needed to support data bridges and cross-walks while applications are being adjusted to the comparate data resource.

DATA TRANSFORMATION

Data transformation is the process of transforming disparate data to comparate data, or comparate data to disparate data, within the context of a common data architecture. The data subject-relation diagram for data transformation is shown in Figure 13.2. The transformation process is shown in the center of the diagram consisting of Data Transform Process, Data Transform Step, and Data Transform Unit. Organization Unit and Data Steward qualify the Data Transform Process. Data Transform Unit identifies the Data Product Unit that is being transformed.

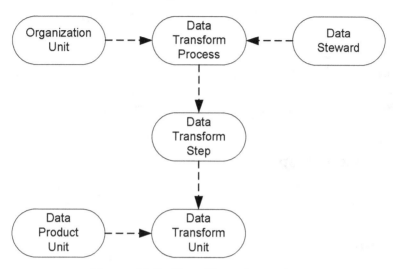

Figure 13.2. Data Transformation.

Data Transform Process

A Data Transform Process is any major effort for transforming disparate data to comparate data, or comparate data to disparate data, based on the preferred data designations. The scope for a Data Transform Process may be a database, a data subject area, a set of applications, a major business function, and so on.

The Data Transform Process is target data driven, meaning that the Data Transform Process, its Data Transform Steps, and the Data Transform Units all represent the target data for a comparate data resource. They do not represent, nor are they structured by, the source data.

The detail data for a Data Transform Process can be created anytime that a Data Transform Process is initiated. The parent Data Steward and Organization Unit must be documented before the Data Transform Process can be created.

> Data Transform Process. Begin Date (R)
> Data Transform Process. Comment
> Data Transform Process. Description

143

Data Transform Process. End Date
Data Transform Process. Name (R)

Data Steward. Name Complete (R)
Organization Unit. Name (R)

Scenario 13.3. Data Transform Process.

Data stewards complete the data cross-referencing for a subject area and have identified the preferred data. The business professionals agree to the preferred data designations, and along with database professionals and application developers, desire to move ahead with transforming the disparate data and realigning the applications to the comparate data. A single Data Transform Process is defined for all the data transformation within the scope of that subject area.

Data Transform Step

A Data Transform Step represents a major grouping of data within a Data Transform Process that is involved in data transformation. A Data Transform Process may have a single Data Transform Step or it may have many different Data Transform Steps for different groupings of data that are being transformed, for different teams involved in data transformation, or for different sets of applications involved in using the data.

The detail data for a Data Transform Step can be entered anytime a Data Project Step is identified within a Data Transform Process. The Data Transform Process must be documented before the Data Transform Step can be created.

Data Transform Step. Comment
Data Transform Step. Description (R)
Data Transform Step. Name (R)

Data Transform Process. Name (R)

Scenario 13.4. Data Transform Step By Data Group.

The data stewards determine that several Data Transform Steps will be defined for relatively isolated groups of data within the subject area, although no group of data is totally independent of other groups of data in the subject area. A team will be formed to work on each of the Data Transform Steps and the teams will coordinate their efforts to ensure that the data are properly transformed and the applications are aligned with the transformed data.

Scenario 13.5. Data Transform Step By Task.

Data stewards on another data transformation process have made the data cross-references, designated the preferred data, and established a Data Transform Process for a subject area. They decide that with the number of bridges and cross-walks between databases and applications that Data Transform Steps will be established for the data pertaining to each individual application.

Disparate data for an application will be extracted and transformed to comparate data for that application, and placed in a temporary database while the application is adjusted to the comparate data. Data will also be transformed from the comparate data produced by the application back to the disparate data until the disparate data are no longer needed by other applications. Eventually, all of the Data Transform Steps will be completed, the comparate data will be supporting the applications, and the disparate data can be eliminated.

Data Transform Unit

A Data Transform Unit is any Data Product Unit that is involved in the Data Transform Step. It describes the specific data transform rules that are applied to the Data Product Unit. It does not describe how those rules are physically implemented.

Data transformation is target data driven, meaning that the preferred data in the comparate data resource drive the data transformation process. In other words, the Data Transform Units are Data Products Units that represent the preferred data that will be used to build the comparate data resource. The rules specify which disparate Data Product Units are needed to produce the comparate Data Product Units.

The detail data for a Data Transform Unit can be entered anytime a Data Product Unit is identified within a Data Transform Step. The parent Data Product Step and Data Product Unit must be documented before the Data Transform Unit can be created.

> Data Transform Unit. Comment
> Data Transform Unit. Data Derivation Rules
> Data Transform Unit. Data Recast Rules
> Data Transform Unit. Data Reconstruct Rules
> Data Transform Unit. Data Restructure Rules
> Data Transform Unit. Data Source Rules
> Data Transform Unit. Data Translate Rules
> Data Transform Unit. Description (R)
> Data Transform Unit. Name (R)

Data Product Unit. Name (R)
Data Transform Step. Name (R)

Scenario 13.6. Data Transform Units.

Data stewards work through each Data Transform Step to determine the Data Product Units that are involved in that Data Transform Step. The process is target data driven, meaning that the target data for the compare data resource are identified and then the existing Data Products Units needed to provide the data for the target Data Product Units are identified. A Data Transform Unit is created for each of the target Data Product Units and the rules for transforming the disparate Data Product Units to the target Data Product Units are defined and documented.

When all of the transformation rules have been defined, the data transformation process can begin. Any errors or discrepancies found during the data transformation process usually result in changes to the data transformation rules. That process continues until the data transformation process produces the desired target Data Product Units.

Scenario 13.7. Detailed Data Transform Units.

Data stewards find that the existing Data Product Data are so disparate that a many-to-many transformation exists between the existing disparate Data Product Units and the preferred Data Product Units. In other words, the data in an existing disparate Data Product Unit can be used to create a preferred Data Product Unit, which can be in the same Data Transform Step, in a different Data Transform Step within the same Data Transform Process, or in a different Data Transform Step in a different Data Transform Process. The data stewards realized the need for the data transform process to be target data driven.

SUMMARY

The Data Transform Function includes the definition of data translation algorithms for converting data values and data transformation rules for creating the compare data resource from the disparate data resource. It's the culmination of the process of thoroughly understanding the existing data resource, designing the desired or to-be data resource based on business needs, and actually making the transformation from the disparate data resource to a comparate data resource.

The Data Transform Function covers only the transformation of the data resource. However, the data resource and the applications are intricately related, and one cannot be changed without changing the other. Careful planning needs to be done to thoroughly understand the business processes as well as the data resource in order to have a successful transformation. Doing one without the other will only lead to disaster for both.

Eventually all of the disparate data will be transformed to comparate data and the disparate data can be flagged as obsolete. However, the disparate data are seldom deleted because they represent an understanding of the data resource at a point in the organization's history. They should be retained to preserve that historical understanding.

The documentation of the Data Transform Function was never intended to drive the data transformation process. It is only intended for thoroughly understanding and documenting the existing disparate data, the desired comparate data, and the transformation of the disparate data to the comparate data. In other words, the code for performing the data transformation process must be developed, using the data transformation specifications, for the operating environment in which the data resource and applications reside.

Chapter 14

DATA RESOURCE REALITY

Simplicity is the fast track to understanding business reality.

Understanding business reality and creating a comparate data resource that accurately depicts the data needed to support that business reality is not an easy task. However, that task is far from impossible if a few basic concepts, principles, and techniques are followed. The problem is that those basic concepts, principles, and techniques have not been followed in the past, leading to large quantities of disparate data that do not support business reality.

Data Resource Reality describes the data resource plague that exists in most public and private sector organizations today. It describes how to cure that plague by using power rather than force, seeking simplicity, understanding an organization's perception of the business world, and promoting agility. It sets the stage for how to achieve business reality and build a comparate data resource to support that business reality.

DATA RESOURCE PLAGUE

Most public and private sector organizations have a serious plague running through their data resource. The *data resource plague* is the situation where an organization's data resource is disparate, that disparity is growing and is getting worse, and it's adversely impacting the business. The situation is serious and needs to be resolved if the organization is to be successful in its business endeavors. However, organizations continue staking their future on their pervasive disparate data.

The *business information demand* is an organization's continuously increasing, constantly changing, need for current, accurate, integrated information, often on short notice or very short notice, to support its business activities. It is a very dynamic demand for information that constantly changes to support business activities that constantly change.

Disparate data are any data that are essentially not alike, or are distinctly different in kind, quality, or character. They are unequal and cannot be readily integrated to meet the business information demand. They are low quality, defective, discordant, ambiguous, heterogeneous data. *Massively disparate data* is the existence of large quantities of disparate data within a large organization, or across many organizations involved in similar business activities.

A *data resource* is a collection of data (facts), within a specific scope, that are of importance to the organization. It is one of the four critical resources in an organization, equivalent to the financial resource, the human resource, and real property. A *disparate data resource* is a data resource that is substantially composed of disparate data that are dis-integrated and not subject-oriented. It is in a state of disarray, where the low quality does not, and cannot, adequately support an organization's business information demand.

A disparate data resource is the result of three major trends in data resource management—prolific hype-cycles, a burgeoning lexical challenge, and the five horsemen. The first two trends, hype-cycles and the lexical challenge, are the attitudes that people have which result in a disparate data resource. The five horsemen are the actions being taken by people that directly cause a disparate data resource.

Hype-Cycles

The first attitude contributing to the data resource plague is prolific hype-cycles. A *hype-cycle* is a major initiative that is promoted in an attempt to properly manage an organization's data resource, but often ends up making the data resource more disparate and impacting the business. A hype-cycle runs its course when the income from conferences, books, consulting, training, and software declines. Then a new hype-cycle begins and the process starts all over. The current hype-cycles in data resource management are described in *Data Resource Simplexity* and *Data Resource Design*, and won't be repeated here.

Hype-cycles are a form of silver bullets that usually become tarnished silver bullets, making the disparate data situation worse. Hype-cycles have not helped data resource management become professional, and lead to most of the lack of respect for data management. Data management professionals must be actively involved in stopping the perpetuation of hype-cycles, or at the very least transcending hype-cycles that are in progress.

Lexical Challenge

The second attitude contributing to the data resource plague is a burgeoning lexical challenge. The *lexical challenge* is the situation where words and terms are created, often used interchangeable, misused, abused, corrupted, and discarded without regard for their real meaning or any impact on the business. The words and terms often have no definitions, minimal definitions, poor definitions, conflicting definitions, unclear definitions, or multiple definitions. Many words and terms have been defined and redefined to the point they are meaningless. Many synonyms and homonyms have been created, adding to the problem.

The burgeoning lexical challenge must be stopped and the existing lexical challenge must be resolved before formal data resource management can be achieved. Formal terms must be established based on roots, prefixes, and suffixes for a language (such as English, German, French, and so on), must have a comprehensive and denotative definition, and must be used consistently throughout the data resource management. Data management professionals must be actively involved in creating a lexicon of formal terms and must be willing to use those formal terms.

The Five Horsemen

The five actions contributing to the data resource plague are brute-force-physical, paralysis-by-analysis, warping-the-business, suck-and-squirt, and process-structured-design, which are referred to as the five horsemen of disparate data. The five horsemen must be avoided to achieve formal data resource management. Data management professionals must avoid all five horsemen if they ever hope to achieve a high quality data resource that fully supports an organization's current and future business information demand.

Brute-Force-Physical

The first horseman is a *brute-force physical* action that goes directly to the task of developing the physical database. It skips all of the formal analysis and design activities, and often skips the involvement of business professionals and domain experts. Those taking such an action consider that developing the physical database is the real task at hand and any other tasks are unnecessary.

Brute-force-physical actions include creating the database code without any formal analysis or design of the business needs. The primary purpose of most data modeling tools, in spite of how they are advertised and marketed, is to cut the code for the physical database. Physical data models are developed and the database is created from those physical data models. Business professionals are seldom involved in any review. If they are involved, the review is superficial because the data models are seldom readily understood by the business professionals.

Although many data modeling tools appear to produce both logical and physical data models, in most situations the data models are really physical. They may show formal names and definitions, or may show abbreviated names and formats. However, the structure is physical, leading to the terms *logical-physical* and *physical-physical* data models.

Brute-force-physical actions often include a conceptual data model as a high level (generalized) data model to gain high level consensus, so that physical development of the database can proceed. However, they were not developed with formal logical design techniques, seldom have formal data names, seldom have comprehensive data definitions, seldom have a data structure related to the organization's perception of the business world, and seldom have precise data integrity rules. The objective is to get a database in place quickly to keep the business happy, yet the result is often an unhappy business. These brute-force-physical, and sometimes supper-brute-force-physical, actions simply lead to increased data disparity.

People often react, sometimes violently, to the mention of any brute-force-physical actions. But, the truth is that brute-force-physical actions are prominent in data management today, and the truth often hurts.

Paralysis-By-Analysis

The second horseman is a *paralysis-by-analysis* action that is an ongoing analysis and modeling effort to make sure everything is complete and correct. Data analysts and data modelers are well known for analyzing a situation and working the problem forever before moving ahead. They often want to build more into the data resource than the organization really wants or needs at that time. The worst, and most prevalent, complaint about data modeling today is its tendency to paralyze the development process by exacerbating the analysis process. Prolonging analysis to get the data model totally complete and accurate delays the project and forces the business to proceed with development, often creating disparate data.

Another frequent complaint about data modeling is that the project is stalled because all the business rules have not been captured or documented. However, some business rules relate to designing a data resource, while others relate to designing processes. Only the business rules that relate directly to data resource design need to be captured for data modeling.

A third frequent complaint about data modeling is that all data have not yet been documented and database development cannot proceed. In many situations the data that have not yet been documented are way beyond the scope of the current project. Data modelers seem to want to include all data that may ever be needed, rather than including just the data currently needed and adding additional data when they are needed.

Paralysis-by-analysis is the opposite of brute-force-physical, and is often used as an excuse to justify brute-force-physical actions. Some database developers encourage paralysis-by-analysis simply to justify moving directly to physical database development.

Warping-The-Business

The third horseman is a *warping-the-business* action that warps the design of the organization's data to the fixed data design of a purchased application. Each organization has a data design that fits their perception of the business world where they operate. That data design often does not match the data design of a purchased application. The result is that an organization's way of doing business becomes warped to fit the application.

Many organizations are serially warping their data design from one purchased application to the next, without any consideration for how the business operates. Many organizations have parallel warping of their data design where part of the design is warped for one purchased application, another part is warped another way for another purchased application, and so on. Both of these actions ultimately lead to the data being warped in a manner that does not represent the way the organization desires to do business.

Suck-And-Squirt

The fourth horseman is a *suck-and-squirt* action that designates a single record or system of reference, sucks the data out of that record or system of reference, performs superficial cleansing, and squirts the data into a target database, and claims data integration. Other records or systems of reference are largely ignored. The action is usually part of an ETL process where little attention is paid to the conditional sourcing of data, the data integrity, or the data meaning. Such transient data integration usually results in the creation of additional disparate data, and little progress is made toward formal data resource integration.

Process-Structured-Data

The fifth horseman is a *process-structured-data* action that structures the data resource according to the processes using the data rather than according to formal data design techniques. Many business professionals describe their data needs in terms of business processes. Many data modelers and data architects tend to structure the data resource according to those processes claiming the data model is more easily understood by the business professionals and the database is easier to build. Event driven data structures are simply another name for process structured data.

Process-structure-data actions means that data files are designed to support specific business processes rather than being designed according to formal data management concepts and principles. Data are stored redundantly in different data files to support specific business processes requiring bridges and feeds to keep those data in synch. The result is redundant data and an increase in disparate data.

Data Manipulation Industry

The data resource plague is perpetuated by a continuous cycle that creates disparate data. The *disparate data cycle* is a self-perpetuating cycle where disparate data continue to be produced at an ever-increasing rate because people do know about existing data or do not want to use existing data. People come to the data resource, but can't find the data they need, don't trust the data, or can't access the data. These people create their own data, which perpetuates the disparate data cycle. The next people that come to the data resource find the same situation, and the cycle keeps going.

The disparate data cycle is driven by prolific hype-cycles, the growing lexical challenge, and the five horsemen. It's a result of attitudes and actions that knowingly create a disparate data resource. It's a result of not formally planning and designing the data resource to support the organization's current and future business information demand, according to established, concepts, principles, and techniques, and based on the organization's perception of the business world.

Looking deeper into the disparate data cycle shows that it is also driven by a data manipulation industry that is based on the attitudes and actions described above. The situation is very similar to health care.

Considerable progress has been made toward health care during the last 100 years. However, a health care program does not currently exist. What does exist is an illness treatment industry where minimal emphasis is placed on a wellness program to prevent illness and major emphasis is placed on treating illnesses after they occur. Even major health initiatives like weight reduction, exercise, stress reduction, and so on, are oriented toward resolving health issues that have already occurred.

Considerable progress that has also been made toward recognizing and treating mental illness in the last 50 years. However, the approach is toward allowing the mental illness to happen and then proceeding to treat the illness.

Minimal effort has been made to ensure mental wellness, let alone establish any formal mental wellness program.

A similar pattern exists with the way organizations manage their data resource. Organizations are physically manipulating the data, for short term needs, without any formal design, or any consideration for long term needs. They are physically manipulating the data according to the attitudes and actions described above. The result is a physical data manipulation industry rather than a formal data resource management program.

Most data modeling tools are used to physically design and implement the database without any formal logical design. The physical design is often oriented toward the data used by specific business processes, without normalizing the data for use by other business processes. The primary objective of most data modeling tools seems to be cutting the code to develop a physical database for a set of business processes.

Many purchased applications have a physical orientation toward a fixed way of doing business and managing data for organizations, without regard for how organizations conduct their business as they perceive the business world. The result is an organization's way of doing business becomes warped to fit the application.

Many applications and databases have very few physical data edits and seldom have extensive logical data integrity rules. Many applications and databases lack formal data names and comprehensive data definitions that are meaningful to the business. Many applications actively create data disparity and many software tools are developed to resolve that disparity. Many data integration and ETL activities intended to resolve disparity actually make the disparity worse.

Another analogy exists between an illness treatment industry and a data manipulation industry. In the illness treatment industry a class of illnesses known as nosocomial infections runs rampant in many medical facilities. A nosocomial infection is an infection that a person did not have when they entered a medical facility, but had when they left the medical facility. It's an infection that was acquired at the medical facility that was not related to the illness that person had when they entered the medical facility.

A nosocomial infection follows the *principle of unintended consequences*, which states that any intervention in a complex system may or may not have the intended result, but will inevitably create unintended and often undesirable outcome. In actuality, a nosocomial infection is a result of not following established sanitary techniques in medical facilities. Had the medical facility followed established concepts, principles, and techniques,

155

most nosocomial infections would not have occurred.

The data resource in many public and private organizations has a nosocomial infection known as disparate data. The result of an illness treatment industry is a high probability of nosocomial infections. The result of a physical data manipulation industry is a high probability of disparate data. Nosocomial infections impact the patient's wellbeing and hamper their pursuit of a productive life. Disparate data impact an organization's wellbeing and hamper their pursuit of a productive business.

Many medical professionals admit, usually in private, that the illness treatment industry is profit motivated. Keeping people healthy and preventing illness is not as profitable as treating illnesses. The profit is in medical procedures and medications, not in prevention. More profit exists from reactive treatment of illnesses than from proactive prevention of illnesses. In addition, more satisfaction comes from solving a problem than from preventing a problem.

The same situation appears to be true for the physical data manipulation industry. Physical data manipulation seems to have a greater profit motive than formal data resource management. More profit exists for being reactive than for being proactive. More profit exists in software application and software tool sales than in formal planning and design.

More satisfaction is gained from getting a database up and running to support current business processes than in following formal concepts, principles, and techniques. More satisfaction is gained from building and implementing than from planning and designing. More satisfaction is gained from playing with tools than from making hard decisions about a high quality data resource that provides long term support to the business.

The existence of a data manipulation industry, rather than a data resource management program, should be obvious. The question becomes what can be done to resolve the situation? What needs to be done to turn a physical data manipulation industry into a data resource management program? What needs to be done to stop the stop the creation of disparate data—the nosocomial infection of databases?

CURING THE DATA RESOURCE PLAGUE

The answer is almost too obvious—cure the plague and create a program that formally manages data as a critical resource of the organization! Support that program with formal data resource design, and support that design with formal data resource modeling.

Power Versus Force

Sounds easy, but the problem is one of power versus force. The attitudes and actions are the force, and the data resource plague is the result of that force. The power is formal concepts, principles, and techniques, and the desire to use that power. Stopping the plague and creating formal data resource management comes only with power, and never with force.

Look into your own organization, or the organization of your clients. Does the organization follow established and proven concepts, principles, and techniques for formal data resource management? Or is it oriented toward the attitudes and actions that create disparate data? Does it have disparate data that are impacting the wellbeing of the business?

Stopping data disparity is like stopping nosocomial infections. Cleaning up existing data management practices to stop data disparity is like cleaning up medical facilities to stop nosocomial infections. The theme of a physical data manipulation industry is the attitudes and actions, and they must be cleaned up.

A strong case can be made that formal data resource management is just as profitable as a physical data manipulation industry, and far better for the wellbeing of the organization. Both business professionals and data management professionals must start a formal data resource management program that replaces the current physical data manipulation industry.

Use the power of established and proven concepts, principles, and techniques to stop the hype-cycles or transcend the hype-cycles, resolve the lexical challenge and prevent it from happening again, and stop the charge of the five horsemen. Stop creating any further data disparity and clean up the existing data disparity. Create a data resource that adequately meets the current and future business information demand of the organization.

Comparate Data

Power begins with the design and development of a comparate data resource. *Comparate data* are data that are alike in kind, quality, and character, and are without defect. They are concordant, homogeneous, nearly flawless, nearly perfect, high-quality data that are easily understood and readily integrated.

A *comparate data resource* is a data resource composed of comparate data that adequately support the current and future business information demand. The data are easily identified and understood, readily accessed and shared, and utilized to their fullest potential. A comparate data resource is an integrated, subject oriented, business driven data resource that is the official record of reference for the organization's business.

Simplicity

Power is used to create an understanding of business reality through simplicity. The theme is *elegance is simplicity*. Taking the simplest approach leads to a simpler data resource that is both comparate and elegant.

Albert Einstein's *simplicity principle* states that *Everything should be as simple as possible...but not simpler*. It's the simplest approach to designing a comparate data resource to support the business information demand.

Albert Einstein also made the statement *We are seeking for the simplest possible scheme of thought that will bind together the observed facts*. That statement readily applies to designing a comparate data resource based on an organization's perception of the business world in which they operate.

Occam's Razor (originally Ockham's Razor), as initially translated, means *Entities should not be multiplied more than necessary. That is, the fewer assumptions an explanation of a phenomenon depends on, the better it is*. Occam's Razor simply means the simpler the explanation, the better; if you have two equally likely solutions to a problem, choose the simplest, and keep things simple.

Many people believe that these statements about simplicity are meaningless and cannot be achieved. However, the statements are quite meaningful in the context of understanding and comprehension.

Simple means not complicated, or being not complicated. Simple can certainly be very detailed, but must also be readily understandable. Simple is achieving full understanding and comprehension regardless of the level of detail. Being too complicated means not fully understandable and comprehensible. Being overly simple means a loss of understanding and comprehension.

Understanding and comprehension resolve uncertainty. As long as uncertainty exists, there is no simplicity. Simplicity is easily identified by the *aha syndrome*, meaning the light dawns. When the light dawns, understanding and comprehension has been achieved, and uncertainty has been resolved.

In many situations, the decrease of input leads to a better understanding and comprehension of reality. If the input creates an overload that does not lead to a better understanding and comprehension of reality, then simplicity has not been achieved. Any overload, meaning not relevant or timely to the intended audience, creates confusion. Therefore, to be simple, the input must be relevant to the understanding and comprehension of the intended audience.

Simplicity is the state of being simple or uncompounded, having a lack of subtlety or penetration, freedom from pretense or guile, directness of expression, and maintainable. Simplicity is plain and uncomplicated. *Data resource simplicity* is the state of an organization's data resource being simple, uncomplicated, and maintainable. It's free from pretense and subtlety. An organization's data resource must be simple if it is to adequately represent business reality.

Reality

Power can be used to achieve business reality and data resource reality. *Reality* is the quality or state of being real; a real event, entity, or state of affairs; the totality of real things and events; something that is neither derivative nor dependent, but exists necessarily. Reality is something that is true, actual, genuine, or authentic.

Business reality is the reality according to the organization's perception of the business world where it operates. It's the simplest understanding and accurate description of that reality, not an abstraction which warps that reality. Any warping of the reality destroys that reality and any simplicity associated with that reality.

Data resource reality is the reality that only formal design of an organization's data resource, according to established theory, and based on sound concepts, principles, and techniques can lead to a comparate data resource that fully supports the organization's current and future business information demand. Data resource reality supports business reality.

Reality is what's in a person's mind. The mind is what perceives the business world, and an architecture is only a representation of what's in the mind. In other words, an architecture is a representation of the business world as perceived in a person's mind. A data architecture is representation of the data perceived to be needed by the organization to achieve the reality of a comparate data resource.

Perception

Business reality is achieved through an understanding of an organization's perception of the business world where they operate. The *organization perception principle* states that the comparate data resource developed to support an organization's business must be based on the organization's

159

perception of the business world. If a comparate data resource is to support an organization's business activities, that comparate data resource must be based primarily on the organization's perception of the business world and how the organization chooses to operate in that business world.

Umwelt is a German word meaning the environment or the world around. It's the world as perceived by an organism based on its cognitive and sensory powers. It's the environmental factors collectively that are capable of affecting an organism's behavior. It's a self-centered world where organisms can have different umwelten, even though they share the same environment. It's an organism's perception of the current surroundings and previous experiences which are unique to that organism. It's the world as experienced by a particular organism.

The *organization umwelt principle* states that each organization has a particular perception of the business world in which they operate based on previous experiences that are unique to that organization. Those experiences affect the organization's behavior in the business world, and determine how the organization adapts to a changing business world and operates in that business world. The organization umwelt principle supports the organization perception principle and emphasizes the importance of understanding both the business environment and the data supporting the business in that environment.

The organization umwelt principle emphasizes that each organization has a unique perception of the business world and chooses to operate according to that perception without being judged right or wrong. An organization can change their perception of the business world and how they operate in it based on experiences that are unique to that organization. One perception of the business world that is suitable for all organizations does not exist. Each organization has its own unique perception of the business world.

Data resource reality emphasizes that the organization perception principle and the organization umwelt principle are followed. The data resource must represent and support the way an organization perceives the business world and operates in that business world. Data resource design must be based on the way the organization perceives the real world and must include the data necessary to operate in that business world.

Organizations create their own business reality based on their perception of the business world where they operate and then define that reality. However, the very act of observing the organization's perception of the business world could change that perception. In other words, the act of observing and documenting the business reality can easily change that reality.

Observation Can Influence Reality

Both the business world and the organization's perception of that business world can be influenced by the act of observation. The observation could be filtered by the observer, it could be confined by the method of observation, or it could be confused by many different observations. The observation could also influence the business world or the organization's perception of that business world.

Heisenberg's uncertainty principle states that both the momentum and the location of an object cannot be measured at the same time. The very act of observation changes the object being observed. Although that uncertainty principle applies to quantum mechanics, it can be applied to understanding business reality.

The question becomes how is an organization's perception of the business world understood in order to document business reality when the act of observation can change either the business world or the perception. The answer is to take a simple approach to understanding and documenting business reality, and to follow established and proved concepts, principles, and techniques. The answer is to cycle through the observations to understand the existing business reality, and to possibly create a better business reality.

Agility

Creating a better business reality helps an organization be agile in a dynamic business world. An organization must be agile to survive and be successful. However, the data resource plague does not support agility by any stretch of the imagination.

Agility is the quality or state of being agile; marked by ready ability to move with quick easy grace, mentally quick and resourceful; marked by speed and flexibility. It's the ability to respond quickly, be nimble, be alert, and be adaptable to change.

Organization agility is the state where an organization is agile enough to remain successful in their business endeavor in a dynamic business world. It's how well the organization perceives the dynamic business world and how well the organization adjusts to that dynamic business world. It's how well the organization understands the business world, how quickly the organization perceives changes in that business world, and how quickly the organization can respond to those changes.

161

The business world is constantly changing. The only thing constant today is the increasing rate and magnitude of change. Organization agility is the name-of-the-game if an organization is to survive and remain successful in its business endeavors.

One major aspect of organization agility is being able to obtain the information it needs to operate successfully. In other words, supporting the business information demand is critical for organization agility. Supporting the business information demand requires data resource agility.

Data resource agility is the state where an organization's data resource is agile enough to support the changing business information demand resulting from organization agility. It depends on how quickly the data resource can change to reflect changes in the dynamic business world where the organization operates.

Data resource agility directly supports organization agility and an intelligent learning organization (the I-organization). A disparate data resource cannot be agile, but a comparate data resource has the ability to be very agile and directly support a changing business information demand. An organization cannot get the information they need if they have disparate data. It must have comparate data to be agile.

Data resource project agility is the state where the management of a data resource project is agile enough to produce a comparate data resource, using formal data resource design techniques, without unnecessary delay. It's performing every task in proper sequence, in due time, with the appropriate people, using formal concepts, principles, and techniques. It's fast, but it's also effective and efficient.

Data resource project agility doesn't mean that eliminating certain tasks, or choosing which tasks to perform and which tasks to skip. It doesn't mean following current hype-cycles or using the lexical challenge as an excuse to rapidly develop a database. It doesn't mean performing the actions of the five horsemen to build databases in the shortest possible time.

Data resource project agility does mean doing everything in the proper sequence—doing the right things at the right times. It does mean developing a comparate data resource that can be easily adjusted to a changing business information demand. It does mean proper management of data as the raw materials to produce information on relatively short notice.

Data resource project ability is not a project management method or a system development cycle. It's the attitude about managing a data resource project that understands business risk and the data needed to mitigate that risk. It's the ability to work directly with business professionals to develop data resource models that directly support the organization's business information demand. It's being business driven.

ACHIEVING DATA RESOURCE REALITY

Resolving the data resource plague and achieving data resource reality is not easy, but it's far from impossible. Organizations must recognize that what exists today is artificiality, not reality, and that no silver bullets exist to automatically resolve that artificiality. They must recognize that change is persistent and business reality is not stable over time. They must recognize that proven approaches to achieving data resource reality are not mainstream and create a paradox.

Reality Versus Artificiality

Reality is how well a comparate data resource directly supports an organization's business activities, as they perceive the business world. Artificiality is any data resource that does not directly support an organization's business activities, as they perceive the business world. Artificiality results from the two attitudes and the actions of the five horsemen.

Many people claim that what exists today, specifically a disparate data resource and mainstream hype, is reality. They claim that the mere existence of a disparate data resource constitutes reality. However, what exists today is artificiality because it does not directly support an organization's business reality.

Many people claim that the data resource plague is reality. These people contribute to the illusion of a comparate data resource, then claim that the illusion is reality, then use that self-proclaimed reality to do the same thing they have been doing in the past. Well, *Those that don't understand history are bound to repeat it* and *If you keep doing what you're doing, you'll keep getting what you're getting.*

The data resource plague is artificiality, meaning that the illusion of proper data resource design is artificial. The situation does exist, but it's an artificial situation. Any alteration or warping of the organization's perception of the business world is artificiality. Reality is a data resource that supports business reality.

Statements are often made that brute-force-physical actions do work and are reality. But those statements depend on the meaning of *work*. If *work* means the data resource functions, then brute-force-physical actions do

163

work. However, if *work* means that the data resource fully supports the current and future business information demand of the organization according to their perception of the business world where they operate, then brute-force-physical actions do not work. The latter case is most often true, and brute-force-physical actions are artificiality.

An organization is not destined to continue with artificiality. Every public and private sector organization has the opportunity, and the responsibility, to choose understanding business reality and developing data resource reality. Organizations need to move from artificiality to reality.

No Silver Bullets

Many organizations are looking for quick fixes and silver bullets to resolve the existing artificiality. They are relying on these quick fixes to solve the data resource plague. Much of the hype in the data manipulation industry today is toward finding quick fixes to current problems.

The sad news is that quick fixes and silver bullets do not exist. Any attempt to find silver bullets only leads to tarnished bullets. An organization cannot buy a solution to their problems. They cannot buy business reality or a comparate data resource. It's just not going to happen.

Too many tools oriented toward current hype are available today. However, those tools alone cannot cure the data resource plague because tools cannot understand the problem. Only people can understand the problem and implement a cure. Tools can support that understanding and assist with implementing a cure.

The only approach is a real hard thinking kind of work that uncovers and documents business reality, and builds a comparate data resource to support that business reality. That hard thinking kind of work leads to change that cures the data resource plague. But, change only comes with pain, and the organization must face that pain to understand business reality and create a comparate data resource.

I'm frequently asked how the pain can be increased so an organization starts the real hard thinking kind of work to cure the data resource plague. The answer is that the pain can't be increased, and doesn't need to be increased. Most organizations already have enough pain. The pain that exists must be known. The real secret in getting started with understanding business reality is to identify the pain and make that pain known. Then the real hard thinking kind of work can begin.

When Is Reality Achieved?

I am frequently asked when is reality achieved? When is a comparate data resource complete? When does an organization have full and complete data resource support for its business reality?

The answer is that complete business reality is never achieved and a complete comparate data resource that supports business reality is never achieved. The reason is the constant and relentless change in the business world, and in the way that organizations perceive the business world. Organizations may not like change, but change doesn't care.

Change is persistent and will never cease. Organizations can only accept change, and plan for change, and manage change when it arrives. Change creates a hidden business reality that can only be understood by constantly seeking to understand current business reality and adjusting the data resource reality accordingly.

SUMMARY

The data resource plague is a disparate data resource that's growing and is adversely impacting an organization's business. That plague is caused by prolific hype-cycles, a growing lexical challenge, and the actions of the five horsemen. These mainstream attitudes and actions are fueling a data manipulation industry.

The data resource plague can only be cured by recognizing the attitudes and actions, and taking corrective action. Corrective action begins with the use of power rather than force. Business reality and data resource reality are achieved through simplicity. An organization's perception of the business world leads to understanding business reality and developing data resource reality. Business reality and data resource reality lead to an agile organization.

The artificiality that exists today must be changed to reality. However, stable reality is never achieved due to the constant change in the business world and the organization's perception of that business world. Silver bullets do not offer any quick fix to current mainstream approaches. Only fresh, sound, proven approaches offer a chance to achieve reality. However, the clash between mainstream approaches and fresh approaches often create a paradox for most organizations that must be resolved before they can move ahead.

Immanuel Kant said that *Science is organized knowledge. Wisdom is organized life.* Isaac Asimov said that *The saddest aspect of society right now is that science gathers knowledge faster than society gathers wisdom.* What's happening with data resource management, design, and modeling today is that *We are gathering techniques faster than we are gathering the wisdom to manage those techniques.*

The data resource plague can only be resolved by avoiding the things that cause the plague and implementing the things that cure the plague. Curing the plague requires using power not force, seeking reality based on the organization's perception of the business world where they operate, documenting that reality in as simple manner as possible (but no simpler), and developing a comparate data resource that directly supports business agility. That's the task ahead.

John F. Kennedy said *We do these things not because they are easy, but because they are hard.*

Chapter 15

DATA RESOURCE DEVELOPMENT

Formal data resource development achieves the reality.

The data resource reality is achieved through the formal development of an organization's data resource. The formal development continually builds toward a thorough understanding of all the data needed by the organization to achieve its business goals. The thorough understanding is achieved through the Data Resource Development Cycle, the data resource components that are developed in that cycle, and the Data – Information – Knowledge Cycle that results from that understanding.[6]

DATA RESOURCE DEVELOPMENT CYCLE

The Data Resource Development Cycle is a formal sequence of events that begins with an organization's perception of the business world where it operates and ends with the data resource that is needed to support their successful operation in that business world. The description of that Cycle includes an overview, a description of the business world perception, the formal development of data schemas, the use of the data resource to support the organization's business information demand, the Data Resource Data that document the data resource, the integration of disparate data, and the relationship between data resource quality and disparity.

Development Cycle Overview

The Data Resource Development Cycle is a sequence of events that leads from an organization's perception of the business world to the data needed by the organization to operate successfully in that business world, as shown in Figure 15.1. The upper left of the diagram shows the organization and the business world in which that organization operates. The center, right, and lower portion of the diagram show the actual development and documentation of the data resource, which is represented by the symbols with dashed lines. The left center of the diagram shows the use of the data resource to meet the current and future business information demand, which

---

[6] Some material adapted from articles by the author on Dataversity.net.

supports the organization's successful operation in the business world.

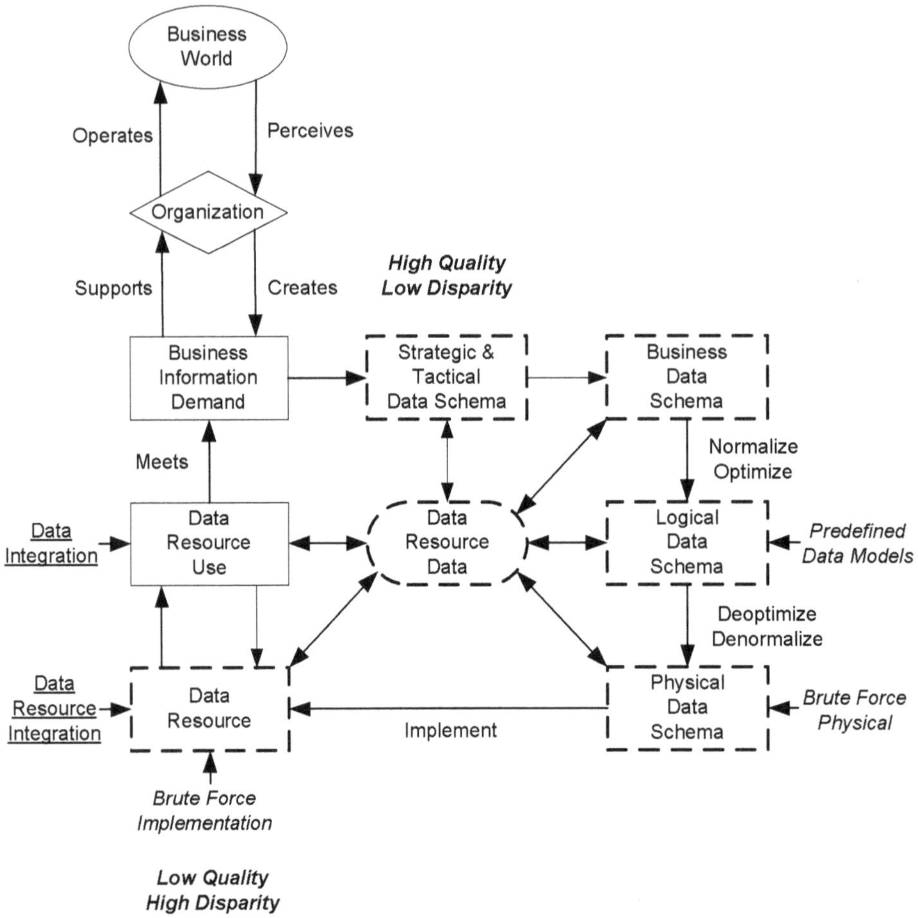

Figure 15.1. Data Resource Development Cycle.

Business World Perception

The development of an organization's data resource begins in the upper left of the diagram. Each organization perceives the business world according to its business goals and how it chooses to operate in that business world to achieve those goals. That perception creates a business information demand that must be met for the organization to operate successfully in the business world. Failure to meet both the current and the future business information demand leads to a less than fully successful business.

The formal development of an organization's data resource must begin with its perception of the business world to assure that the data needed for the organization to operate successfully in the business world are available. All too often data resource development begins later in the development cycle, such as with the logical data schemas or physical data schemas, which is usually to the detriment of the organization's success.

Each organization does have its own perception of the business world, and they have the right to that perception and to build a data resource according to that perception. However, most organizations belong to a major subject, area, such as health care, criminal justice, education, and so on, and they need to recognize certain conventions general perceptions within that subject area. In other words, a major subject area has certain general perceptions of the business world and can develop conventions within that major subject area to be followed for the exchange of data. An organization does not have to follow those conventions for developing its data resource, but it does need to translate their data according to those conventions for exchanging data between organizations.

The issue is one of rights and responsibilities. Each organization has the right to create their data resource according to their perception of the business world, but they have the responsibility to share data according to certain conventions for major subject areas. To go a step farther, major subject areas can overlap, such as geographic areas, political areas, and so on. These more universal subject areas have their own conventions for sharing data. Each organization's rights and responsibilities also apply to these more universal subject areas.

Each organization has the right to design its data resource as it deems necessary for its business, which may be according to conventions for major subject areas or more universal subject areas, or may be according to its own perception of the business world. If the design is according to its own perception of the business world, then the organization is responsible for translating the data. The bottom line is that sharing common data does not mean having a common data resource.

Changes In Perception

Three major events can happen that will change an organization's perception of the business world, which results in a change to its data resource to adequately support that change in perception.

First, the business world changes which causes changes in an organization's perception. Regulations change, other organizations start business and go out of business, citizens and customers change their habits, and so on. Any of these changes result in changes to an organization's perception.

Second, the organization adjusts its lines of business, adds new lines of business, or discards lines of business which causes changes in its perception. Public sector organizations usually have their lines of business changed by legislative action. Private sector organizations can choose to change their lines of business, or may be regulated to change their lines of business. Any of these changes results in changes to an organization's perception.

Third, and most important, the act of observing and documenting an organization and its perception of the business world changes both that organization and its perception. In other words, any observation interferes with the very thing that is being observed. In addition, the act of observation allows the thing being observed to better understand and evaluate itself, which leads to changes.

Collectively, these changes result in ongoing changes to the data resource that supports the organization. Therefore, the Data Resource Development cycle must begin with the organization's perception of the business world, and must constantly adjust to changes in the perception over time. To do otherwise seriously compromises the data resource and the organization's success.

Data Schema Development

Based on the organization's perception of the business world, the business information demand is developed which identifies the data needed to support the organization's business activities. That business information demand starts the development of formal data schemas that will lead to implementation and improvement of the organization's data resource. That data resource, in turn, supports the business information demand.

First, the strategic data schemas and tactical data schemas are developed. The strategic data schemas provide a generalized 30,000 foot view of the data for executives. The tactical data schemas provide a more specialized 10,000 foot view of the data for managers which is more detailed than the strategic data schemas. Collectively, these two data schema provide an overview of the data needed to support the business information demand.

Next, the business data schemas are developed that provide a detailed ground level view of the data for knowledge workers that are performing the business activities. The business data schemas include all the documents, reports, screens, and so on, that the organization uses to conduct its business activities or to evaluate its business activities.

The logical data schemas are developed from the tactical data schemas and the business data schemas, as modified by formal data normalization and formal data optimization. Data normalization assures that the data are properly structured and grouped according to how the organization perceives the business world. Data optimization assures that the data are not unnecessarily fragmented beyond that proper structuring and grouping.

The physical data schemas are developed from the logical data schema according to formal data optimization and data denormalization techniques. Data deoptimization represents the distribution of the logical data schemas to different physical operating environments. Data denormalization represents the adjustment of the logical data schemas to the physical operating environment for optimum performance without compromising the logical data schemas. The physical data schemas are used to design and implement the physical data resource, and populate that data resource with the data.

Pre-empting Data Schema Development

The formal sequence from the strategic and tactical data schemas, to the business data schemas, to the logical data schemas, to the physical data schemas, to implementation can be pre-empted in several ways.

First, development might begin with the logical data schemas, shown in italics on the upper right of the diagram in Figure 15.1. Beginning with the logical data schemas eliminates the benefits of the organization's perception of the business world, the strategic and tactical data schemas, and the business data schemas. The elimination of these benefits seriously compromises the ability of the data resource to support the business information demand.

In addition, the use of predefined data models to develop the logical data schemas imposes a predefined perception on the organization that may not match its perception of the business world. Developers of the predefined data models cannot impose their perception of the business world on an organization. Also, the predefined data models are often incomplete with only a data structure. They seldom have formal data names, comprehensive data definitions, or precise data integrity rules.

Predefined data models can be used to kick-start or support the development of logical data schemas. They can be used to provide suggested logical data schemas that represent the organization's perception of the business world. However, they cannot be used to force an organization into a fixed perception of the business world that limits its ability to be successful in that business world.

Similarly, data modelers cannot impose their perception of the business world on an organization, no matter how experienced they might be. They

171

must seek to uncover and understand how the organization perceives the business world, and then develop the appropriate data models to portray that perception.

Second, development might begin with the brute-force development of the physical data schemas, shown in italics on the right side of the diagram in Figure 15.1. Beginning with the physical data schemas eliminates all the benefits of the logical data schemas and its predecessors, and severely compromises the ability of the data resource to support the business information demand.

The primary drivers for brute-force development of physical data schemas is most of the data modeling tools and the desire of organizations to quickly implement a database so they can begin processing the data. What's really happening is that the organization is knowingly letting the data modeling tools drive the business perceptions and how the organization conducts business. The result is massive, and growing, data disparity.

Data modeling and design tools can, and should, be used to support the Data Resource Development Cycle. However, those tools should support every step from the organization's perception of the business world, through all the data schemas, to implementation of the database storing the data. They must follow the business, to logical, to physical, to implementation sequence.

Third, development might begin with brute-force implementation of the physical databases, shown in italics on the bottom of the diagram in Figure 15.1. Brute-force physical implementation is absolutely the worst place to begin. It eliminates all the benefits of the organization's perception, development of the logical data schemas, and development of the physical data schemas. It devastates the ability of the data resource to support the business information demand.

The basic problem with pre-empting the formal development cycle is that what people know frames what they see, what they see frames what they understand, and what they understand frames what they implement. People pay little attention to unfamiliar objects in front of them if they focus too strongly on the familiar ones. When people focus on predefined data models, brute-force physical design, and brute-force implementation, they fail to see the benefits of beginning with the business world perception and proceeding through the formal development process.

Therefore, the best approach is for people to focus on the formal development cycle. When they know that cycle, it frames what they see, which frames what they understand, which frames what they implement. The result is a data resource that adequately supports the business information demand and helps support a successful organizational.

Data Resource Use

After the data resource has been developed it is used by a wide variety of applications to meet the business information demand. Although the actual use of the data resource appears small with only one symbol on a diagram of the entire Data Resource Development Cycle, use of the data resource is by far the largest portion of the entire Cycle. The use is where all of the operational, evaluational, and predictive processing occurs.

Use of the data resource is limited only by people's imagination. Their imagination is maximized with the formal Data Resource Development Cycle that creates and maintains a data resource that is thoroughly understood. When that understanding is not readily available, the imagination is limited and the organization's business activities suffer.

Use of the data resource includes drawing existing data from the data resource and storing new data in the data resource. Those new data must be formally documented to ensure that they are as readily understood as the existing data. Otherwise, the data resource slowly deteriorates, becomes disparate, and does not fully support the organization's business activities.

In a broad sense, the development and maintenance of the data resource is data resource management and use of the data resource to produce information for the business activities is information management. Sometimes the two processes are referred to as data engineering and information engineering, which are appropriate. However, management is a broader and more inclusive term than engineering.

Data resource management produces and maintains a data resource that supports the business information demand. Information management produces information from that data resource to meet the business information demand. The quality of the information produced can be no higher than the quality of the data resource used to produce the information, and may be lower depending on the quality of the information management process.

Data Resource Data

The Data Resource Data, shown in the center of the diagram in Figure 15.1, play a critical role in understanding and documenting the organization's data resource. The Data Resource Data connect to nearly everything in the Data Resource Development Cycle. The business information demand connects to the Data Resource Data. The strategic, tactical, business, logical, and physical data schemas connect to the Data Resource Data. The data resource and use of the data resource connect to the Data Resource Data.

Data Resource Data are the heart of the Data Resource Development Cycle and contain the understanding necessary to fully utilize the data resource. Data Resource Data are what the current book and the previous book are all about. They are the critical piece of the Data Resource Development Cycle.

Disparate Data Integration

Most organizations have an existing disparate data resource, or massively disparate data resource, that needs to be formally integrated and documented.

The traditional approach to integrating data is data integration as the data are extracted from the data resource for use by applications to meet the business information demand, shown in underlined Data Integration in Figure 15.1. However those integrated data are often stored for later use, without proper documentation, which further increases the data resource disparity. Even if those integrated data are not stored, the data integration process and the meaning of those integrated are seldom documented, which puts the quality of the information produced in question.

The preferred approach is to formally integrate the entire disparate data resource one time, as shown in the underlined Data Resource Integration in Figure 15.1. The resulting comparate data resource is formally documented and the need for multiple undocumented traditional data integrations is eliminated. The result is a higher quality data resource that fully supports the business information demand.

Quality and Disparity

What has become clear over the years is that when the Data Resource Development Cycle begins with the organization's perception of the business world and goes through the entire cycle, the data resource has high quality and low disparity, as shown by the bold italics in the upper center of the diagram in Figure 15.1. When the process begins later in the Data Resource Development Cycle, such with the logical data schemas, the physical data schemas, or direct implementation, the data resource has lower quality and higher disparity, as shown by the bold italics on the lower left of the diagram in Figure 15.1.

As the data resource quality decreases and the disparity increases, the information quality is lower, and the business information demand is impacted and compromised, which impacts business activities. However, when the data resource quality increases and the disparity decreases, the information quality is higher, the business information demand is met, and the business activities are adequately supported.

DATA RESOURCE COMPONENTS

Thoroughly understanding an organization's data is a primary consideration for supporting the business information demand. A thorough understanding includes the three major components of data description, data structure, and data integrity. These three components must be balanced and support each other to provide a complete and meaningful understanding of the data.

The Missing Descriptive Component

The problem is that the data description component has been largely neglected in favor of the structural and integrity components. The neglected descriptive component began in the early days of data processing when the orientation was primarily toward a physical structure and data manipulation. The neglected descriptive component was quite likely the beginning of the massive data disparity that exists today in most organizations.

In 1966 Ann Rand presented man's precepts; the concept of an existence, be it a thing, attribute, or action; perceptual entities and attributes as characteristics of entities; motions of entities; and relationship among entities. Her presentation was the first real insights into approaches to designing an organization's data resource. However, the presentation did not emphasize a strong need for describing the data.

In the late 1940s Claude Shannon developed his communication theory consisting of syntactic information and semantic information. Syntactic information was the raw data and semantic information was the meaningful, timely, and relevant information. He did not present data-in-context, which is data wrapped with meaning. He relied on an individual's connotative meaning of the words, the intonation in the message, and the individual's interpretation of timeliness and relevance based on that connotative meaning.

In 1970 Dr. Edgar F. 'Ted' Codd presented the Relational Model that consisted of structural, integrity, and manipulative components. He extended it to the Relational Model / Tasmania in 1979, and along with Chris Date presented the techniques of data normalization. The structural and integrity components were used for physical data resource development, and the manipulative component was for data resource use. No descriptive component was presented, which limited a thorough understanding of the data meaning.

In 1976 Dr. Peter Chen presented formal entity-relationship modeling, which began to emphasize logical data modeling based on a business orientation and the understanding of relationships. He used more meaningful data names with few abbreviations, which was the beginning of a descriptive component. Although he referred to possible semantic issues, he did not provide any formal definitions for fully understanding the data, or any denormalization criteria for developing a physical data model from a logical data model.

ANSI provided an initial two-schema concept with internal and external data schema, and later a revised three-schema concept with an internal data schema (physical storage), external data schema (physical use), and conceptual data schema. The conceptual data schema was a common denominator between the internal and external data schemas, and emphasized the need for a logical business orientation. However, the approach was still physically oriented and did not emphasize a descriptive component for thorough data understanding.

The canonical synthesis approach was presented to solve the problems of increasing data disparity by stating that if the canons were followed for developing data models, then those data models could easily be combined into a seamless data architecture that provided a full understanding of the data resource. The approach was valid as presented. However, no formal canons were provided and no descriptive component was emphasized.

Many people use the lack of emphasis on a descriptive component as an excuse that any detailed description of the data is not important and is not needed for data resource development. If it wasn't emphasized, then why was it needed? Informal data names and vague data definitions were used, resulting is limited understanding. Even more important, the relevance and timeliness of the data couldn't be accurately determined, resulting in a confusion between the terms *data* and *information*.

The lack of a descriptive component is a major contributor to the burgeoning disparate data for several reasons.

First, when people don't understand the meaning of existing data, they can't interpret the timeliness or relevance of the data, and they create their own data. Usually, the newly created data does not have a descriptive component other than in the creator's mind, which often leads to additional disparate data.

Second, the strong physical orientation without a descriptive component leads to brute-force-physical development of the data resource based on physical data schemas without any supporting logical data schemas or business perception, and to brute-force implementation of the data resource without any supporting physical data schemas.

Third, the emphasis on physical structural integrity led to the documentation of structural integrity on the data structure. The result is often incomplete, unclear, and difficult to understand. Even worse, the emphasis on structural integrity limits the specification of all the other types of data integrity.

Fourth, data modeling tools fail to provide good support for the descriptive component. The tools are often oriented toward physical database design and implementation. Consistent data names are not enforced within and across data models. Normalized data definitions are not provided within and across data models. Data model development is not done within a single organization wide data architecture.

Fifth, predefined data models generally lack a robust descriptive component. The data names and definitions often do not match the way an organization perceives the business world or the way the organization chooses to do business. The orientation is often toward a one-size-fits-all data model for rapid physical implementation.

Adding The Descriptive Component

Emphasis on development of a descriptive component slowly evolved as data disparity burgeoned. The descriptive component consists of formal data names that provide precise unique labels for data and comprehensive data definitions that provide denotative meanings for data so they can be readily understood. Both data names and data definitions are based on semiotic theory, which includes syntax, semantics, and pragmatics.

The use of a descriptive component is mandatory for thoroughly understanding the data, reducing data disparity, and supporting the business information demand. Business professionals know what information they need to operate the business and to evaluate the business. But if the proper data can't be found, whether those data exist or not, to produce that information, then business professionals cannot adequately perform their business activities or gain business insight.

A data name is a label for a fact or a set of related facts contained in the data resource, appearing on a data model, or displayed on screens, reports, or documents. A formal data name readily and uniquely identifies a fact or group of related facts in the data resource, based on the business, and using formal data naming criteria. Formal data names follow semiotic theory by providing a formal structure to the data name (syntax), a meaningful data name with respect to the business (semantic), and a practical and useful data name (pragmatic). Formal data names must be normalized within a single organization wide data architecture to prevent synonyms and homonyms, and to ensure uniqueness.

Data names and data definitions are often treated lightly, confused, used interchangeably, and misused. A short data name may be meaningless and have a definition that is a tautology. A long data name is often considered to be a short data definition with no additional definition to provide meaning. Both rely on an individual's connotative meaning, and interpretation of timeliness and relevance.

Adding a comprehensive definition to a formal data name provides maximum understanding. A comprehensive data definition is a data definition that provides a complete, meaningful, easily read, readily understood definition that thoroughly describes the content and meaning of the data with respect to the business. It helps people thoroughly understand the data and use the data efficiently and effectively. A comprehensive data definition provides a denotative meaning that is direct and explicit. It avoids connotative meanings that are ideas or notions that a person interprets in addition to what is explicitly stated.

Comprehensive data definitions follow semiotic theory by providing a formal structure for data definitions (syntax), meaningful data definitions with respect to the business (semantic), and practical and useful data definitions (pragmatic). They provide both semantic meaning with respect to the business and structural meaning with respect to relationships. They must be meaningful, thorough, accurate, current, and synchronized with the data name.

Data definitions must be normalized within a single organization wide data architecture to ensure thorough understanding of the data. Each data resource component must have one, and only one, comprehensive data definition that is based on the normalized formal data name. As the degree of data structuring increases, the data definitions need to be more comprehensive for people to fully understand the intricacy of the data structures.

Balancing The Components

The addition of a descriptive component consisting of formal data names and comprehensive data definitions provides the three primary components for understanding an organization's data resource. These three primary components are shown in Figure 15.2. The descriptive component consists of two sub-components for formal data names and comprehensive data definitions. These two sub-components of the descriptive component provide a formal description of the data resource architecture.

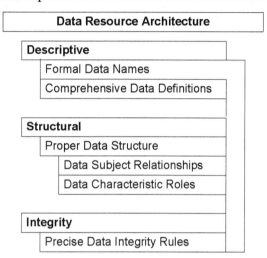

Figure 15.2. Data Resource Components.

The formal data names, in addition to contributing to the descriptive component, provide the glue that ties the comprehensive data definitions, proper data structure, and precise data integrity rules together. The lack of formal data names results in a loss of that tie between components, often resulting in weak data normalization, overloading of the data relation diagrams, general confusion about the meaning of the data, and increased data disparity. The lack of formal data names also leads to tautological data definitions, which at best provide an indication of a meaningful data name for an abbreviated data name.

The structural component consists of proper data structures, which has two sub-components for the relationships between data subjects, and the data characteristics contained in each data subject and their roles with respect to the data resource architecture. The data subjects and the relationships between those data subjects are shown on a data subject-relation diagram. The data characteristic list supports the data subject relationships with a list of all the data characteristics in each data subject and the roles that each play, such as primary keys and foreign keys. The data characteristic list also provides the construct for specifying all of the data integrity rules.

The integrity component consists of precise data integrity rules that specify constraints on the data and actions to be taken when the data integrity rules are violated. The constraints include data value integrity, data structure integrity, data derivation, data retention, data selection, and data conversion rules. The actions when data integrity rules are violated include violation actions and notification actions.

The three components of the formal data resource architecture must be balanced to provide maximum denotative understanding about the data resource architecture with minimum detail and minimum confusion. The best way to achieve the proper balance is through the Data Architecture Trinity, shown in Figure 15.3.

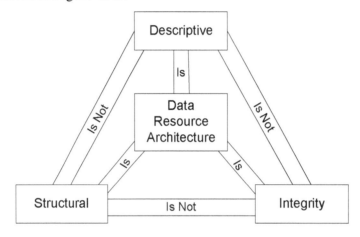

Figure 15.3. Data Architecture Trinity.

Trinity is the number 3; a tripod; triple; a set of three. The Data Architecture Trinity, like the Holy Trinity, the Alchemical Trinity, and so on, is a trinity representing the three components of a formal Data Resource Architecture and the relationships between those components. Each point in the Trinity is separate and distinct, but collectively the three points contribute to a single, formal, organization wide Data Resource Architecture for the organization.

The balance between the three components must be simple and understandable, and must follow semiotic theory. Specifically, the balance is between the Descriptive and Structural components, the Descriptive and Integrity components, and the Structural and Integrity components.

The data definitions do not explain the data structure, except for a very general description that provides an overview of the structure that is not readily obvious from the data subject relation diagram.

Similarly, the data structure does not contain any descriptions of the data, only the relationships between the data subjects, and the data characteristics within each data subject and their roles. Placing data definitions with the

180

data structure on the data subject-relation diagram only overloads the diagram making it confusing and very difficult to comprehend and understand. It also leads to short tautological definitions.

The data descriptions do not explain the data integrity rules, except for a very general description that provides an overview of the integrity that is not obvious from the data integrity rules.

Similarly, the data integrity component does not contain any data definitions. It contains only the integrity criteria placed on the data structure and the data values, and the actions when those criteria are violated.

The data structure does not contain any data integrity rules, except for the general data cardinality shown on the data subject-relation diagram.

Similarly, the data integrity rules do not contain any explanation of the data structure, only the constraints on the data structure and the actions to be taken when the constraints are violated.

The two sub-components of the data structure must not be combined, meaning the data characteristics and their roles must not be placed on the data subject-relation diagram. Combining those components only overloads the data subject-relation diagram making it confusing and very difficult to understand.

The Data Architecture Trinity supports development of a single, organization wide Data Resource Architecture. If the Data Architecture Trinity is not followed, then traditional data architectures are developed which eventually lead to a disparate or a massively disparate data resource. The result is failure to fully support an organization's current and future business information demand.

Similarly, data resource models either contribute to development and enhancement of a Data Resource Architecture, referred to as a model driven architecture, or provide selected details from a Data Resource Architecture for an intended audience, referred to as architecture driven models. The Data Resource Architecture represents the whole of an organization's data resource and data resource models contribute to development of that Data Resource Architecture, or portray portions of that whole for an intended audience.

Data resource models are developed according to the Data Architecture Trinity, subject to the detail needed by the intended audience. In other words, if the intended audience does not need the detail, it's not placed on the data resource model. Presenting the proper details for the intended audience ensures that audience can fully understand the data resource from their perspective.

If a data model is not developed within the Data Resource Architecture according to the Data Architecture Trinity, then it's a traditional data model which eventually leads to a poor understanding of the data resource, and disparate data or massively disparate data. The result is a failure to fully support an organization's current and future business information demand.

When the Data Architecture Trinity is followed, a formal Data Resource Architecture and data resource models are developed and the pitfalls of a traditional data architecture and data models are avoided.

THE DATA – INFORMATION – KNOWLEDGE CYCLE

The Data Resource Development Cycle has an imbedded cycle of data, information, and knowledge. However, the definitions of these three terms need to be reviewed before presenting the Data – Information - Knowledge Cycle.

Data are the individual facts that are out of context, have no meaning, and are difficult to understand. They are often referred to as raw data. The term *data* is plural, equivalent to *facts*, while *datum* is singular, equivalent to *a fact*. Although some people continue to use the term *data* as singular, a comprehensive, denotative definition of *data* in the singular form, beginning with *Data is ...* is not available. Most definitions of data in the singular are really definitions of a data resource.

Data could be considered an irregular noun, like *deer* or *sheep*, where the meaning is in the context. *Data* could be used to represent an individual fact the same as *datum*, and *data* could be used to represent a set of facts. However, the data management discipline has a huge lexical challenge without treating *data* as an irregular noun. Therefore, *datum* is singular and *data* is plural.

Data in context are individual facts that have meaning and can be readily understood. They are the raw facts wrapped with meaning, but they are not yet information. *Datum in context* is a single fact wrapped with meaning.

Information is a set of data in context with relevance to one or more people at a point in time or for a period of time. Information is more than data in context—it must have relevance and a time frame. Information is considered to be singular.

Knowledge is cognizance, cognition, the fact or condition of knowing something with familiarity gained through experience or association. It's the acquaintance with or the understanding of something, the fact or condition of being aware of something, or apprehending truth or fact. Knowledge is information that has been retained with an understanding about the significance of that information. Knowledge includes something gained by experience, study, familiarity, association, awareness, or comprehension.

Knowledge can be either tacit or explicit. *Tacit knowledge*, also known as *implicit knowledge*, is the knowledge that a person retains in their mind. It's relatively hard to transfer to others and to disseminate widely. *Explicit knowledge*, also known as *formal knowledge*, is knowledge that has been codified and stored in various media, such as books, magazines, tapes, presentations, and so on, and is held for mankind, such as in a reference library or on the web. It is readily transferable to other media and capable of being readily disseminated.

Organizational knowledge is information that is of significance to the organization, is combined with experience and understanding, and is retained by the organization. It's information in context with respect to understanding what is relevant and significant to a business issue or business topic – what is meaningful to the business. It's analysis, reflection, and synthesis about what information means to the business and how that information can be used. It's a rational interpretation of information that leads to business intelligence.

Knowledge management is the management of an environment where people generate tacit knowledge, render it into explicit knowledge, and feed it back to the organization. The cycle forms a base for more tacit knowledge, which keeps the cycle going in an intelligent learning organization. It's an emerging set of policies, organizational structures, procedures, applications, and technology aimed toward increased innovation and improved decisions. It's an integrated approach to identifying, sharing, and evaluating the organization's information. It's a culture for learning where people are encouraged to share information and best practices to solve business problems.

Several misperceptions exist with information. One misperception is that information is the same as data in context. Whenever raw data are wrapped with meaning, those data become information. However, if information is considered to be data in context, then the question becomes What are the terms for information that is relevant and timely and information that is not relevant and timely?

The answer might lead to relevant information and non-relevant information. However, only relevant information leads to knowledge and non-relevant information does not lead to knowledge. Therefore, raw data are wrapped with meaning to become data in context, which can become either relevant or non-relevant information. Only relevant information can become knowledge.

Another misperception is that information is any summary data or derived data. That misperception is not valid because whether data are primitive or derived, they are still data. They have not yet become relevant or timely and, therefore, are not yet information.

If data in context are not relevant or timely, then they are not information. However, data may not be relevant or timely to one person, but could be relevant and timely to another person. Therefore, the definition of information can be expanded. *Specific information* is a set of data in context that is relevant and timely to one or more people at a point in time or for a period of time. *General information* is a set of data in context that could be relevant to one or more people at a point in time or for a period of time.

Now that these basic terms are defined, the Data-Information-Knowledge Cycle can be described. The Data-Information-Knowledge Cycle is the cycle from data, to data in context, to relevant information (specific or general), to knowledge, and back to data when that information or knowledge is stored, as shown in Figure 15.4.

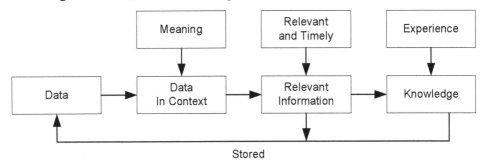

Figure 15.4. Data – Information – Knowledge Cycle.

When information and knowledge are stored, they become part of the organization's data resource and are managed according to formal data resource management concepts, principles, and techniques. Whether those data were once raw data, specific or general information, or knowledge makes no difference. Everything stored is part of the organization's data resource, is considered data, and is formally managed as data.

When specific information and general information are stored, they become part of the data resource, they are treated as data, and are managed like any other data. Those data will only become information again when they become relevant and timely. The same is true for knowledge. Stored knowledge becomes data and is managed like any other data. Those data will only become knowledge again when they are extracted as information, combined with experience, and retained.

A book on the shelf, a document on a server, raw data, a stored form or document, a stored report, and so on, are all considered data and managed as part of the organization's data resource. The storage of information or knowledge is still data to other people, and may or may not become information or knowledge to those people.

Looking at the situation the other way around, all information and knowledge were data at one time, whether or not they were stored in the organization's data resource. By becoming relevant and timely, those data became information. By being combined with business experience and retained, that information becomes knowledge.

Based on these definitions, there is no *information resource*, because timeliness and relevancy cannot be managed or stored. There can be information resources (plural) which are the set of resources used to produce information from data and present that information to the business. Knowledge resource is the tacit and implicit knowledge within an organization or available to the organization, and most of that knowledge is stored in the human resource.

SUMMARY

Data resource reality is achieved by building a thorough understanding of an organization's data resource through the Data Resource Development Cycle, the data resource components that make up that development cycle, and the Data – Information – Knowledge Cycle that is imbedded within the Data Resource Development Cycle.

The Data Resource Development Cycle is a formal sequence of events that begins with the organization's perception of the business world, proceeds through the business information demand, through the development of strategic and tactical data schemas, business data schemas, logical data schemas, and physical data schemas, to implementation of the data resource. The data resource is then used to meet the business information demand and support the organization in its business endeavors. Data Resource Data support that development cycle by storing the understanding that has been gained.

The three primary data resource components are data description, data structure, and data integrity. Data description consists of formal data names

185

and comprehensive data definitions. Formal data names are the glue that binds the other components together and provide an initial meaning. Comprehensive data definitions provide the full denotative meaning. Proper data structure and precise data integrity rules rely heavily on formal data names and comprehensive data definitions.

These three primary components of an organization's data resource represent the detail that provides the thorough understanding of the data in an organization's data resource. They must be balanced to provide maximum understanding and support for development of a high quality, low disparity data resource. The balance is achieved through a Data Architecture Trinity.

The Data Resource Development Cycle has an imbedded Data-Information-Knowledge Cycle that is the cycle from data, to data in context, to relevant information (specific or general), to knowledge (tacit and explicit), and back to data when that information or knowledge is stored.

The Data Resource Development Cycle, the primary data resource components of that cycle, and the Data – Information – Knowledge Cycle emphasize the management of data as a critical resource of the organization. They lead to a change in terms from data to data resource, from data models to data resource models, from data architecture to data resource architecture, from data integration to data resource integration, from data quality to data resource quality, and from data management to data resource management.

Chapter 16

RELATIONSHIPS

Data resource development is driven by relationships.

Data resource development is basically about identifying, understanding, and documenting relationships, and ultimately processing those relationships to produce information that supports business activities. Relationships begin in the business world, and are captured, adjusted, and documented throughout the entire Data Resource Development Cycle as part of data resource management. Those relationships are processed to support the business information demand as part of information management.[7]

THE DATA RESOURCE IS ABOUT RELATIONSHIPS

Relationships exist from the organization's perception of the business world, to business data schema, through data normalization to logical data schema, through data denormalization to physical data schema, to implementation and use of the data resource to provide information to the organization to meet their business information demand. They exist in operational data evaluational data, and predictive data, and through all the degrees of data structuring. The organization's data resource is substantially based on relationships.

Relationships Are Pervasive

Relationships have been around from the ancient philosophers to modern times. Notable people, like Ann Rand, Claude Shannon, Dr. Edgar F. Codd, Dr. Peter Chen, John Zachman, and many others, have talked about relationships as part of everyday personal and organizational life. Identifying, understanding, and documenting relationships are crucial for designing and developing a high quality data resource.

Many people consider that the relational concept is dead and often use the phrase *Now that (fill in the blank) is here, relational is dead.* However, that statement depends on what people mean by *relational*. *Relational* with reference to relational databases should not be confused with *relational*

---

[7] Some material adapted from articles by the author on Dataversity.net.

pertaining to understanding and managing relationships for building and using an organization's data resource.

Even though relational databases may not adequately handle all types of data, the identification, understanding, and management of relationships is crucial for developing a high quality data resource. Therefore, the meaning of relationships with respect to the business world as perceived by the organization is the important task.

Business World Relationships

The business world has always had relationships and will always have relationships. The business world is full of relationships, many of which are meaningful to an organization and become part of the organization's data resource, and many of which are not meaningful to the organization and will not become part of the organization's data resource.

The business world consists of many business objects, such as drivers, cities, vehicles, and accounts, and many business events, such fires and purchases. Note that these business objects and events are not the same as information system objects, which includes both business objects and events. The two concepts must be kept separate when designing and developing the organization's data resource.

When an organization is interested in a business object or event, an interest relationship is established between the business world and the organization. The business objects and events in that interest relationship become the initial data subjects in the business data schema of the organization's data architecture. When an organization has no interest in a business object or event, no interest relationship exists and no initial data subjects are established.

Many business relationships exist between business objects and events in the business world. When an organization is interested in a business relationship, that relationship becomes an initial data relation between the initial data subjects in the business data schema of the organization's data architecture. When an organization has no interest in a business relationship, it does not become and initial data relation.

Business objects and events are characterized by various business facts, such as size, name, date, location, and so on. When an organization is interested in a business fact, it becomes an initial data characteristic in the business data schemas of the organization's data architecture. When an organization has no interest in a business fact, it does not become an initial data characteristic.

An organization is part of the business world in which it operates. As part of that business world, an organization perceives how it chooses to operate the same as it perceives the external business world. Any business objects and events, business relations, and business facts within the organization become initial data subjects, initial data relations, and initial data characteristics in that organization's data architecture.

Data Schemas Represent Relationships

When the business data schemas have been established, they are normalized to logical data schemas following formal data normalization principles and techniques. Initial data subjects may be split or combined, initial data characteristics may be split or combined, and data relations may be adjusted. Data subjects, data characteristics, and data relations may be added, and primary and foreign keys are established. The result is the logical data schemas in the organization's data architecture that represent the normalized way the organization perceives the business world independent of any physical implementation.

The development of logical data schemas is based on relationships, the same as the development of the business data schemas. Relationships between data subjects are defined as data relations. Relationships between data characteristics and data subjects identify home and foreign data characteristics, and identify primary and foreign keys. Relationships between data characteristics within and between data subjects identify elemental and combined data characteristics and data reference sets. The entire formal data normalization process is based on identifying and understanding relationships.

When the logical data schemas have been established, they are denormalized to physical data schemas following formal data denormalization principles and techniques. Data subjects become data files / tables, logical data relations become physical data relations, and data characteristics become data items / columns. The result is the physical data schemas in the organization's data architecture that represent the way the organization chooses to implement its understanding of the business world.

The development of the physical data schemas is based on relationships, the same as the development of the logical data schemas. The relationships are physical in nature depending on how the organization chooses to operate its databases to support business processes. Specifically, the relationships between the data in the databases and the data used or developed by business processes are identified and understood.

The primary principle for formal data denormalization is that physical data schemas are developed for optimum processing without compromising the logical data schemas. When the logical data schemas are compromised, the flow of identifying and understanding relationships is broken, and the resulting databases will not likely fully support the organization's current and future business information demand.

Multiple physical data schemas may be developed from the logical data schemas depending on the types of processing that may be performed, as long as the primary principle is followed. However, the development of multiple physical data schemas from the logical data schemas creates redundant data, and those redundant data must be kept in synch if they are volatile operational data. Keeping those redundant data in synch leads to higher maintenance, and failure to keep the redundant data in synch leads to a low quality data resource.

Operational, Evaluational, and Predictive Data

Derived operational data have relationships with their contributors. These relationships are defined with data integrity rules, specifically data derivation and data re-derivation rules. Derived evaluational data from the extensive analysis results in large quantities of hierarchical data. These hierarchical derived data have very detailed relationships that must be understood to fully benefit from the analysis. Even predictive data have very intricate relationships involving variations and influences that need to be thoroughly understood.

Degrees Of Data Structuring

The degrees of data structuring are directly related to relationships. Unstructured data, by definition, are an unstructured amorphous mess that have no definable relationships and are difficult to process. Structured data have definable relationships that can be easily displayed in tabular form and can be easily processed by structured query languages. Highly structured data, such as text, have more intricate definable relationships that often stretch the capabilities of structured query languages. Complex structured data, such as voice or pictures, have even more intricate relationships and may have relationships between relationships. Ultra-structured data, such as biochemistry or quantum mechanics, have very intricate relationships that are near or exceed the limits of human comprehension.

As the degree of data structuring increases, relational databases begin to fail and other database technologies will evolve. However, even though relational databases fail, relationships are still of primary importance and must be identified and understood. In addition, as the degree of data structuring increases, formal data denormalization techniques will evolve to handle the more intricate relationships and support evolving database technologies.

Single Data Architecture

All relationships from the organization's perception of the business world through database implementation and use to support business activities must be managed within a single organization wide data architecture. Any time that an organization develops more than one data architecture, the quality of the data resource rapidly deteriorates. Similarly, any time that an organization relies solely on predefined data models to define relationships, the quality of the data resource deteriorates.

The identification, understanding, and management of relationships flow from the organization's perception of the business world, through business data schema, through normalization to logical data schema, through denormalization to physical data schema, to physical database implementation and use. One fact that has become very obvious is that the farther upstream (organization perception of the business world) the process begins, the greater the chance for a high quality data resource. The ultimate data resource quality is how well the data resource supports the current and future business information demand.

RELATIONSHIPS AND COMPUTATIONAL SPACES

Identifying, understanding, and managing relationships are crucial to the proper design and development of an organization's data resource. However, most data management professionals don't consider the importance of the wide range of relationships in an organization's business and very few consider relationships with respect to the mathematical or computational spaces. The result is often a less than optimum data resource design.

Basic Computational Spaces

The four basic computational spaces are the data space, aggregation space, influence space, and variation space. Computational spaces are sometimes referred to as computational complexity, where the complexity increases from the data space, through the aggregation space, influence space, and variation space. That complexity is due to more intricate relationships.

The data space is a set membership with business objects and events, facts, and relationships. Business objects and events lead to data subjects. Business facts lead to data characteristics that have a defined set of values documented as data integrity rules, specifically data value and conditional data value rules. Business relationships lead to a wide variety of data relations. Operational data represent the data space.

The aggregation space is arithmetic and multi-dimensional. Multi-dimensional does not refer to spatial dimensions. It refers to data dimensions surrounding a central data focus within a specific data perspective. It builds on the data space to produce aggregated data that provide a better understanding of the operational data. Analytical data represent the aggregation space.

The influence space uses logic and pertains to identifying the influencing relationships by searching for and discovering hidden or unknown patterns and trends. The exploratory phase finds hypotheses through fixed or free roaming approaches, and the confirmatory phase confirms or refutes those hypotheses. The influence space builds on the aggregation space and often requires additional data not already available.

The variation space uses differential calculus and other techniques to identify the type, relative influence, and rate of change of the influences. It builds on the influence space and often requires additional data not already available.

Both the influence space and the variation spaces are used for discovery to further the organization's understanding of the past and current business. They form the base for making future predictions about the business.

Additional Computational Spaces

Two additional computational spaces that cross the four basic computational spaces are the time space containing temporal data and temporal relationships, and the spatial space containing spatial data and spatial relationships. The complexity of the four basic computational spaces is increased by the addition of the time space and the spatial space.

The time space contains temporal data and temporal relationships pertaining to time. Temporal data can range from 10^{-37} seconds for the early formation of the universe to 13.75×10^9 years for the age of the universe. It typically ranges from seconds to geologic eras, systems, and epochs.

The spatial space contains spatial data and spatial relationships pertaining to distances and directions in the three basic dimensions of space, excluding the six or seven additional dimensions of quantum mechanics. It is often referred to as geometric space, but geometric refers only to the Earth (geo meaning Earth). Geospatial data refer to Earth, selenespatial data refer to the moon, ariespatial data refer to Mars, and so on.

Spatial data can represent a point, line, area (two dimensional polygon), or volume (three dimensional set of polygons). Spatial data can range from the Planck length of 1.6 x 10^{-35} meters to the size of the universe calculated at 44 x 10^9 light years or 26.4 x 10^{22} miles. All spatial data have a spatial base, geospatial represents the various coordinate systems for Earth. Structosatial represents buildings, biospatial represents biological organisms and the biological environment, astrospatial represents astronomy, and so on.

Relationships exist between the spatial data tiers and between the data schemas in each spatial data tier. Operational data in the data space are usually obvious based on the organization's perception of the business world and data needed to operate the business. Aggregation data are based on renormalization of the operational data to better understand the business. Influence and variation data in the predictive data tier are not as obvious as operational and analytical data, and are based on the organization's need to analyze and understand the business world.

Computational Space Relationships

A variety of other relationships exist across all six computational spaces.

Relationships between the degrees of data structuring become more intricate in the progression from unstructured data, to structured data, to highly structured data, to complex structured data, to ultra-structured data.

Relationships exist with normal data and special data. Normal data are non-temporal / non-spatial data that use formal data relations defined by the organization. Special data are temporal and spatial data that use informal data relations inherent in the data.

Relationships exist between general data and detailed data. General data are strategic (30,000 foot view) and tactical (10,000 foot view) data that have general data relations. Detailed data are operational, analytical, and predictive data that have detailed data relations.

Relationships exist between primitive data and derived data. Primitive data are generally obtained from the business world. Derived data are generally created from primitive data based on a derivation algorithm documented as data derivation and re-derivation rules.

Relationships exist between elemental data and combined data, like the components of a person's name and the person's complete name. Elemental data cannot be further subdivided and retain their meaning. Combined data result from the combination of one or more closely related elemental facts into a group that are managed as a single unit. Valid combined data have a strong relationship between the components. Invalid combined data have a very weak or no relationship between the components.

Relationships exist between fundamental data and specific data. Fundamental data provide basic names and definitions that are inherited by specific data. Fundamental data are not stored in databases and are not used in application, but support the definition of specific data. Specific data are stored in databases and are used by applications. A few fundamental data can support many specific data, providing stability in data definitions and understanding.

Relationships exist with aggregated data hierarchies consisting of nested sets of data. Fixed data hierarchies are natural hierarchies, such as time and geography (political subdivisions), where the nested data sets represent relationships that cannot be rearranged. Variable data hierarchies are formed at the organization's discretion based on relationships perceived by the organization and can be rearranged based on changing perceptions.

Fixed and variable data hierarchies should not be confused with fixed and variable data characteristics. The latter deal with the format and content of data values that are important for data resource integration. All data characteristics should have fixed data characteristics to achieve a high quality data resource.

Relationships And Quality

Data resource quality is a measure of how well the data resource supports the current and future business information demand. One very obvious fact is the farther upstream that the understanding and management of relationships begins, the higher the data resource quality. Similarly, the farther downstream the understanding and management of relationships begins, the lower the data resource quality.

Beginning farther upstream in the Data Resource Development Cycle means beginning closer to the organization's perception of the business world and the relationships in the business world. Beginning farther upstream results in fewer anomalies and a lower cost for quality. Data resource quality is not free, but it's far less expensive if built in beginning with the organization's perception of the business world.

Beginning farther downstream means beginning closer to physical implementation and use, and losing the benefits of understanding the relationships through the upstream data schemas. Beginning farther downstream results in more anomalies and a higher cost to achieve quality. Brute-force physical refers to development beginning with physical data schema followed by database implementation. Brute-force implementation refers to development beginning with database implementation. Both create massive anomalies and devastate data resource quality.

RELATIONSHIPS AND DATA NORMALIZATION

Data normalization is the process of identifying, understanding, and documenting relationships within the data that an organization needs to both operate and evaluate their business. Data normalization encompasses everything from normalizing the business data schema to data view schema, optimizing data view schema to logical data schema, deoptimizing logical data schema to deployment data schema, to denormalizing deployment data schema to physical data schema. It also includes renormalizing the logical data schema between data tiers.

Data Normalization

Many data management professionals have forgotten the full scope of data normalization and only use a few formal techniques, or no formal techniques, to develop databases. The result is an increase in data disparity and a failure to meet the organization's business information demand.

Properly normalizing data begins with the organization's perception of the business world in which they operate. That perception is typically documented as business data schemas. Those business data schemas are then formally normalized, denormalized, and renormalized according to a formal set of concepts, principles, and techniques.

Data normalization is the process of identifying relationships in the data and adjusting the data structure according to those relationships to minimize redundancies and keep anomalies from entering the data resource. Some approaches number these techniques, such as first normal form, second normal form, etc., and formally define each technique based on a specific sequence. However, two problems exist with numbering the techniques.

First, numbering the techniques does not provide a clear meaning about what the techniques represent. Lack of a denotative label limits the proper use of the techniques when developing a data resource. Second, numbering implies a sequence that must be followed. In practice, a specific sequence does not need to be followed. Any of the techniques can be used at any time when specific relationships are identified. Therefore, proper data normalization uses formally named techniques that are meaningful and sequence independent.

Data Normalization Techniques

The data normalization techniques used to identify relationships are repeating groups, partial key dependencies, inter-attribute dependencies, derived data, inter-entity dependencies, temporal data, and spatial data.

Repeating groups is a technique to identify a relationship between a subordinate set of one or more data characteristics that repeat two or more times for a parent set of one or more data characteristics. The repeating group becomes a separate subordinate data subject.

Partial key dependencies is a technique to identify the relationship where the data values of one or more data characteristics uniquely identify a data occurrence, and those data characteristics comprise a primary key. More specifically, it's the identification of no relationship between a data characteristic's data values and the unique identification of a data occurrence. The lack of a relationship results in the removal of the data characteristic from a primary key.

Inter-attribute dependencies are a technique to identify a relationship between data characteristics where one is independent and the others are dependent. A common example is a data reference set where a coded value or name is independent and the definition, dates, and so on, are dependent.

Derived data is a technique to identify the relationship between a derived data characteristic and its primitive or derived contributing data characteristics. The relationship is documented as a data integrity rule, specifically a data derivation rule and possibly a data re-derivation rule. The primary reason for identifying derived data is to ensure that their data derivation and re-derivation rules are documented.

The management of derived data has changed over the years. When storage was expensive, derived data were prepared from their contributors when they were needed. As storage became less expensive, more derived data were stored to be readily available.

Inter-entity dependencies is a technique to identify relationships between data subjects where the data value of a data characteristic in one data subject is dependent on the data value of a data characteristic in another data subject. A common example is a hierarchy of geographic areas.

Temporal data is a technique to identify data characteristics that represent time. These temporal data characteristics represent time relationships between data subjects. A common example is a temporal relationship used in criminal investigations where all facts and events are organized with respect to time.

Spatial data is a technique to identify data characteristics that represent space. These spatial data characteristics represent space relationships between data subjects. A common example is a spatial relationship between different public works infrastructures to ensure that one organization does not compromise another organization's infrastructure.

Temporal And Spatial Relationships

Temporal and spatial data characteristics use informal relationships between data subjects that are inherent in the data, but are only defined as needed by the organization. The informal relationships are not shown as formal data relations in the data structure. They use neutral keys rather than primary and foreign keys, because neither key is a parent or child. More specifically, either key can be used as parent or child depending on the relationship. In addition, the relationships usually involve a range of values based on proximity criteria rather than exact value matches.

Data Optimization and Deoptimization

Data optimization is the process of identifying data subjects that have the same relationship between the business world and the organization, but have different names, and combining them into a single data subject. Data normalization typically separates data and creates data subjects. Data optimization ensures that identical data subjects are combined. Many data management professionals include data optimization as part of formal data normalization, many treat it as a separate task, and many completely ignore it leading to increased data disparity.

Data deoptimization is the process of identifying deployment relationships between the data and data sites where those data are stored. Data may be stored in one data site, in multiple data sites, or split across multiple data sites based on optimum utilization. When redundant volatile operational data are created, a synchronization mechanism must be implemented to keep those data in synch. Many data management professionals include data deoptimization as part of formal data deoptimization, many treat it as a separate task, and many completely ignore it leading to increased data disparity.

Data Denormalization

Data denormalization is the process of identifying relationships between the logical data as understood by the business and the physical data that will be implemented for optimum processing. The logical data schemas are adjusted to physical data schemas, according to formal data denormalization rules, without compromising the logical data schemas.

Data denormalization has changed over the years as technology progressed from flat files, to index sequential, direct index sequential, hierarchical, network, network with full inversion, relational, and so on. Data denormalization will continue to change as new technology evolves. Many pre-relational data denormalization rules existed, relational data denormalization rules exist, and many post-relational data denormalization rules will likely exist.

Each organization should have only one set of logical data schemas within a single organization wide data architecture. Those logical data schemas can be denormalized multiple times for different processing platforms or purposes. However, multiple denormalizations of volatile operational data create redundant data that require a synchronization mechanism to keep those data in synch.

Data Renormalization

Data renormalization is the process of performing data normalization on data that has already been normalized for one purpose based on relationships identified for a different purpose, such as renormalizing operational data to analytical data (analytical data normalization), or renormalizing analytical data to predictive data (predictive data normalization). Data renormalization adjusts the data relations between data subjects and the data characteristics within data subjects.

Data renormalization is not a data denormalization process, because denormalized data cannot be further denormalized. In other words, physical data schemas cannot be further denormalized to other physical data schemas. The proper sequence is to renormalize the logical data schemas, and then denormalize the new logical data schemas to physical data schemas.

Data renormalization is not the same as multiple data denormalizations because different relationships are being represented. Data renormalization represents logical relationships between different purposes for the data and multiple data denormalization represents physical relationships between data and the data sites where those data are stored.

TEMPORAL DATA

Temporal data are often treated lightly, and sometimes not at all, during data resource design and development. However, temporal data can be extremely important to an organization and must be considered in a well-designed data resource. The three aspects of temporal data that must be considered are briefly described below.

Temporal means of or relating to time; of or relating to the sequence of time or to a particular time. *Chronological* means of, relating to, or arranged in or according to the order of time. *Temporal data* are any data that represent time in some form, and allow other data to be placed in a chronological sequence, or to be analyzed chronologically. The term *temporal* is used when referring to the chronological component data resource design. The term *time* is used when referencing time as hours, minutes, seconds, and fractions of seconds.

Temporal Granularity

Granularity is the coarseness or fineness of something. It's the extent to which something is broken down into smaller parts. Granularity applies to temporal data ranging from astronomical time to chronons. The coarsest granularity of time is astronomical time, which is measured in millions or billions of years. It's the time in our universe that started with the Big Bang some 13.7 billion years ago. It's the time used by astronomers and theoretical physicists in their study of the birth and expansion of the universe, the birth and death of galaxies, and the life cycle of solar systems.

Geologic time is the next most coarse granularity of time and is used to measure time with respect to the Earth. The Geologic Time Scale consists of Geologic Eras, Geologic Periods, Geologic Epochs, and Geologic Series. It's the time used by geologists studying evolution of the Earth.

Calendar time is the next most granular form of time. It is typically based on the Gregorian Calendar, which is based on the equinoctial year. However, other calendars exist, such as Julian, Chinese, etc., and other years exist, such as sidereal and anomalistic years. Calendar time has four components for century, year, month, and day. Most organizations use calendar time for their business activities.

The most granular form of time is clock time, which is typically based on the Gregorian Calendar and a 24-hour day. Clock time has four components for hours, minutes, seconds, and *chronons*. A chronon is a clock tick to the precision that is relevant to the organization. Normal business activities may not use clock ticks, but particle physics is interested in very small fractions of a second. For example, the Large Hadron Collider at CERN impacts atoms every 25 millionths of a second and the resulting particles last for about a trillionth of a second.

Temporal granularity is the degree of granularity of time that ranges from astronomical time to chronons. *Temporal relevance* is the smallest unit of temporal granularity that is acceptable or relevant to an organization. Geological studies have a temporal relevance of geologic time, business has a temporal relevance of calendar time, and particle physics has a temporal relevance of trillionths of a second. Each organization determines their own temporal relevance and uses that temporal relevance in their data resource design.

Temporal Data Aspects

The first aspect of temporal data is tracking the states of a business event from its happening to its availability in the organization's data resource. It is commonly referred to as bi-temporal data. However, up to five different states could exist in the pathway from its happening to its availability in the data resource.

The *business change state* is the point in time that the business change actually happened in the business world, such as a vehicle collision. The *organization notification state* is the point in time that the business change was reported, such as a driver sending a vehicle collision report to their insurance company. The *organization receipt state* is the point in time that the change was first received by the organization, such as the receipt of the vehicle collision report. The *change entry state* is the point in time that the change was entered into the organization's data resource. The *change availability state* is the point in time that the change entered into the data resource was actually available to applications and queries.

The term *bi-temporal data* is often used for tracking the business change state and the change entry state. From a database perspective, these appear to be the only two states that are important. However, from a business perspective, tracking only the business change state and change entry state could have serious legal and financial implications for the organization. Therefore, all five states must be considered when designing a data resource.

The terms *tri-temporal data, quadri-temporal data,* and *quinti-temporal data* are useful for many organizations, based on their business needs. *Tri-temporal data* track the business change state, the organization receipt state, and the change entry state. *Quadri-temporal data* track the business change state, the organization receipt state, the change entry state, and the change availability state. *Quinti-temporal data* track all five states. Each organization must choose the states they need to track in their data resource.

The second aspect of temporal data is the tracking of subjects through their life cycle, which is commonly referred to as *multi-temporal data*. However, the term *multi-temporal data* is often confused with bi-temporal data, tri-temporal data, quadri-temporal data, and quinti-temporal data. *Longitudinal* means running lengthwise; dealing with the growth and change of an individual or group over a period of years. *Longitudinal data* are data that track business objects and business events over time according to an organization's temporal relevance.

For example, geologists track continental drift on the Earth. A person's growth and health are tracked over their lifetime. Students are tracked longitudinally during their time in the public school system. Particles are tracked over billionths or trillionths of a second. Longitudinal data have a wide variety of uses as organizations move into analytics and business intelligence.

The third aspect of temporal data is navigation through the data resource based on time components, which are commonly referred to as time relational data. *Time relational data* are any data subjects that are connected by time. Time relational data uses navigation based on time ranges, rather than navigation based on primary key and foreign key values. Referential integrity is not enforced for time relational data, because the connection between subordinate data occurrences and a parent data occurrence is based on a specific time or a time range, not on the value in primary keys and foreign keys.

Temporal Integrity And Navigation

Referential integrity is the situation where the value of a foreign key in a subordinate data subject must have a matching value in a primary key in a parent data subject. A data occurrence cannot be added in a subordinate data subject without a corresponding parent data occurrence in the parent data subject. Similarly, a data occurrence in a parent data subject cannot be deleted while a subordinate data occurrence still exists in a subordinate data subject. Referential integrity ensures that data relations remain viable.

Temporal integrity is the situation where temporal data characteristics must exist in a parent data subject and a subordinate data subject to allow temporal navigation, although those data characteristics may not exist in primary or foreign keys. Referential integrity is an existence dependency based on values in primary keys and foreign keys, and temporal integrity is a temporal dependency based on temporal ranges.

Temporal navigation is the technique for navigating between data subjects based on the temporal data values. A specific parent data occurrence is not known for time relational data. However, temporal data characteristics must be present to support the navigation. A *temporal relation* is an association between data occurrences in different data subjects based on time ranges. It provides the capability for temporal navigation between data subjects. It is different from a data relation because it does not depend on fixed values in primary keys and foreign keys. *Temporal normalization* is the technique that ensures the existence of temporal data characteristics in a parent and subordinate data subject to support temporal navigation. It ensures temporal dependency.

For example, a question might arise whether the person voted in the proper precinct based on their address. Since no direct link exists between the date of the election and the effective dates of the addresses, a data relation doesn't work. A search needs to be made of the effective data ranges for the addresses based on a temporal relation to determine which address was active at the time of the election.

SPATIAL DATA

Spatial data are often treated lightly, and sometimes not at all, during data resource design and development. However, spatial data are extremely important to an organization and must be considered in a well-designed data resource. The breadth of spatial data is described below to show how important they can be to an organization.

Spatial means relating to, occupying, or having the character of space. The term is used when referring to the location component of data. *Spatial data* are any data with a spatial component that allows an object or event to be precisely located on some base, such as the surface of the Earth.

The problem with spatial data is the same as with any other data—the disparity is growing. The data are not readily understood and cannot be readily integrated. The independent creation and storage of spatial data within and across organizations prevents those data from being readily shared. Spatial data need to be understood and managed with the same techniques and intensity as the tabular data.

Spatial Data Systems

Spatial data systems are an organized collection of computer hardware, software, and spatial data designed to capture, store, update, manipulate, analyze, and display all forms of spatial data. They provide a repository for spatial data and tools for manipulating spatial data to produce electronic maps. They can be used to establish trends, make projections, and predict the future outcome of various alternative plans, such as the spread or recession of pollution with various abatement efforts. They can perform what-if analyses to reduce errors of guessing, such as the environmental impacts of population growth, strip mining, clear cutting, hazardous waste disposal, volcanic eruptions, earthquakes, and so on. They can store aerial photo images and satellite images to support traditional map information.

Geographic is derived from *geo* meaning Earth and *graphein* meaning to write or to describe. Literally, it means describing the Earth. *Geographic data* are any data that locate, identify, or describe objects on, about, or within the Earth.

A *geospatial object* is any natural feature, constructed feature, or boundary, on, above, or below the Earth's surface. The object may be a point, line, area, or three-dimensional. A geographic event is any happening on, above, or below the Earth's surface. *Geospatial data* are any data that represent the geographic location and identifying characteristics of a geospatial object or geographic event. They place objects on, above, or below the surface of the Earth and uniquely identify those object.

However, spatial data are much broader than just Earth-based data. They can include structures, biology, astronomy, physical sciences, and so on. They can store, manipulate, and display all types of one-dimensional, two-dimensional, three-dimensional, and time series data. Their use is limited only by one's imagination.

Demographic is derived from *demos* meaning population and *graphein* meaning to write or to describe. Literally, it means describing populations. *Demographic data* are any data that locate, identify, or describe populations, and are typically related to the Earth, but could be based on other locations.

A *structure* is an object with elements arranged in a definite pattern or organization that bear a relationship to each other. *Structographic* is derived from *structus* meaning structure and *graphein* meaning to write or to describe. Literally, it means describing a structure. *Structographic data* are any data that locate, identify, or describe objects on, in, or about a structure. A *structographic data layer* contains structographic data.

Structospatial is derived from *structus* meaning structure and *spatium* meaning of, relating to, involving, or having the nature of space. Literally, it means spatial locations on, in, or around a structure. A *structospatial object* is any feature or boundary on, in, or around a structure. *Structospatial data* are any data that represent the location and identifying characteristics of a structospatial object. They place structospatial objects on, in, or around a structure and uniquely identify those objects. A *structospatial data layer* contains structospatial data.

Similar terms can be used for biological objects and events, such as *biospatial data*, *biospatial object*, *biospatial event*, *biospatial data layer*, and so on. Similar terms can be used for astronomical objects and events, with *astrospatial data*, *astrospatial object*, *astrospatial event*, *astorspatial data layer*, and so on. The terms can be adapted to quantum mechanics with *quantumspatial data*, *quantumspatial object*, *quantumspatial event*, *quantumspatial data layer*, and so on.

Spatial Data Layers

A *data layer* is a separate and distinct set of related spatial data that are stored and maintained in a spatial database. It represents a particular theme or topic of interest to the organization and is equivalent to a data subject for a given area. A *geospatial data layer* contains geospatial data.

A *data layer extent* is the outer boundary, or the limits, of a data layer. The *data layer coverage* is the portion of a data layer extent for which data are captured and stored. It is always within the data layer extent. A *data layer exclusion* is the portion of a data layer extent for which data are not captured or stored. It is the opposite of a data layer coverage.

A *primitive data layer* is a data layer that represents one set of objects or events. A *derived data layer* is a data layer that is built by combining two or more primitive or derived data layers to meet a specific business need. It represents two or more sets of objects or events.

A *spatial reference system* provides the horizontal (x and y) and sometimes vertical (z) control necessary for accurately positioning spatial objects and events on some base. It also provides control for accurately combining spatial data from different spatial layers. A *geospatial reference system* provides control for geospatial data, and similar terms can be used for structospatial data, biospatial data, astrospatial data, quantumspatial data, and so on.

Georeferencing is derived from *geo* meaning Earth and *referre* meaning to carry back. It is the process of accurately locating geospatial objects. Similar terms can be used for structoreferencing, bioreferencing, astroreferencing, quantumreferencing and so on,

A *framework data layer* is a primitive data layer that is basic to many other data layers. It is based on a spatial reference system and provides the base for developing specific data layers and business data layers. A *specific data layer* is any primitive data layer, other than a framework data layer, that is of interest to the organization. It has a more specific, limited interest than a framework data layer. A *business data layer* is any derived data layer resulting from an aggregation of framework or specific data layers.

A *datum* is something used as a base for calculating or measuring. Sea level is a traditional datum for measuring, elevations on the Earth, and latitude / longitude is a traditional datum for location objects on the Earth's surface. A *geodatum* is a datum for aligning objects on, above, or below the Earth's surface. Similar terms can be used for other bases, such as *structodatum, biodatum, astrodatum, biodatum*, and so on.

Spatial Data Referencing

A linear referencing system is a technique for measuring the length along a linear object. A *geolinear referencing system* is a linear referencing system for geospatial objects. Similar terms can be used for other reference systems, such as *structolinear referencing system, biolinear* reference system, *astrolinear reference system, quantumlinear reference system,* and so on.

A *linear addressing system* is a technique for establishing locations along linear objects that do not change over time. Terms like *Geolinear addressing* can be used for postal addresses, *strctolinear addressing* can be used for wiring systems in a structure, *biolinear addressing* can be used for sequencing along a DNA chain, and so on. Linear object segmentation is a technique where an object or event can be located on segments of a linear object or across segment boundaries of adjacent linear objects.

A *grid referencing system* is a technique for establishing locations on a grid basis. Common georeferencing grid systems are postal addresses, and geographic coordinate systems, such as latitude / longitude, Universal Transverse Mercator, Army Map Grid, and so on. Similar systems exist for structures, biology, astronomy, and the physical sciences.

Derived Spatial Data

A *spatial data hierarchy* is a hierarchy of operational or derived spatial data layers. Specific terms could be *geospatial data hierarchy, structospatial data hierarchy, biospatial data hierarchy, astrospatial data hierarchy*, and so on.

Data layers can be combined vertically (multiple data layers), horizontally (edge matched), and chronologically. Vertical data layer aggregation is the aggregation of two or more contributing data layers. Horizontal data layer aggregation (often referred to as tiling) is the edge matching of two or more data layer extents to provide an expanded data layer. Chronological data layer aggregation is the aggregation of successive time periods for a specific data layer extent.

Data layers usually have a specific scale that is the data layer size relative to the actual size, such as 1:100,000 or 100:1. Data layer generalization, known as zooming out, is the process of reducing the scale of a data layer extent from the scale at which the data were captured by a formal algorithm. Data layer specialization, known as zooming in, is the process of increasing the scale of a data layer extent, but the scale should not be larger than the scale at which the data were collected.

Spatial Data Documentation

Spatial data are based on relationships, the same as any other data. They are named and defined the same as any other data according to the Data Naming Taxonomy and supporting vocabulary. Data layers are named and defined the same as data subjects and the characteristics for data layers are named and defined the same as any other data characteristic. Data relations and data keys are named and defined the same as for data subjects.

Spatial data can be processed, derived, analyzed, and integrated the same as any other data. Spatial integrity, spatial navigation, spatial relations, and spatial normalization serve the same function as their equivalents for temporal data. Spatial data are documented as Data Resource Data the same as any other data.

The above description of spatial data, albeit brief, provides an idea of the type and expanse of spatial data that might be captured, stored in the data resource, and used by an organization to support its business activities.

PROCESSING RELATIONSHIPS

Data in the data resource are used by applications to provide information that supports an organization's business activities. Although it's commonly perceived that those applications are processing the data to produce information, they are actually processing relationships represented by the data to produce information about those relationships. The information is then used to carry out the business activities.

For example, a patient visits their physician for a physical exam, which represents several relationships. The physician orders several lab tests on the patient's blood from a specific lab, which represents several more relationships. The patient goes to the lab, where a technician draws several vials of blood for the lab tests, which represents more relationships. Other lab technicians using specific equipment perform the tests, based on standard clinical procedures, and record the results, which represents more relationships. The lab results are sent to the patient and the physician, which closes the loop on the relationships. Note that some of these relationships are temporal and some are spatial.

The example above shows the processing of existing operational relationships. However, processing can be performed on existing relationships to create new relationships, such as the analysis of operational data to create evaluational data. The results of the analysis can be placed in a table with horizontal and vertical headings and subheadings with cross-footed totals. That table can be displayed as a data hierarchy where the data sets in that hierarchy have relationships with each other, resulting in evaluational relationships.

Processing can also be performed on operational and evaluational relationships to identify possible future relationships. The result of such processing produces predictive relationships, such as storms, earthquakes, floods, and so on. These predictive relationships also have temporal and spatial components.

Temporal and spatial data can be processed to identify different, often rapidly changing, relationships. For example, air traffic control, highway traffic flow management, and battlefield tactics have rapidly changing relationships. Tectonic plate movement, continental drift, comet and asteroid paths, and so on, have slower changing relationships.

A whole new perspective emerges when the development of a data resource is based on relationships and the processing is based on relationships. The new perspective promotes a better understanding of both data and business processes, and a better integration of data and applications. It also promotes a reduction in the disparity of both data and business processes.

SUMMARY

The design and development of an organization's data resource must follow the sequence from business world perception, thorough development of business data schemas based on that perception, to formal normalization for the logical data schemas, to formal denormalization for the physical data schemas, to implementation into databases that support business processes. Data management and business professionals must learn to identify, understand, and manage a collection of relationships that flows from the business world, through logical and physical design, to implementation and use, to support business activities.

Relationships exist across the six computational spaces. The data space represents operational data, the aggregation space represents evaluational data, the influence and variation spaces represent predictive data, temporal represents time data, and spatial represents location data. Relationships also exist between normal and special data, general and detailed data, primitive and derived data, elemental and combined data, fundamental and specific data, and in fixed and variable data hierarchies. Data management and business professionals must learn to identify, understand, and use these relationships.

Relationships are refined through the processes of normalizing the business data schemas to the data view schemas, optimizing the data view schemas to the logical data schemas, deoptimizing the logical data view schemas to the deployment data schemas, and denormalizing the deployment data schemas to the physical data schemas. They are also refined through the process of renormalization from the operational data to evaluational data, and from evaluational data to predictive data. Data management and business professionals must learn to refine relationships through formal processes.

Temporal and spatial data are crucial for understanding and managing relationships. Many organizations depend on both temporal and spatial data to conduct their business activities. Data management and business professionals must learn to identify, understand, and document temporal and spatial relationships to adequately support those business activities.

Relationships also exist in the business processes. Learning to identify, understand, and document those process relationships, and to work with both data relationships and process relationships, will improve the efficiency and effectiveness of using the data resource and business processes to support an organization's business activities.

Chapter 17

ARCHITECTURES AND MODELS

Data architectures and models are crucial to the understanding process.

The process of understanding, documenting, and developing an organization's data resource involves the use of data architectures and data models to portray those data architectures. The results of that process are documented as Data Resource Data that are readily available to anyone in the organization who wants to understand and use the data resource.

All data in an organization's data resource must be formally modeled at some level of detail within a single organization-wide data architecture to thoroughly understand and fully utilize the data resource.[8]

DATA MODEL DETAIL

Traditional data models cover the extremes from generality and commonality to detail and specificity. They also range from providing a full understanding of the data based on the business to rapid physical implementation for immediate use. Such extremes lead to data that are not thoroughly understood and a disparate data resource.

The understanding of a ubiquitous data model, a detailed ubiquitous data model, formal strategic and tactical data models, predefined data models, and the need to share data between organizations provides a base for developing robust data resource models.

Ubiquitous Data Model

The most extreme of generality and commonality is the ubiquitous data model consisting of one data entity with a single many-to-many recursive data relations, shown in Figure 17.1. It contains about 200 data attributes that have very general definitions and about 5000 very detailed data integrity rules. The data resource of any organization, regardless of their size or business activities, whether public or private sector, can be modeled with the ubiquitous data model.

---

[8] Some material adapted from articles by the author on Dataversity.net.

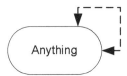

Figure 17.1. Ubiquitous Data Model.

However, when a data structure is very general, the data definitions by nature are very general, and the data meaning is limited. The data integrity rules must be very detailed to provide data quality, which is the reason a few hundred data attributes require a few thousand data integrity rules. When the detailed data integrity rules are not defined, then the quality suffers and support to the organization's business information demand suffers.

Detailed Ubiquitous Data Model

The problem with the ubiquitous data model is that the meaning is limited, and the data quality is generally limited because very few organizations make the effort to develop detailed data integrity rules. A thorough understanding of the data requires both detailed meanings and detailed data integrity rules. That problem can be somewhat resolved with a detailed ubiquitous data model.

The detailed ubiquitous data model consists of five data entities and fifteen many-to-many data relations between those data entities, as shown in Figure 17.2. The detailed ubiquitous data model consists of about 500 data attributes and about 5,000 very detailed data integrity rules. Although it provides a little more detail and is still applicable to all organizations, it suffers the same basic problem as the ubiquitous data model.

The detailed ubiquitous data model expands the single data entity for Anything to five more detailed data entities for Person (individual or organization), Thing (real or virtual), Event (happening or service), Location (spatial), and Time (temporal). These are the five basic data entities in any organization's data resource. The single recursive many-to-many data relation becomes 15 many-to-many data relations between the five basic data entities.

The traditional data entities for Person, Place, Thing, Event, and Concept arose from business objects and events in the business world. The business objects became Person, Place, Thing, and Concept, and the business events became Event. Time was never included, probably since it was not an object or event and was pervasive throughout the data. The detailed ubiquitous data model combines Concept into Thing, making it real and virtual, and

210

adds Time.

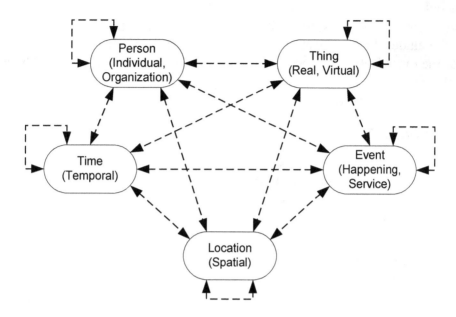

Figure 17.2. Detailed Ubiquitous Data Model.

The problem with the detailed ubiquitous data model is that it is still too general to be of much use to an organization for thoroughly understanding their data resource. The structure is slightly more detailed, but the data definitions are only marginally more detailed. The data integrity rules still need to be very detailed to provide the quality.

Strategic And Tactical Data Models

The next level of detail below the detailed ubiquitous data model is the strategic data model, which is an executive view (30,000 foot view) of the organization's data resource. It is based on the organization's perception of the business world and the major data subjects within that perception. The data are formally named, the data structure and data definitions are more detailed and the data integrity rules are fewer and more relevant to the structure and definitions.

The next level of detail below the strategic data model is the tactical data model, which is a management view (10,000 foot view) of the organization's data resource. It's an enhancement of the strategic data model and is based on a more detailed perception of the business world. The data are formally named, the data structure and data definitions are more detailed, and the data integrity rules match the structure and definitions.

The next level of detail below the tactical data model is the detailed data model, which is the knowledge worker's (ground level) view of the organization's data resource. It is an enhancement of the tactical data model and includes the organization's entire data resource based on the data needed for the organization to operate successfully in the business world. The data structure, data definitions, and data integrity rules are balanced and provide a thorough understanding of the data resource.

Predefined Data Models

The problem with developing strategic, tactical, and detailed data models is that many organizations are looking for a quick development of their data resource, to answer their immediate questions, without consideration for a thorough understanding or answers to future questions. These approaches usually end up as failures with increased data disparity.

Support for these quick development efforts often include predefined data models. A *predefined data model* is any standard model, generic model, universal architecture, model template, model pattern, and so on, developed outside the organization. They are usually incomplete, seldom have formal data names, seldom have comprehensive data definitions, usually contain only the data structure, and seldom have any data integrity rules. They often do not represent any type of organization wide data architecture based on an organization's perception of the business world.

Predefined data models seldom qualify as data resource models. They are typically data structure models, are seldom normalized within a single organization wide data architecture, and are usually physically oriented. When questioned about these weaknesses, the respondents usually state that those are specific details that can be added by the organization later, or are details that are not necessary for a basic structural understanding.

Predefined data models are popular because they are easy for the designer, developer, consultant, and software vendor. They avoid the hard work of understanding how each organization perceives the business world. They avoid the hard work of developing databases and applications that support an organization's perception of the business world.

The problem is that predefined data models often force an organization into that predefined data model without any regard for the way the organization perceives the business world where they operate. Such action is simply warping-the-business. Even if the predefined data model was a perfect fit, the organization loses the benefit of going through the data modeling effort to thoroughly understand their business and the data needed to support that business. A far better approach is to use the predefined data models as insight to guide the organization in developing data resource models.

Established standards should not be confused with predefined data models. For example, standard railroad gauges, standard electrical voltages, standard nut and bolt sizes, and so on, are necessary. Many such legitimate established standards are encountered when an organization does business, and those standards need to be considered during data modeling. However, many other pseudo-standards, like discipline or subject area standards, are often established and forced on organizations. If these pseudo-standards do not match the way an organization desires to do business, they should not be used.

Sharing Data

Many reporting requirements are established for sending data from one organization to another. These requirements are for reporting purposes only and may not represent the way an organization desires to do business. They should not be used to influence an organization's data resource design, other than to assure that the data are available to meet the reporting requirements. If the data are available, it's quite easy to transform or translate the organization's data to meet the reporting and reporting requirements.

The need to share common data does not mean that the organizations sharing those common data must have a common data resource. Sharing data is not the same as sharing a common perception of the business world. Organizations can share common data, and need to share common data, but those common data can reside in the organization's unique data resource. Each organization can build a data resource that best suits their perception of the business world and best supports their business information demand.

A ubiquitous data model doesn't work. A detailed ubiquitous data model doesn't work. Predefined data models don't work. They all warp the organization's business perception in some manner and compromise support of the business information demand, and should not be used.

DATA RESOURCE ANOMALIES

An *anomaly* is a deviation from the common rule; an irregularity; something different, abnormal, peculiar, or not easily classified. A *data resource anomaly* is a deviation of an organization's data resource from the common rule of being based on the organization's perception of the business world and how it chooses to operate in that business world. It's an irregularity or abnormality that occurs when the data resource does not match the

213

organization's perception of the business world. It's a warping of the organization's business to fit a predefined perception that is contrary to the organization's perception.

Party Anomaly

The most prominent data resource anomaly today, other than the massive and burgeoning data disparity, is the use of Party in logical data models. Party evolved from the basic data entity for Person that includes individuals and organizations, which are groups of individuals. Any data about individuals or organizations are forced into a Party structure that is touted to be uniform for all organizations.

Vendors have forced Party into logical data models because they need something generic for their applications. Data modelers and data architects have forced Party into logical data models because it is easier for them to model and design the data resource compared to a variety of different perceptions of the business world from different organizations. Technical people have forced Party into logical and physical data models because it is easier to implement than a variety of different perceptions.

Party was intended to include all individuals and groups of individuals within and without the organization that the organization deals with in their business activities. However, that scope often becomes too complex to manage because it includes all customers / citizens, all employees and teams, all vendors / suppliers / contractors, drivers, business owners, suspects / inmates, and so on. Party would have dozens of relationships with itself and with other data entities, and a variety of different data attributes for each of those relationships. Numerous data integrity rules are needed to ensure data quality.

Some organizations have limited Party to only prominent entities, but no clear distinction is made between prominent and minor entities. Some organizations have limited Party to external individuals and groups of individuals, and some organizations have limited Party to only legal parties involved in legal and financial transactions. As a result, Party has become a multi-defined term, and in some situations an undefined term, depending on the organization.

In addition, Party might be the wrong word because of connotative meanings, such as political party, legal party, ceremonial events, and so on. The result is that Party is not well defined in logical data models and is not consistent across an organization or between organizations, which causes difficulty understanding and fully utilizing the data resource.

Creating a physical data file for Party might be acceptable if 1) it leads to physical optimization of the database and 2) the data are received from and presented to business professionals in a manner that is consistent with their perception of the business world and how they choose to operate in that business world. If these two criteria are not met, then the creation of a physical file for Party is not acceptable.

In other words, the logical data model should include data entities based on the organization's perception of the business world and how they choose to operate in that business world. The logical data model is based on formal data normalization of the organization's perception of the business world. The physical data model is then based on formal data denormalization for optimum operational efficiency without compromising the logical data model. The data are then received from and presented to business professionals according to the logical data model.

A better approach for logical data models is to create a strategic data model for Party, which is a high level grouping of people and groups of people. The strategic Party can then be further defined with Legal Party, External Party, Internal Party, and so on, in a tactical data model. Finally, the detail data model is developed with the specific data entities according to the organization's perception of the business world, which are the working data entities for conducting business.

Note that any physical data files resulting from formal data denormalization may or may not match the strategic or tactical data models. One of the problems with data modeling is that high level 'conceptual' data models have been developed and then, when accepted, become the pattern for developing physical data files. The leap from 'conceptual' to physical implementation generally does not provide a data resource that fully supports an organization's information need.

Other Anomalies

Data resource anomalies can also occur with the other four basic data entities. A Location data entity could be created for all locations that are relevant to an organization depending on their particular business activities, creating a location anomaly. These locations may be two dimensional or three dimensional and may vary over time. They may be based on a variety of different coordinate systems, such as grid addressing, linear addressing, latitude – longitude, altitude / elevation / depth, and so on.

However, like the Party anomaly, a Location anomaly often becomes too complex resulting in distinctions between locations internal to the organization and locations external to the organization, or locations based on different identification systems. Location then becomes multi-defined and is not consistent within or across organizations. Multiple data relations need to be defined with a variety of data attributes pertinent to each data relations, and numerous data integrity rules are needed to ensure data quality.

An Event data entity could be created for all events that are relevant to an organization depending on their particular business activities, such as fires, floods, collisions, purchases, exams, repairs, and so on, creating an event anomaly. An Event data entity could easily become more complex than a Location data entity and could be divided into smaller data entities for groups of related events. Again, the result is multiple data relations, a wide variety of data attributes, and numerous data integrity rules.

A Thing data entity could be created for all real and virtual things relevant to an organization depending on their particular business activities, such as vehicles, rivers, pipelines, buildings, accounts, and so on, creating a thing anomaly. A Thing data entity could easily become complex with multiple data relations, a variety of data attributes, and numerous data integrity rules.

Finally, a Time data entity could be created for the entire continuum of time that ranges from the smallest unit of time that could be measured to the longest known time, creating a time anomaly. Each organization would use the segment of that continuum that is relevant to their particular business activities, including points in time and time periods. Note that Time is a basic data entity that is typically not identified in most logical or physical data models.

The shortest unit of time that can be measured is Planck Time, which is the time it takes light to travel one Planck Length (10^{-35} Meters), or about 10^{-43} seconds. However, the shortest unit of time that has actually been measured is only 10^{-26} seconds. The time continuum progresses through seconds, minutes, hours, days, weeks, months, quarters, years, decades, and centuries; to geologic ages and epochs; to astronomical time periods for precession cycles of 26,000 years, birth and death of planets, solar systems, and galaxies; up to the ultimate age of the universe calculated by theoretical physicists to be $10^{10^{120}}$ years.

The five data resource anomalies for Party, Location, Event, Thing, and Time are simply GRLs – Gigantic Retrogressive Leaps from a formal logical data resource model that is based on an organization's perception of the business world back to the Detailed Ubiquitous Data Model with the five basic data entities that provide a generic design to suit designers and developers. The data resource anomalies carry all the disadvantages of the Detailed Ubiquitous Data Model and ultimately lead to a low quality data resource that is not well understood by business professionals, and is not fully utilized to support an organization's current and future business information demand.

DATA ARCHITECTURE AND MODEL DEVELOPMENT

The development of a single data resource architecture and data resource models to portray that architecture mandatory for development of a high quality data resource. Existing data models are plagued with problems. Formal data resource models are based on specific criteria and require robust software support.

Data Resource Architecture And Models

Data resource models are used to build the Data Resource Data which are then stored in a Data Resource Guide, and data resource models can be developed from the Data Resource Data that have been stored in a Data Resource Guide.

The diagram in Figure 17.3 shows the relationship between the Data Resource Data contained in a Data Resource Guide and data resource models. Organizations have a business information demand (upper left) that could be data captured, acquired, or created by the organization. The data defined by the business information demand go through a data resource design process and are portrayed as data resource models. Those data resource models are then stored as Data Resource Data in the organization's Data Resource Guide.

Organizations also have disparate data (upper right) that go through a disparate data analysis process and are portrayed as data resource models. Those data resource models are also stored as Data Resource Data in the organization's Data Resource Guide.

The Data Resource Data can be extracted from the Data Resource Guide to develop data resource models, covering a specific business subject area, using a preferred data modeling technique, for an intended audience. The development of data resource models and the maintenance of Data Resource Data are done within a single organization-wide data architecture. Looking at it the other way around, the Data Resource Data represent the single organization-wide data resource architecture.

Model driven architectures is the concept where data resource models are developed to identify and document the data needed to support the business

217

information demand and the existing disparate data, and are stored as Data Resource Data in the Data Resource Guide.

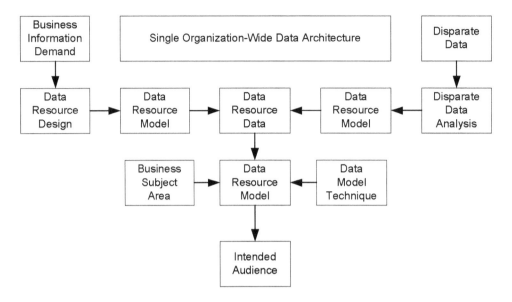

Figure 17.3. Data Architecture And Data Resource Models

Architecture driven models is the concept where data resource models are prepared by extracting the appropriate Data Resource Data from the Data Resource Guide, for a specific business subject area, using appropriate data modeling techniques for the intended audience, and then presented to that intended audience.

The benefits of a model driven data architecture and architecture driven models is the avoidance of large quantities of data models, the tedious check-in / check-out process for individual data models, and the huge effort to maintain those data models as the data architecture changes. Data model disparity is eliminated and the understanding of an organization's data resource through the Data Resource Data is maximized.

Traditional Data Model Problems

Data modeling has evolved over many years and will continue to evolve. A few of the prominent problems with data modeling today are listed below. These problems lead to a poor understanding of the data in the organization's data resource, and incomplete or inappropriate use of the data resource to support an organization's business activities.

Data models are often oriented toward one person's perception of the business world where the organization operates and the data need by

218

the organization to operate successfully in that business world. That person is often a data modeler whose perception is independent of the organization's perception and is often quite different from the organization's perception.

Data models often start with the physical data model so the organization can "cut the code" and get on with building the database. Such brute-force-physical orientation does not provide the benefits achieved from the business world perception or the logical data schemas.

Data models are often ignored for the brute-force-implementation of databases. The databases are usually developed without benefit of a physical data model, logical data model, or business world perception. The likelihood of the database fully supporting the business information demand is poor.

Data models are usually incomplete. They lack formal data names, comprehensive data definitions, and precise data integrity rules. Data names are usually inconsistently abbreviated and data definitions are not comprehensive or denotative, and are often tautologies. Data integrity rules seldom exist and are often shown on the data structure.

Data models are not developed within a single organization-wide data architecture, leading to disparate data models, multiple data models of the same data, conflicting data models, and competing data models. These disparate data models lead to the creation of disparate data and a disparate data resource and create confusion rather than understanding about the data resource.

Data models are seldom normalized within a single organization-wide data architecture. Data names, definitions, and integrity rules are disparate and conflicting, leading to a disparate data resource.

Data models are seldom oriented toward an intended audience. They are usually physically oriented toward the audience that develops the databases with little concern for executives, managers, and knowledge workers. They do not have the proper detail to encourage active involvement from business professionals.

Data models are often developed from predefined data models that likely do not accurately or adequately represent the organization's perception of the business world. They actually warp the business to fit a predefined perception.

Data models seldom represent the entire data resource of the organization. Typically, about fifteen percent of an organization's data are modeled in any form. Those data are typically the easiest to model, and are often modeled multiple times by different people using different data modeling tools.

Data models are seldom developed for any derived data, evaluational data, or predictive data. These data represent a large segment of the organization's data resource and need to be understood the same as basic operational data.

Data models are seldom developed for data integration. Data integration is typically done with a brute-force physical approach using ETL software tools. The integration process is seldom documented, leaving doubt about how the data were integrated.

A more meaningful term for these traditional data models might be *limited data structure models* or *physical data structure models*. These traditional data model problems must be resolved so that an organization's complete data resource can be modeled, documented, and readily understood by anyone in the organization.

Data Resource Models

A far better approach for an organization desiring to build and maintain a high quality data resource is to develop formal data resource models that are characterized by twelve primary criteria. If a data model does not meet all of these primary criteria, it is simply a data model.

1. Data resource models are based on the organization's perception of the business world in which the organization operates. Further, understanding and documenting that perception often changes the perception.

    The Hawthorne Effect, also known as the observer effect, is the situation where workers' productivity improved when changes were made to their working environment. The productivity improved when the workers' knew they were being evaluated, and was not due to changes to the environment.

    The Heisenberg uncertainty principle states that the location and the momentum of a quantum object cannot be measured at the same time. By measuring the momentum, the location changes, and by measuring the location, the momentum changes. It's similar to the observer effect in physics which states that measurement of a system cannot be made without affecting the system.

The observer effect applies to developing data resource models. The act of observing an organization's perception of the business world can change that perception, which can lead to changes within the organization and to the data resource model. Those changes must be expected and represented in data resource models.

2. Data resource models are a model of the organization's reality. Stephen Hawking states "We never have a model-independent view of reality. But that does not mean there is no model-independent reality." An organization's view of business world reality is a model-dependent reality as perceived by the organization. However, the business world reality, independent of an organization, is not model-dependent--it's a model-independent reality.

   Organizations can never have a model-independent view of reality, because there is no model-independent test of reality. There may be an underlying reality, but the organization's perception of that reality is based on their perception and is model-dependent. The question is whether a model agrees with observation (perception), not whether it is real. Therefore, data resource models are a model-dependent view of reality based on the organization's experience, and is the only reality the organization knows.

3. Data resource models follow a business – to – logical – to – physical development sequence. Business data schemas are identified based on the organization's business information demand as they perceive the business world. The business data schemas are then normalized to logical data schemas using formal data normalization rules. The logical data schemas are then denormalized to physical data schemas using formal data denormalization rules. Data resource models can represent any of the data schemas in the Four-Tier Five-Schema Concept or the Five-Tier Five-Schema Concept.

4. Data resource models are developed within a single organization-wide data architecture that becomes the single version of truth about the organization's perception of the business world. The data resource singularity is that one version of truth about the business world as perceived by the organization. It's a single set of high quality data that fully supports the current and future business information demand of the organization. The prime directive for data resource modeling is to achieve the data resource singularity.

5. Data resource models must have formal data names, comprehensive data definitions, proper data structures, and precise data integrity rules. These

four components comprise a complete data resource model and must be balanced according to the Data Architecture Trinity. However, these four components do not need to appear on a single diagram, because that diagram would become too large and confusing to be readily understood. The four components are better represented and more understandable when presented in separate documents.

6. Data resource models are documented as fully normalized data resource data within a Data Resource Guide. Data resource models either draw from or contribute to the data resource data stored in the Data Resource Guide using the model driven architecture concept and the architecture driven concept. That Data Resource Guide is a data resource data singularity that provides a single version of truth about the organization's data resource. The prime directive for a Data Resource Guide is to achieve a data resource data singularity.

7. Data resource models contain material that is relevant to the intended audience, and is presented in a manner that is acceptable for that intended audience. Multiple data resource models can be prepared for different intended audiences by drawing only the relevant data resource data for that audience from the Data Resource Guide. Data resource data that are not relevant are not drawn from the Data Resource Guide or presented to the intended audience.

8. Data resource models can contain any degree of data structuring, including structured, highly structured, complex structured, and ultra-structured data. All degrees of data structuring are part of the organization's data resource and must be represented by data resource models.

9. Data resource models maximize the interaction between data modelers and data architects, and the involvement of business professionals and data management professionals. Data architects are responsible for developing a single organization-wide data architecture. Data modelers are responsible for documenting the data representing the organization's perception of the business world. Business professionals are responsible for providing the input for the organization's perception of the business world and the data needed to support the business information demand. Data management professionals are responsible for designing, developing, and maintaining the data resource.

10. Data resource models are not, and must not, be predefined data models. Predefined data models predefine an organization's perception of the business world, and the data the organization needs to operate in that

business world. They preclude understanding the organization's perception and any changes to that perception, and force an organization to warp their business according to a perception that is unrealistic. However, predefined data models can be used as input for identifying and documenting data resource models.

11. Data resource models can, and should, use model development tools, and promote development of more sophisticated model development tools. Model development tools have evolved a long way since pencils and templates, but still have a long way to go. They need to evolve to the point where they can handle all models in a Four-Tier Five-Schema Concept or Five-Tier Five-Schema Concept, and automatically generate data resource models from existing data resource models with the input of a few parameters.

12. Data resource models rely on cognitive thinking. *Cognitive* means capable of being reduced to empirical factual knowledge. Cognitive data resource modeling is constantly thinking about formal data resource modeling, not just data modeling or data structure modeling. It's the habit of deliberately practicing formal data resource modeling until it becomes such a habit that there is no other way to design a high quality data resource.

Data Resource Model Support

Data modeling software tools have evolved a long way since the days of plastic templates and hand-drawn models. However, they have a long way to go to provide increased support for developing data resource models within a single organization wide data architecture. A few of the major advancements that could be made are listed below.

All data resource models and model components normalized within a single organization-wide data architecture.

All models stored as Data Resource Data within a Data Resource Guide.

Support for the model driven architecture concept and the architecture driven model concept.

Development of data resource models with detail relevant for specific audiences and proper presentation to that specific audience.

No length limitations or format limitations on formal data names, comprehensive data definitions, or data integrity rules.

Automated data normalization, data optimization, data deoptimization, data denormalization, and data schema generation based on parameters.

Automated arrangement of data subjects on data structure diagrams for easy understanding.

Automated segmentation of data structure diagrams for ready review and easy understanding

Automated feedback identifying possible problems to the data resource models or data resource architecture.

Use of voice commands and voice feedback for developing data models and the data resource architecture.

Voice commands – interactive modeling software.

And so on, limited only by one's imagination and the ability of software to support that imagination.

SUMMARY

Identifying, understanding, and documenting an organization's data to build a high quality data resource is crucial for that organization's success. Developing a single organization-wide data resource architecture with data resource models and presenting that architecture to various audiences with data resource models is the heart of that process. Without the understanding portrayed by data resource models, people cannot thoroughly understand the data resource and fully utilize that data resource.

Ubiquitous data models and detailed ubiquitous data models must be avoided. Instead, strategic, tactical, and detail data resource models need to be developed to represent different levels of detail. Predefined data models should be avoided in favor of the organization's perception of the business world. Sharing common data between organizations should be considered, but not to the extent that organizations develop a common data resource.

Data resource anomalies, such as Party, Event, Thing, Time, and Space, must be avoided, particularly in logical data models. Those generalizations may be made in a physical data model as long as the business professionals can interface with the data resource according to their perception of the business world. To do otherwise seriously compromises the organization's chance of being successful in their business endeavors.

Traditional data models have numerous problems that impact their effectiveness for understanding the data in an organizations data resource.

Those problems can be resolved by following twelve specific criteria for developing data resource models. If those criteria are not met, then traditional data models will continue to be developed. Data modeling software support has gone a long way since the days of template and pencil, but can be further enhanced with a few major improvements.

Data resource modeling is not a mindless routine, it isn't always fun, and it doesn't always come easily. It requires high motivation and persistence, but it is achievable and can become routine with practice.

Immanuel Kant said "Science is organized knowledge. Wisdom is organized life." *Critique of Pure Reason,* 1781.

Isaac Asimov said "The saddest aspect of society right now is that science gathers knowledge faster than society gathers wisdom."

Michael Brackett said "We are gathering techniques faster than we are gathering wisdom to manage those techniques." Opening Keynote Address, Data Modeling Zone 2014, Baltimore, Maryland.

Chapter 18

ACHIEVING DATA UNDERSTANDING

Understanding the data resource is an organization's choice.

Thoroughly understanding the data in an organization's data resource requires a persistent effort by everyone in the organization involved with developing, maintaining, or using the data. Achieving that thorough understanding involves a look at a data manipulation industry, the agenda of many organizations, a perspective of the data management profession, and the discretion that an organization has to become professional and manage their data as a critical resource.

DATA MANIPULATION INDUSTRY

Data management today is largely a data manipulation industry, rather than a data management program. That fact is substantiated by heath care analogies, software support orientation, and profit motivation. These situations show a need for a formal data resource management approach.

Health Care Analogy

A recent article about health care in the United States made the case that although considerable progress has been made toward health care in the last 100 years, that a health care program does not exist in the United States— only an illness treatment industry exists. Minimal emphasis is placed on a wellness program to prevent illness. Instead, major emphasis is placed on treating illnesses after they occur. Even major health initiatives like weight reduction, exercise, stress reduction, and so on, are oriented toward resolving health problems that have already occurred.

A similar article describes the tremendous progress that has been made treating mental illness in the last 50 years. To be sure, progress has been made toward both recognizing mental illness and treating mental illness. However, the article also emphasized that the approach is toward allowing the mental illness happen and then proceeding to treat the illness. Minimal effort has been made to ensure mental wellness, let alone establish any formal mental wellness program.

These two articles described a pattern that is similar to the way organizations manage their data resource. That pattern is a physical data manipulation industry rather than a data resource management program. Organizations are physically manipulating the data, for short term needs, without any formal design, or any consideration for long term needs. They are physically manipulating the data according to the business processes using those data rather managing the data according to formal data management concepts and principles.

Software Support

Most data modeling and design software tools are used to physically design and implement the database without any formal business perception or logical design. The physical design is often oriented toward the data used by specific business processes, without normalizing the data for use by other business processes. The primary objective of most data modeling tools seems to be an orientation toward cutting the code to develop a physical database for a set of business processes.

Many purchased applications have a physical orientation toward a fixed way of doing business and managing data for organizations, without regard for how organizations conduct their business as they perceive the business world. The result is an organization's way of doing business becomes warped to fit the application. Many organizations are serially warping their business from one purchased application to the next without any consideration for the way the business operates. Many organizations have parallel warping of the business where part of the business is warped one way to fit a purchased application and another part of the business is warped another way to fit another purchased application.

Many predefined data models appear to be doing the same thing—forcing organizations to manage their data in a set manner without any regard for the way the organization perceives business world. Many data files are oriented toward supporting specific business processes rather than being designed according to formal data management concepts and principles. Data are often created redundantly in different data files to support specific business processes. The redundant data require bridges and feeds to keep those data in synch, which are seldom fully effective.

Most applications and databases have very few physical data edits and seldom have extensive logical data integrity rules. Most applications and databases lack formal data names and comprehensive data definitions meaningful to the business. Many applications actively create data disparity requiring the development of many software tools to resolve that disparity.

Most data integration and ETL activities intended to resolve disparity actually make the disparity worse.

All of these situations, and many others, fall into the category of brute-force-physical data manipulation without any formal design or regard for the way an organization does business. Brute-force-physical data manipulation is the theme of a physical data manipulation industry. People react, sometimes violently, to the term 'brute-force-physical', but it's true and the truth often hurts.

Another Analogy

In the illness treatment industry a class of illnesses known as nosocomial infections runs rampant in many medical facilities. A nosocomial infection is an infection that a person did not have when they entered a medical facility, but had when they left the medical facility. It's an infection that was acquired at the medical facility that was not related to the illness that person had when they entered the medical facility.

Many people claim that a nosocomial infection follows the principle of unintended consequences, which states that any intervention in a complex system may or may not have the intended result, but will inevitably create unintended and often undesirable outcome. In actuality, a nosocomial infection is a result of not following established sanitary techniques in medical facilities. Had the medical facility followed established concepts, principles, and techniques, most nosocomial infections would not have occurred.

The data resource in many public and private organizations has a nosocomial infection, known as disparate data. Disparate data are any data that are essentially not alike, or are distinctly different in kind, quality, or character. They are unequal and cannot be readily integrated to meet the business information demand. They are low quality, defective, discordant, ambiguous, heterogeneous data. The disparate data resulted from not planning and designing the data resource to support the current and future business information demand of the organization according to established, concepts, principles, and techniques.

The result of an illness treatment industry is a high probability of nosocomial infections. The result of a physical data manipulation industry is a high probability of disparate data. Nosocomial infections impact the patient's wellbeing and hamper their pursuit of a productive life. Disparate data impact an organization's wellbeing and hamper their pursuit of a productive business.

Profit Motivation

Health care professionals respond to questions about an illness treatment industry by stating that it's profit motivated. Keeping people healthy is not as profitable as treating illnesses. The profit is in medical procedures and medications—more profit exists for being reactive than for being proactive. Even after the case was made that a formal health care program oriented toward the proactive prevention of illness could be profitable, most health care professionals respond that it would not be as profitable as the reactive treatment of illnesses. In addition, more satisfaction comes from solving a problem than from preventing a problem.

The same response appears to be true for the physical data manipulation industry. Physical data manipulation has a greater profit motive than formal data resource management. More profit exists for being reactive than for being proactive. More profit exists in software application and software tool sales than in formal planning and design. More satisfaction is gained from getting a database up and running to support current business processes than in following formal concepts, principles, and techniques. More satisfaction is gained from building and implementing than from planning and designing. More satisfaction is gained from playing with tools than from making hard decisions about a high quality data resource that provides long term support to the business.

A Data Resource Management Approach

Do organizations follow established and proven concepts, principles, and techniques for formal data resource management? Are they oriented toward brute force physical development of databases to support current business processes? Are they warping your business into one or more applications? Do you have disparate data that are impacting the wellbeing of the organization?

The fact that a physical data manipulation industry exists today rather than a data resource management program should be obvious. The question becomes what can be done to resolve the situation? What is needed to turn a physical data manipulation industry into a data resource management program? What needs to be done to stop the stop the creation of disparate data—the nosocomial infection of databases.

The answer is almost too obvious—create a data resource management program that formally manages data as a critical resource of the organization! Follow established and proven concepts, principles, and techniques to build a data resource that adequately meets the current and future business information demand of the organization. Stop warping the business to fit applications. Stop building databases that directly support specific business processes, because the structure of data is orthogonal to the structure of business processes. Stop creating any further disparity in the data resource and clean up the existing disparity.

Stopping data disparity is like stopping nosocomial infections. Cleaning up existing data management practices to stop data disparity is like cleaning up medical facilities to stop nosocomial infections. A strong case can be made that formal data resource management is just as profitable as a physical data manipulation industry, and far better for the wellbeing of the organization. Both business professionals and data management professionals must start a formal data resource management program that replaces the current physical data manipulation industry.

THE AGENDA

Developing a data resource management program requires understanding perceptions like industry standard and mainstream, recognizing the profit motive of many organizations, and dealing with a paradox that exists between software vendors and software purchasers.

Industry Standard

The term *industry standard* is most often used in a defensive context, such as *What I'm doing is industry standard.* The term is also used in a confrontational context, such as *That's not industry standard, That's not recognized by the industry,* or *That's not industry approved.* People use industry standard to defend what they are doing or to question what someone else is doing. The term is obviously part of the lexical challenge in data resource management.

When asked what *industry standard* means, the most frequent response is along the lines of *Industry standard means it's standard for the industry.* That's not a definition—it's a tautology. Data resource management is fraught with many tautologies, particularly in data definitions, that add nothing to the understanding.

When people that use *industry standard* are asked to provide a reference to the ANSI, ISO, FIPS, IEEE, or other formal standard confirming their statement, the vast majority people ignore the question and never provide a reference to a formal standard. The conclusion, of course, is that no formal industry standard exists.

Then, just who or what is *the industry*? *Industry* is defined as diligence in an employment or pursuit; systematic labor especially for some useful purpose or the creation of something of value; a department or branch of a craft, art, business, or manufacture, especially one that employs a larger personnel and capital; a distinct group of productive or profit-making enterprise, manufacturing activity as a whole; work devoted to the study of a particular subject or author.

The term *industry* could mean professional organizations, standards organizations, certification organizations, research groups, vendors, consultants, educators, thought leaders, visionaries, publishers, authors, practitioners, legislators, educational institutions, public and private sector organizations, and so on. It literally becomes any person or organization that is involved in data resource management.

Standard is defined as constituting or conforming to a standard, especially as established by law or custom; sound and usable but not of top quality; regularly and widely used, available, or supplied; well-established and very familiar; having recognized and permanent value; substantially uniform and well established by usage in the speech and writing of the educated and widely recognized as acceptable. The definition leads to two types of standards – formal standards and de-facto standards.

Formal standards are obligatory or de jure standards established by an organization that has the recognized authority to establish those formal standards, such as IEEE, ANSI, FIPS, SAE, and so on. Formal standards are certainly necessary for many things, such as electric voltages and amperages, nuts and bolts, railroad gauges, wire sizes, dimensional lumber, structures, and so on. Products and practices would be in utter chaos and disasters would happen without these formal standards.

De-facto means in reality; actuality; existing in fact; in practice or actuality, but not officially established. *De-facto standards* are a custom, convention, product, or system that has achieved a dominant position by public acceptance or market focus. They are something that many people or organizations are using.

Statements similar to those for industry standard use the term *mainstream* in in place of industry standard, such as *What I'm doing is mainstream, That's not mainstream, That's not recognized as mainstream*, and so on. These statements lead to the question What does mainstream mean?

Mainstream is defined as a prevailing current or direction of activity or influence; the common current thought of the majority. It means essentially the same as de-facto standard, something that is readily accepted or common practice in data management.

From these definitions and the context within which *industry standard* and *mainstream* are frequently used, it becomes obvious that these terms actually mean whatever the person using those terms wants it to mean based on what they are presenting or what they are refuting. The terms are perpetuating a current hype-cycle in data management. People are hyped by quick fixes or fixes that can be bought, and believe that a quick fix is available for purchase to understand their data resource and resolve disparity. They have become part of the growing lexical challenge in data management.

The Agenda

Terms like *industry standard* and *mainstream* are supporting The Agenda of many organizations which is a profit motivation. Not being industry standard or mainstream means not supporting The Agenda or The Establishment, and being industry standard or mainstream means supporting The Agenda. Although different organizations have different agendas, those agendas are likely based on a profit motive.

Look at situations like Royal Raymond Rife's cancer cure, antigravity, antigravity propulsion, infinite energy technologies, cold fusion, zero point energy, and the efforts of Thomas Townsend Brown, Viktor Schauberger, Nikola Tesla, and others. They are not part of The Agenda and were stifled, discredited, suppressed, bought out and hidden, and so on.

Look at the evidence for ancient civilizations on Earth, the Moon, Mars. Look at evidence the real purpose for many ancient structures. They are not part of the current mainstream and are being ignored or discredited.

The same thing is happening with many data resource management approaches, such as data resource design, data resource development, data resource integration, data resource documentation, and so on. Many of these approaches to thoroughly understand an organization's data resource and how that resource supports the business are being stifled by The Agenda.

Vendor - Customer Paradox

A real paradox exists between what vendors develop and what customers want to purchase. Vendors only develop products and services that will sell, regardless of what may be needed. Customers can only purchase what is available, regardless of what they may need. That paradox is created by the profit motivation of vendors, which requires the ongoing trend of hype-cycles, which are promoted by terms like *industry standard* and *mainstream*.

Organizations want a high quality data resource that supports their current and future business information demand, but often can't achieve that level of quality because of the difficulty understanding the data and documenting that understanding. High quality data and support for the business information demand are not mainstream, and are not readily supported. Physical database development and on-the-fly data integration activities are mainstream and are supported.

Organizations have made a big mistake in the past by not following formal data resource management concepts, techniques, and principles to develop a high quality data resource. The result is large and growing data disparity that is costing the organization. However, organizations are continuing to make the same big mistakes with their current data management practices, and will continue to perpetuate the growing data disparity.

That trend can be reversed and a high quality data resource that is thoroughly understood, and fully supports the current and future business information demand can be achieved. The establishment of a formal data management profession will resolve the problems and will produce a high quality data resource.

PROFESSIONAL PERSPECTIVE

Developing a formal data management profession requires looking at the current situation, the requirements for a formal data management profession, the approaches to achieving that profession, and the current status of efforts in that direction.

Current Data Management

Data management today is a collection of disciplines (plural) that include mathematics, philosophy, logics, sociology, and so on. It has not yet become a formal profession, in spite of what many people declare. Data management professionals cannot self-proclaim that a data management profession exists. They must work hard at building a formal profession, and earning recognition and respect for that profession.

Data management today has a long history of creating disparity and then trying to manage that disparity. It is based on hype-cycles and mainstream agendas supporting those hype-cycles. It is based on quick fixes and automated physical design that does not support a thorough understanding of the data and long term support for the business information demand.

A Data Management Profession

For data management to become a profession, it must be formal, certified, recognized, and respected. Failure to achieve any of these four basic criteria will only result in the data management that exists today.

Formal means having a basic construct for managing data as a critical resource. That construct includes an established curriculum leading to a degree in data resource management, not a degree in information science or information technology. Such a curriculum does not exist.

Formal includes acceptable standards that promote managing data as a critical resource. Some standards do exist, but they are produced by a variety of different organizations, and are often incomplete, confusing, and conflicting. A complete set of formal, clear, non-conflicting data management standards must be developed within one overarching construct.

Formal includes professional publications where articles may be peer reviewed. Some good professional publications currently exist, but are largely about current hype-cycles and day-to-day physical processing details. Few are oriented toward formally managing data as a critical resource. The DAMA-DMBOK and DAMA Dictionary of Data Management are steps in the right direction, but are just a beginning.

Formal includes a prestigious professional organization that boldly leads the initiative to develop a formal data management profession. That organization must have a membership that represents a predominance of people in the data management profession.

Certified means that members of the profession are certified at different skill levels, such as novice, apprentice, journey, and master, and in different areas, such as analysis, design, implementation, and operation. Some progress has been made with certifications, but many different organizations are offering a variety of certifications that often overlap, conflict, or leave gaps. One overarching authority needs to be established for coordinating all data management certifications.

Recognized means that a data management profession, and data management professionals, are recognized by public and private sector organizations and by business professionals. Data management professionals have typically done a poor job at getting themselves properly recognized. Historically, they have created a lexical challenge, caused paralysis by analysis, developed brute force physical databases, created and promoted hype-cycles, and produced massive quantities of disparate data. They have done more damage to themselves than anyone could have ever done to them. They have certainly earned recognition, but it has been the wrong kind of recognition.

Respected means gaining respect from peers, other professionals, and employers. Currently, data management professionals have minimum respect, and are doing little to gain respect. Like recognition, respect must be earned based on performance rather than demanded. Only data management professionals can earn the respect they deserve—no one else can earn respect for them.

Data management professionals might be able to self-proclaim a formal profession. It's questionable if they will be able to self-proclaim a certified profession. It's doubtful if they can self-proclaim a recognized or respected profession.

Data Management Profession Approaches

The primary question has been *How do you go about building a data management profession from a collection of disciplines?* Three basic approaches could be followed.

The first approach is a *current hype-cycle approach* that documents, publishes, and promotes all of the current hype-cycles and terms that exist today. The approach is to join the current hype-cycles, support those hype-cycles, and perpetuate those hype-cycles. When hype-cycles run their course and change, the approach changes to support the new hype-cycles. The profession changes accordingly, the certifications change according, and the classes, books, articles, and consulting change accordingly. Eventually, by a very circuitous route, a formal data management profession may ultimately be achieved, but the cost to organizations along the way is tremendous.

The *current hype-cycle approach* is an easy route to follow. All that needs to be done is to keep track of the current hype-cycles, and the corresponding terms, and continue documenting, publishing, and promoting those current hype-cycles. Organizations and data management professionals look good, because they appear to be right on course with the current trends. However, over time the trends fail to provide the intended benefits, the data resource becomes more disparate, the trends fail, and new trends emerge. In the long run, being trendy and following current hype-cycles only makes the situation worse, and results in data management professionals losing respect.

The second approach is a *persistent hype-cycle approach* that attempts to make the current set of hype-cycles and terms a persistent data management profession. It attempts to establish the current state of hype-cycles and terminology as the persistent state for a formal data management profession. It avoids the long and circuitous route toward developing a formal data management profession.

236

The *persistent hype-cycle approach* is moderately difficult to achieve because most hype-cycles are not well-founded on sound concepts, principles, and techniques. Hype-cycles will eventually wane because they failed to provide the intended benefits, and will be replaced with new hype-cycles regardless of any attempt to make them persistent. The persistence is only temporary, will result in more effort to establish a formal data management profession, and the cost to organizations along the way will be tremendous.

The third approach is a *transcend hype-cycle approach* to establish a basic foundation for formal data management that transcends any past, current, or pending hype-cycles. It drives straight toward developing a formal data management profession based on sound theory, concepts, principles, and techniques. It establishes stability across change, avoids hype-cycles, and resolves the lexical challenge. It's the best approach to achieve a persistent formal data management profession

The *transcend hype-cycle approach* is very difficult to achieve because it involves bucking current hype-cycles, personal agendas, and profit motives. It requires hard thought about establishing a formal set of concepts, principles, and techniques for managing data as a critical resource. It's the least costly approach for organizations and it makes data management professionals look good in the long term. But, it's the least popular approach in the short term and tends to be avoided.

The *transcend hype-cycle approach* is the best and only reasonable approach. It's the approach that will achieve a formal data management profession in the shortest time, at the least cost, and will gain the recognition and respect that is deserved.

Data management professionals must take the initiative to develop a formal data management profession. They must earn the right to be called a profession, and to be recognized and respected professionals. Data management professionals must work extra hard at developing a formal data management profession, clean up the disparity that they have created, and properly manage data as a critical resource. They must stop demanding proper recognition and start earning proper recognition and respect.

Data Management Profession Status

The current status of a formal data management profession is analyzing the collection of disciplines and documenting those disciplines. The real progress of synthesizing a formal data management profession hasn't begun. It's coming, but it's not here yet. The motto is *If we don't do it to ourselves,*

237

someone else will do it to us. So far neither has happened, but the time is coming. Data management professionals have the opportunity to choose working together to develop a formal data management profession.

What's more likely to happen is that business professionals will step up to the task of creating a data management profession. It's the business that's scathing from poor data resource management. It's the business professionals that have knowledge about the business and the data needed to support the business. It's the business professionals that can learn the techniques and skills of managing data as a critical resource. Business professionals may well take over data resource management.

If a data management curriculum were established leading to a degree, the business professionals would likely be the majority registering, followed by the data management professionals. The business professionals have a profound interest, and ability, to manage data as a critical resource.

When the DAMA International Foundation was established in 2004, the primary initiative was to create a formal, certified, recognized, and respected data management profession. The objective for that initiative was to manage data as a critical resource of the organization. The theme was for data management professionals to develop a formal data management profession. That initiative was placed in the first Introduction to DAMA Guide to the Data Management Body of Knowledge (DAMA-DMBOK).

The primary initiative with a full set of objectives and implementation tasks was presented at the DAMA Conferences in the United States and Europe through 2006, and was widely accepted by data management professionals. The professional believed that the initiative could be substantially achieved within 5 years. However, that primary initiative was subsequently seriously compromised and ultimately devastated. The status of a data management profession is substantially the same as it was in the early 2000s, except for the ongoing hype-cycles.

Developing a formal data management profession will have trials and tribulations. It will have successes and failures. It will have differences of opinions and intensive discussions. Some people will support the development and others will attempt to block the development. People will take action according to their own personal and financial agendas. Eventually, a formal data management profession will evolve and become firmly established. That's the ultimate goal that needs to be achieved.

ORGANIZATION DISCRETION

The process of developing a data resource is at an organization's discretion.

They can chose the path they want to follow, whether they want to use the Data Resource Data for understanding their data, develop a Data Resource Guide for documenting that understanding, and how they want to perform their understanding and documentation projects. The discretion is limited only by their imagination and their ambition to do it right.

Organizations have a choice about how professional they want to be when developing their data resource. They can become professional with or without a formal data management profession. The concepts, principles, and techniques exist and have been proven over time. They can be used to identify, understand, document, and develop a high quality data resource.

Organizations have a choice about the degree to which they want to use the Data Resource Data to understand their data. The Data Resource Data architecture can be adjusted and enhanced to meet a particular organization's needs. Additional features can be added to the Data Resource Data and existing features could be eliminated depending on the organization's needs. When features are added, they should be formally documented as part of the Data Resource Data model presented in the previous book.

Organizations have a choice about developing a Data Resource Guide to document their understanding of the data. The Data Resource Guide should implement the Data Resource Data according to the formal data resource model presented in the previous book. However, the actual design and implementation of the Data Resource Guide can be done with and application development tool, in any program language, on any platform that is available to the organization. Organizations do not need to wait for a commercial Data Resource Guide to be developed by a vendor.

A large organization, such as a large Federal agency or a large multi-national company, can initiate multiple projects to understand and document their data resource. Each project can develop its own interim Common Data to understand their particular disparate data. Those independent sets of Common Data are then converted to independent sets of Data Product Data which are cross-referenced to the final Common Data for the organization.

Organizations can make a conscious and cognitive choice to understand their data, document that understanding, and develop a data resource that supports their business needs as they perceive the business world. They can choose to become leaders in managing data as a critical resource of the organization.

SUMMARY

The theme for developing a high quality data resource is to involve people, understand the data, and document that understanding.

239

Since the beginning of data processing, everything has changed, yet nothing has changed. Organizations are still physically manipulating their data to meet current needs without consideration for long term needs. They are still manipulating the data without thoroughly understanding those data from a business perspective. In many respects, the situation has gotten much worse with the increase in data disparity and the loss of a thorough understanding.

Standards for developing a data resource should be like the building codes for developing building. A finite set of building codes, although very detailed, covers a vast array of different buildings, for different purposes, for different occupants. Similarly, a finite set of data resource development standards can cover a vast array of different data resources, for different purposes, by different organizations.

The flip side would be a finite set of standard buildings that must be used for all purposes by all occupants. Occupants would pick the standard building that best fit their needs. No discretion would be allowed for the specific needs of the occupants. The same might be true for bridges, ships, planes, and so on. That situation would be untenable.

The same situation exists for standard data resource designs. Organizations could select one of a finite set of standard data resource designs that they had to use. No discretion would be allowed for the specific business needs of the organization. That situation would be just as untenable. A better approach is the development of a finite set of data resource concepts, principles, and techniques that could be used to develop an infinite variety of data resources that suit an organizations specific need.

The question becomes Who is the industry that is developing those standards? Whether it's the vendors, consultants, trainers, standards organizations, practitioners, they must be professional. If they allow or promote or accept the wrong concepts or the wrong terms, then professionalism does not exist and data management will be in turmoil. If they allow and promote and accept the proper concepts, principles, techniques, and terms, then professionalism exists.

Hopefully, all will rise to the challenge and begin to tell organizations what they need to hear about data resource development, rather than what they want to hear about data resource development. Hopefully, all will seek the achievement of thoroughly understanding the data resource based on business needs and the documentation of that understanding. Hopefully, all will follow a sequence of business, to logical, to physical, to implementation, to use.

The driving force should be the restoration of data resource quality and complete confidence in that data resource for supporting business activities, and the resilience of people desiring to have that confidence in the data resource. The basis for real data science is to understand and utilize the data resource to support each organization's business goals.

Identify – Understand – Document!

APPENDIX A

DATA RESOURCE DATA CHANGES

Appendix A contains data definitions, structure, and integrity rules that were not included in *Data Resource Data*. The material is in alphabetical order by Data Subject with Data Characteristics in alphabetical order within a Data Subject. The material is presented as formal data names, comprehensive data definitions, and precise data integrity rules.

ADDITIONS

The following additions, shown by the underscored text, were made to the Data Resource Data.

Business Process Type

(The Data Reference Items were not listed in *Data Resource Data*.)

The Business Process Type data reference items are suggestions only and may be developed by the organization as they deem necessary.

Automated	The Business Process is automated, but not on a computer.
Computer	The Business Process is performed on a computer.
Manual	The Business Process is performed manually.

Data Characteristic Variation

Data Characteristic Variation. Partial Fact Indicator

(A Data Characteristic added to Data Characteristic Variation)

An indicator showing whether or not the Data Characteristic Variation represents a partial fact of the parent Data Characteristic. A "Y" indicates that it represents a partial fact and an "N" indicates that it does not represent a partial fact.

Need! Required
Unique! No
Domain! {"Y" | "N"} Default "N"
Change! Allowed

Data Product Unit Process

(Data characteristics added to support creation, use, and deletion of data.)

Data Characteristic List:
Data Product Unit Process. Data Create Indicator
Data Product Unit Process. Data Delete Indicator
Data Product Unit Process. Data Update Indicator
Data Product Unit Process. Data Use Indicator

Data Product Unit Process. Data Create Indicator
An indicator showing whether or not the Data Product Unit is created by the Business Process accessing the data. A "Y" indicates that the Business Process created the data and an "N" indicates that it did not create the data.

Need! Required
Unique! No
Domain! {"Y" | "N"} Default "N"
Change! Allowed

Data Product Unit Process. Data Delete Indicator
An indicator showing whether or not the Data Product Unit can be deleted by the Business Process accessing the data. A "Y" indicates that the Business Process can delete the data and an "N" indicates that it cannot delete the data.

Need! Required
Unique! No
Domain! {"Y" | "N"} Default "N"
Change! Allowed

Data Product Unit Process. Data Update Indicator
An indicator showing whether or not the Data Product Unit is updated by the Business Process accessing the data. A "Y" indicates that the Business Process can update the data and an "N" indicates that it cannot update the data.

Need! Required
Unique! No
Domain! {"Y" | "N"} Default "N"
Change! Allowed

Data Product Unit Process. Data Use Indicator

An indicator showing whether or not the Data Product Unit is used by the Business Process accessing the data. A "Y" indicates that the Business Process uses the data and an "N" indicates that it does not create the data.

Need! Required
Unique! No
Domain! {"Y" | "N"} Default "N"
Change! Allowed

Data Step

Data Step. Sequence

The sequence number of the Data Step within a Data Track, numbered from the original data source to its current location. The sequence numbers need not start at 1 and need not be consecutive to allow for the identification of earlier Data Steps in the Data Track, or for additional Data Steps identified within the Data Track

Need! Required
Unique! Yes, within Data Track
Domain! Integer
Change! Allowed

Data Subject Set

Data Characteristic List:
Data Set Hierarchy. System Identifier

(The word 'Hierarchy" was left out of the data characteristic name.)

Data Set Hierarchy. System Identifier

Need! Required
Unique. No
Domain! Long Integer
Change! Allowed

(The word 'Hierarchy" was left out of the data characteristic name.)

Data Subject Set. System Identifier

Need! Required
Unique. Yes
Domain! Long Integer
Change! Prevented

(The data integrity rules did not get entered.)

Data Subject Set Characteristic

___

Data Subject <u>Set</u>. System Identifier
Need! Required
Unique. No
Domain! Long Integer
Change! Allowed

(The word "Set" was left off the data characteristic name.)

Data Track

Data Track is a pathway that data follow from their creation to their current location. It is part of the data provenance process and consists of many Data Steps that can be internal or external to the organization. <u>Each Data Track represents the movement of one unit of data, which at any Data Step in the Data Track may be a single fact or multiple facts.</u>

<u>Data Track. Name</u>

<u>The formal name of the Data Track, which is usually some version of the name of the data being followed along that track. The physical data name may change along the Data Track, so the Data Track. Name should be something meaningful to the organization, such as the formal Common Data Name.</u>

<u>Need! Required</u>
<u>Unique! Yes</u>
<u>Domain! 5 <= character <= 30 & first character <> ' '</u>
<u>Change! Allowed</u>

<u>Jurisdiction Type</u>

(The Data Reference Items were not listed in *Data Resource Data*.)

<u>The Business Process Type data reference items are suggestions only and may be developed by the organization as they deem necessary.</u>

City	The Jurisdiction is an incorporated city.
County	The Jurisdiction is a County within a State.
Federal	The Jurisdiction is a Federal Agency.
State	The Jurisdiction is a State Agency.
Superior Court	The Jurisdiction is a Superior Court.

Organization Unit

<u>Organization Unit. Organization Indicator</u>

(A Data Characteristic added to Organization Unit)

<u>An indicator showing whether or not the Organization Unit is the highest level in the Organization Unit hierarchy and does not have a parent Organization Unit. A "Y" indicates that the Organization Unit is the highest level in the Organization Unit hierarchy and an "N" indicates that it is not the highest level in the Organization Unit hierarchy.</u>

<u>Need! Required</u>
<u>Unique! No</u>
<u>Domain! {"Y" | "N"} Default "N"</u>
<u>Change! Allowed</u>

Data Subject

(Text added to the Data Subject Definition)

<u>Data Subject is recursive to show derived data subjects, such as data occurrence groups, data occurrence roles, data focus for dimensional data, derived spatial data, and so on.</u>

DELETIONS

The following deletions, shown by crossed out text, were made to the Data Resource Data.

Data Subject

(Data Subject Class was removed from the Data Resource Data; however the foreign key in Data Subject to Data Subject Class was not removed.)

~~Foreign Key: Data Subject Class~~
~~Data Subject Class. Name~~

BIBLIOGRAPHY

Al-Khalili, Jim. *Paradox: The Nine Greatest Enigmas in Physics.* New York: Broadway Paperbacks, 2012.

Bara, Mike. *Ancient Aliens on the Moon.* Kempton, Illinois, Adventures Unlimited Press, 2012

Bara, Mike. *Ancient Aliens on Mars II.* Kempton, Illinois: Adventures Unlimited Press, 2014.

Bauval, Robert, and Thomas Brophy. *Black Genesis: The Prehistoric Origins of Ancient Egypt.* Toronto: Bear and Company, 2011.

Blascovich, Jim, and Jeremy Bailenson. *Infinite Reality: The Hidden Blueprint of Our Virtual Lives.* New York: Harper Collins, 2011.

Baggot, Jim. *Higgs: The Invention & Discovery of the 'God Particle'.* Oxford: Oxford University Press, 2012.

Brackett, Michael H. *Developing Data Structured Information Systems.* Topeka, KS: Ken Orr and Associates, Inc., 1983.

_____. *Developing Data Structured Databases.* Englewood Cliffs, NJ: Prentice Hall, 1987.

_____. *Practical Data Design.* Englewood Cliffs, NJ: Prentice Hall, 1990.

_____. *Data Sharing Using a Common Data Architecture.* New York: John Wiley & Sons, Inc., 1994.

_____. *The Data Warehouse Challenge: Taming Data Chaos.* New York: John Wiley & Sons, Inc., 1996.

_____. *Data Resource Quality: Turning Bad Habits Into Good Practices.* New York: Addison-Wesley, 2000.

_____. *Notes from the Back of the Clipboard: Anecdotes from Real Life.* New York: Eloquent Books, 2008

_____. *The Adventures of Bunny and Hare.* New York: Eloquent Books, 2010.

_____. *Data Resource Simplexity: How Organizations Choose Data Resource Success Or Failure.* New Jersey: Technics Publications, LLC, 2011.

_____. *Data Resource Integration: Understanding and Resolving a Disparate Data Resource.* New Jersey: Technics Publications, LLC, 2012.

_____. *Data Resource Design: Reality Beyond Illusion.* New Jersey: Technics Publications, LLC, 2012.

_____. *Data Resource Data: A Comprehensive Data Resource Understanding.* New Jersey: Technics Publications, LLC, 2014.

_____. Monthly articles on Dataversity.net, November 2011 through December, 2014.

Butler, Alan. *The Dawn of Genius: The Minoan Super-Civilization and the Truth About Atlantis.* London: Watkins Publishing, 2014.

Choinard, Patrick. *Lost Race of the Giants.* Rochester, New York, Bear & Company, 2013.

Church, Dawson. *The Genie In Your Genes: Epigenetic Medicine and the New Biology of Intention.* Santa Rosa, California: Energy Psychology Press, 2009.

Collins, Francis C. *The Language of Life: DNA and the Revolution in Personalized Medicine.* New York: Harper Perennial, 2010.

Coppens, Philip. *The Lost Civilization Enigma: A New Inquiry Into the Existence of Ancient Cities, Cultures, and Peoples Who Pre-Date Recorded History.* Pompton Plains, New Jersey: Career Press, Inc., 2013.

Dawkins, Richard. *The Greatest Show On Earth: The Evidence For Evolution.* New York: Free Press, 2009.

Dawkins, Richard. *The Magic of Reality: How We Know What's Really True.* New York: Free Press, 2011.

Eversole, Finley. *Infinite Energy Technologies: Tesla, Cold Fusion, Antigravity, and the Future of Sustainability.* Rochester, Vermont: Inner Traditions, 2013.

Farrell, Joseph P. *Covert Wars and the Clash of Civilizations.* Kempton, Illinois: Adventures Unlimited Press, 2013.

Ferguson, Kitty. *Stephen Hawking: An Unfettered Mind.* New York: Palgrave McMillan, 2013.

Francis, Richard C. *Epigenetics: How Environment Shapes Our Genes.* New York: W.W. Norton & Company, 2011.

Grann, David. *The Lost City of Z.* New York: Vintage Books, 2009.

Greene, Brian. *The Hidden Reality: Parallel Universes and the Deep Laws of the Cosmos.* New York: Vintage Books, 2011.

Hawkins, David R. *Power vs. Force: The Hidden Determinants of Human Behavior.* New York: Hay House, Inc., 2012.

Haze, Xaviant. *Aliens in Ancient Egypt.* Rochester, New York: Bear & Company, 2013.

Joseph, Frank. *Before Atlantis: 20 Million Years of Human and Pre-Human Cultures.* Rochester, New York: Bear & Company, 2013.

Kaku, Michio. *Physics of the Future: How Science Will Shape Human Destiny and Our Daily Lives by the Year 2100.* New York: Anchor Books, 2011.

LaViolette, Paul A. *Secrets of Antigravity Propulsion.* Rochester, Vermont: Bear & Company, 2008.

Livio, Mario. New York: Simon & Schuster Paperbacks, 2013.

Marrs, Jim. *Rule By Secrecy.* New York: Harper, 2001.

McClure, Rusty, and Jack Heffron. *Coral Castle: The Mystery of Ed Leedskakn in and His American Stonehenge.* Ternary Publishing, 2009.

Panek, Richard. *The 4% Universe: Dark Matter, Dark Energy, and the Race To Discover The Rest Of Reality.* New York: Mariner Books, 2011.

Panno, Joseph. *Stem Cell Research: Medical Applications and Ethical Controversies.* New York: Checkmark Books, 2010.

Parker, Andrew. *The Genesis Enigma: Why The First Book Of The Bible Is Scientifically Accurate.* New York: Penguin Group, 2009.

Parsaye, Kamran. *Surveying Decision Support: New Realms of Analysis.* The 2nd Annual Data Mining Summit. 1996.

Penrose, Roger. *Cycles of Time: An Extraordinary New View of the Universe.* New York: Vintage Books, 2010.

Pyle, Rod. *Curiosity: An Inside Look at the Mars Rover Mission.* New York: Prometheus Books, 2014.

Restak, Richard. *Think Smart: A Neuroscientist's Prescription for Improving You5r Brain's Performance.* New York: Riverhead Books, 2009.

Rowland, Wade. *Galileo's Mistake: A New Look at the Epic Confrontation between Galileo and the Church.* New York: Arcade Publishing, 2012.

Schoch, Robert M. *Forgotten Civilization: The Role of Solar Outbursts In Our Past And Future.* Rochester, Vermont: Inner Traditions, 2012.

Taleb, Nassim Nicholas. *The Black Swan: The Impact of the Highly*

Improbable. New York: Random House, 2010.

Tesla, Nicola. *My Invents and Other Writings.* New York: Penguin Books, 2011.

Vedral. Vlatko. *Decoding Reality: The Universe as Quantum Information.* New York: Oxford University Press, 2010.

Wilcock, David. *The Source Field Investigations.* New York: Penguin Group, 2011.

Zubrin, Robert, with Richard Wagner. *The Case for Mars: The Plan to Settle the Red Planet and Why We Must.* New York: Free Press, 2011.

INDEX

www.ingramcontent.com/pod-product-compliance
Lightning Source LLC
Chambersburg PA
CBHW060523060326
40690CB00017B/3365